The Book of
Carshalton

The Book of
Carshalton

AT THE SOURCE OF THE WANDLE

Based on Talks by Michael Wilks
Edited by Stella Wilks & Gordon Rookledge

HALSGROVE

First published in Great Britain in 2002
Reprinted in 2003

THIS BOOK IS DEDICATED TO THE
MEMORY OF MICHAEL WILKS

British Library Cataloguing-in-Publication Data
A CIP record for this title is available from the British Library

ISBN 1 84114 1550

HALSGROVE

Halsgrove House
Lower Moor Way
Tiverton, Devon EX16 6SS
Tel: 01884 243242
Fax: 01884 243325
email: sales@halsgrove.com
website: http://www.halsgrove.com

Frontispiece photograph: *The Windsor Castle, c.1870.*

Printed and bound in Great Britain by CPI Bath Press, Bath

FOREWORD

Carshalton is best known to many for Carshalton Ponds, a surprisingly picturesque spot, complete with ford and swans, ducks and geese, in South-West London. But Carshalton also has many hidden treasures. Professor Michael Wilks made it his life's work to uncover them. *The Book of Carshalton* brings countless local historical gems to the attention of a much greater audience than were able to attend his informative Carshalton Society chats. The photographs, some dating back to the late 1800s, portray a town which is very proud of its heritage.

Whether you are a historian or simply a resident of Carshalton, you will want to own *The Book of Carshalton*. Edited by Professor Wilks' wife, Stella, and Gordon Rookledge, author and publisher, it is a suitable tribute to Professor Wilks' commitment to, and enthusiasm about, Carshalton.

Tom Brake
Member of Parliament for Carshalton and Wallington

General view looking across the Upper Pond showing the Parish Church and Queen's Well before the Second World War.

Carshalton Water Tower, built in 1720, from an early-nineteenth-century watercolour by Gideon Yates. (S.L.S.L.)

Dame Duffin's Cottage, after a painting by W.J.T., 1777.
(S.L.S.L.)

CONTENTS

The King's Arms, High Street, early-twentieth century.

An old comic postcard referring to Carshalton. (M.F.)

ACKNOWLEDGEMENTS

The editors are indebted to Alan Crowe for allowing us to use his map of Carshalton on which to indicate the sites of some of our vanished history. He has also allowed us to reproduce a drawing from his *Inns, Taverns and Pubs of the London Borough of Sutton*. Valuable textual input has been received from Mary Bates (St Helier Hospital and Development of the Estate), Brian Gibbs (Carshalton Choral Society), R. Hodges (Carshalton Cricket Club), Mario Fuller (Carshalton Athletic), Sister Monica McAuley FC of the Daughters of the Cross (St Philomena's School), Elvyn Fowler (Carshalton Tennis Club), Adrian Mann (Holy Cross RC Church), John Thornton (The Carshalton Society), Peter Stroud (Carshalton Camera Club), Anthony Reeves (Cottage of Content) and Theresa Fox (St Margaret's R.C. Church).

Other valuable assistance was received from Graham Gibbs, Jennie Rookledge, David Cobourne, Nesta and Ian White, Diana and David Moore, Jim Bowden, Beryl Smith, Mick Worrall, John Thornton, Andrew Skelton, Adrian Mann, Anne Dodwell and Kath Shawcross (Borough Archivist and Local Studies Manager, London Borough of Sutton), Catherine Webber, Mavis Gee, Derek Lockhart, John Priest and Lesley Barrett.

Acknowledgements for reproduction of photographs are due to:

M.F.	Mario Fuller	K.W.	Keith White
K.N.	Ken Needham	C.W.	Christopher Wheaton
J.H.	Jill Hale	D.Y.	Derek Young
V&A	Victoria and Albert Museum	J.T.	John Thewlis
V.M.	Valerie Moffatt	J.E.	Jean Evans
J.B.	Joyce Broom	G.B.	Geoffrey Brown
E.B.	Ena Bestley	C.C.	Carshalton Cricket Club
M.S.	Michael Slatford	S.L.S.L.	Sutton Local Studies Library
S.M.M.	Sister Monica McAuley	C.M.C.	Carshalton Methodist Church
S.N.	Surrey Newsgroup	H.C.P.M.	*Holy Cross Parish Magazine*

Sources for the illustrations are indicated where appropriate, and our thanks go to the many people who have loaned their old photographs and slides. Every attempt has been made to acknowledge the source of material where appropriate.

The editors are also indebted to the many friends, local and otherwise, whose comments have helped in the preparation of this volume. We hope that readers will enjoy these glimpses of the past as much as we have done in the course of working on the material.

Stella Wilks and Gordon Rookledge

View looking east down Pound Street. Wallace House is on the right.

INTRODUCTION

Michael Wilks lived in Carshalton from 1957 until his death in 1998. He was Professor of Medieval History at London University and taught at Birkbeck College for many years. He became interested in the history of Carshalton and the surrounding area, and did an enormous amount of research on the early history of the village and the River Wandle. For nearly 30 years, beginning in 1966, Michael regularly addressed the Carshalton Society twice a year on a variety of topics, mostly concerned with planning matters, but enlivened with snippets of local history. Some of these historical excerpts have been collated and are presented here as a memorial to him and his work for the Society. An attempt has been made to retain his rather discursive style, as the text was written for the listener rather than the reader and is quite different to his usual academic mode of writing.

Michael drew on many sources: Calendars of Court Rolls, manorial records, *Victoria County History*, cartularies, and many original sources in Record Offices, as well as the invaluable work of previous local historians such as G.B. Brightling, A.V. Peatling and A.E. Jones. Assistance was also received from the archivist Bernard Nurse and the noted local archaeologists Keith Pryer and Andrew Skelton. There was also close collaboration with the late Douglas Cluett, formerly the Borough Heritage Officer. Michael's own considerable research runs to many files and will be an invaluable archive for future local historians.

The present volume does not attempt to be a definitive history of Carshalton but aims to give some insight into the life and times of our forebears. It is a flavour of the past which can be enjoyed by all lovers of Carshalton.

Infants School, Mill Lane, c.1870.

A horse taking a drink outside the Windsor Castle, c.1870.
The horse and cart belonged to English & Sons of Thornton Heath.

Pound Street looking west, c.1870. The lamp for the Fire Station can be seen to the left of the street light.
Wallace House is further up the road on the left.

The former Swan public house, used later by Tom Preen, wheelwright and timber merchant in the early 1900s. (S.L.S.L.)

Tom Preen's House, 14 Carshalton Park Road. (S.L.S.L.)

Top: *Queen's Well, the house fronting the Upper Pond.*
This photograph: *Queen's Well (left) by the*
Ponds in the 1920s. (Both S.L.S.L.)

MICHAEL WILKS

In 1963, at a time when the civic amenity movement was gathering strength throughout the country, one of Carshalton's oldest and most picturesque buildings, Queen's Well, was demolished after falling into what was at that time considered to be irreversible disrepair. The local sense of dismay at the loss of this building, coupled with apprehension over what might replace it, brought together a group of people whose determination that local opinion should be taken into account gave rise to the formation of the Carshalton Society.

Prominent in this group was Dr Michael Wilks, who effectively became the voice of the Society for over 30 years. During this time the Society actively campaigned to preserve and improve the amenities of Carshalton – by protecting its historic buildings from unsuitable development and its open spaces from encroachment, by combating attempts to increase the capacity of its roads, and by encouraging good architecture in new buildings. As a historian, Dr Wilks possessed a sense of the identity of Carshalton which was important at a time when it was about to be subsumed into the newly-formed London Borough of Sutton and as an able propagandist he always insisted that that identity should be respected.

The Society quickly became involved in many matters of public concern and in its early years it produced its own Conservation Area scheme, which laid special emphasis on the need to relieve the congestion of the High Street shopping area by re-routing through-traffic – a vision still unrealised. More successfully, it was closely associated with the scheme to maintain water in the Ponds and the campaign to prevent parts of the 'Lodge Land' being sold off for housing. The Society was also instrumental in reviving the historic Carshalton Charter Fair which is held in September.

The members of the Society meet five times a year to hear reports and discuss current planning matters and it was at these meetings and in the newsletter which precedes them that Dr Wilks would incorporate into his discourse the brief historical essays which are featured in this volume. Between meetings, the administrative work of the Society is carried on by an annually elected executive committee whose Secretary is Mr John Thornton of 25 Lavender Road, Carshalton SM5 3EF (020-8647 2574) to whom applications for membership and general enquiries should be addressed.

Stella Wilks, widow of Michael, was born in Carshalton and knows it well. She assisted her husband with his work for many years. Gordon Rookledge, author and publisher, is a past Chairman of the Carshalton Society and has a great interest in local history. *Rookledge's Architectural Identifier of Conservation Areas*, Sutton edition, by Gordon Rookledge and Andrew Skelton, was published in September 1999.

Michael Wilks in 1992.

OS Map, 1934

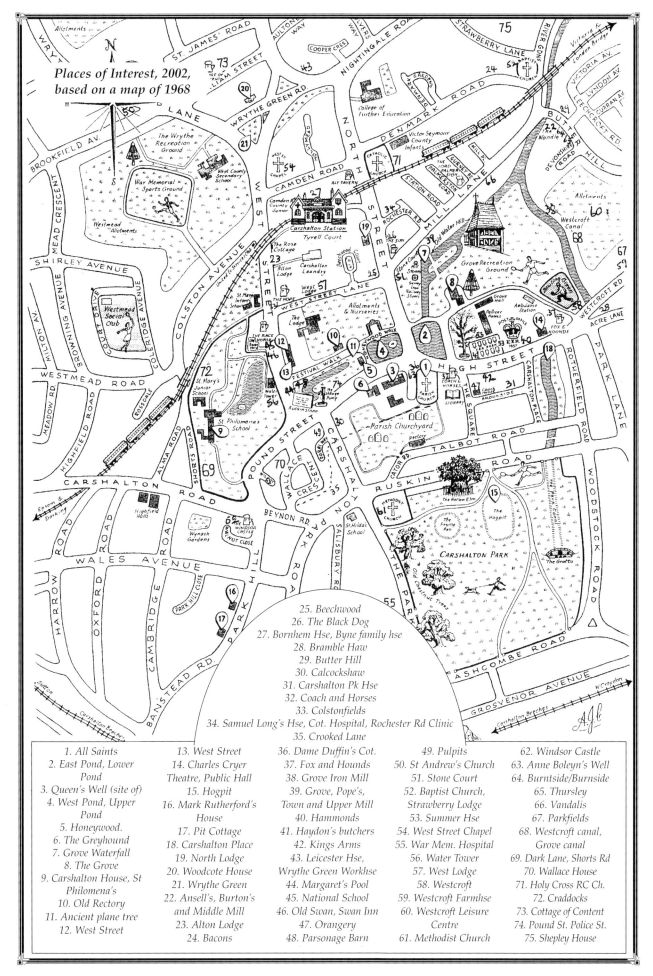

Places of Interest, 2002, based on a map of 1968

25. Beechwood
26. The Black Dog
27. Bornhem Hse, Byne family hse
28. Bramble Haw
29. Butter Hill
30. Calcockshaw
31. Carshalton Pk Hse
32. Coach and Horses
33. Colstonfields
34. Samuel Long's Hse, Cot. Hospital, Rochester Rd Clinic
35. Crooked Lane

1. All Saints	13. West Street	36. Dame Duffin's Cot.	49. Pulpits	62. Windsor Castle
2. East Pond, Lower Pond	14. Charles Cryer Theatre, Public Hall	37. Fox and Hounds	50. St Andrew's Church	63. Anne Boleyn's Well
3. Queen's Well (site of)	15. Hogpit	38. Grove Iron Mill	51. Stone Court	64. Burntside/Burnside
4. West Pond, Upper Pond	16. Mark Rutherford's House	39. Grove, Pope's, Town and Upper Mill	52. Baptist Church, Strawberry Lodge	65. Thursley
5. Honeywood.	17. Pit Cottage	40. Hammonds	53. Summer Hse	66. Vandalis
6. The Greyhound	18. Carshalton Place	41. Haydon's butchers	54. West Street Chapel	67. Parkfields
7. Grove Waterfall	19. North Lodge	42. Kings Arms	55. War Mem. Hospital	68. Westcroft canal, Grove canal
8. The Grove	20. Woodcote House	43. Leicester Hse, Wrythe Green Workhse	56. Water Tower	69. Dark Lane, Shorts Rd
9. Carshalton House, St Philomena's	21. Wrythe Green	44. Margaret's Pool	57. West Lodge	70. Wallace House
10. Old Rectory	22. Ansell's, Burton's and Middle Mill	45. National School	58. Westcroft	71. Holy Cross RC Ch.
11. Ancient plane tree	23. Alton Lodge	46. Old Swan, Swan Inn	59. Westcroft Farmhse	72. Craddocks
12. West Street	24. Bacons	47. Orangery	60. Westcroft Leisure Centre	73. Cottage of Content
		48. Parsonage Barn	61. Methodist Church	74. Pound St. Police St.
				75. Shepley House

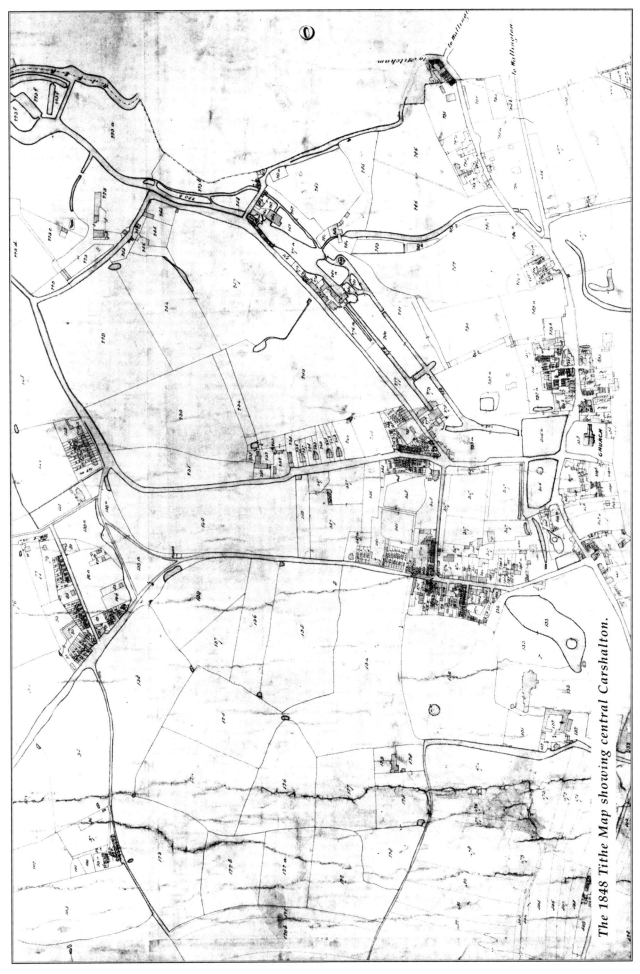

The 1848 Tithe Map showing central Carshalton.

Chapter One

EARLY DAYS

EARLY LORDS OF THE MANOR

Officially, throughout the thirteenth century, the manor of Carshalton belonged to the Fiennes family (who obtained it by marriage from the de Boulognes, holders since the Norman Conquest). The Fiennes family may not have lived in Carshalton at all, but the Colevilles certainly did.

About the middle of the twelfth century one of the old Norman Tregoze family of Lydiard Tregoze near Swindon, a lady called Aubrey de Tregoze, married a Norman lord, Robert de Beseville. De Beseville, for reasons which are still not clear, possessed, amongst other places, something like a quarter or a third of Carshalton. He had enough land to keep three ox-ploughs busy for a year, a water mill, and a manor house, a 'capital messuage'. It is thought that he had the area of the Grove, the so-called manor of Stone Court. It is not clear whether Aubrey de Tregoze and Robert de Beseville actually lived in Carshalton but their daughter Maud certainly did. Maud de Beseville was born about 1158, and she was quite a girl! By the time she was 15 she had married one of the King's judges, Gilbert de Coleville – who gave her eight children at least in the course of the next 12 years (two boys and six girls) and then died of his exertions about 1185. But there was no stopping Maud. By the end of the century she had married again, to a Belgian, Guillaume le Fleming, William of Flanders, and they had at least three more children, two boys and a girl.

One of the problems of getting married twice was that on the occasion of the second wedding one's parents tended to reclaim the dowry which they'd paid for the first marriage – in Maud's case a manor at Carshalton. Meanwhile one's first husband's family didn't want you to keep what you'd inherited from him, in case you gave it to your second husband. So all the families concerned – the de Tregozes, the de Besevilles and the de Colevilles – started telling Maud to cast off and let slip her worldly goods, to them. But Maud was a spirited woman. In 1200 she had sued her mother's family, the Tregozes, for the estates they had promised her in Suffolk; and she sued her father, old Robert de Beseville, for

Carshalton. She got the Suffolk property from the Tregozes eventually in 1207/8. But she had to agree to a complicated compromise with her father and with the eldest son by the first marriage, William de Coleville. She let her father have half of the land and the mill at Carshalton, so long as she kept the house and the other half of the land: Carshalton, we are told, was her favourite home, and she wasn't going to give it up. That was in 1200. But seven years later she had to come to terms with her son, William de Coleville. By 1207 Maud seems to have been dying and she wanted to sort things out and make peace between her son and her second husband. So there was another agreement by which he had to agree to look after her for the rest of her life, in return for which he got the manor of Carshalton. But as well as looking after his mother, or paying her second husband William the Fleming £5 a year to do it for him, he had to agree to look after their children as well; also to give his stepfather, William of Flanders, 32 acres of plough-land, pasture for six oxen and two horses, and to have him as a guest free of charge in the manor house for 13 weeks in every year. So William of Flanders really did very well out of the arrangement. He got free lodgings for a quarter of the year; he had his own little farm; he didn't have to pay for his children; and, above all, he either didn't have to look after Maud or else he got paid for doing so. It is an arrangement which many husbands and fathers may have envied since. And all he had to do was pay his stepson 64 shillings, and give him a horse, a palfrey worth two marks. Nevertheless, the son, William de Coleville, got the manor of Stone Court. And although there were further arrangements between the de Besevilles and the de Colevilles in the late 1220s and '30s about who had the mill and who had the manor house, this part of Carshalton seems to have remained de Coleville territory during the thirteenth century.

William doesn't seem to have been so keen on Carshalton after this. He was here around 1220, but preferred to spend his time on his other estates in Suffolk; and his two sons (William and Ralph) weren't very interested in it either. They were offered it, but refused. By 1240 William was over 60, and he

THE CARSHALTON SOCIETY

CARSHALTON CHARTER FAIR

12 59

Saturday 8th September

in The Square, Carshalton

Craft and Charity stalls   Pennyroyal Clog Dancers

Enquiries: 020 - 8647 2574

10 am — 5 pm • Free admission

Handbill for the Charter Fair since its revival in 1983.

still wanted to provide for his family, so he arranged for his elder grandson, Gilbert de Coleville, to have Carshalton when he was old enough – but for the time being young Gilbert was to be a ward. The wardship of young Gilbert was held first by the King's brother, Richard, Earl of Cornwall (brother of Henry III), and then by a very prominent royal official, John de Gatesden. A most powerful person indeed, John de Gatesden was one of the leading figures at the royal court – in fact he'd arranged the King's marriage; he was Sheriff of both Surrey and Sussex; and had the job of defending the coast of Sussex against French attack. He was an astute financier and a very able administrator; and he made so much money from his various court jobs that he was able to buy up vast estates. At the time he was a cleric, like most royal officials, but he hadn't much time for apostolic poverty, and in 1244 created a scandal by resigning from the clergy and being knighted instead. Worse still, he seized possession of Carshalton and said that he was going to keep it for himself, and not let his ward, the heir, Gilbert de Coleville, inherit. He justified this by saying that Gilbert's uncle Ralph had agreed to this and that Ralph supported him. So poor young Gilbert, the handsome but penniless heir, was left in the classic situation of having been swindled out of his inheritance by his wicked uncle Ralph and the

unscrupulous royal official, Sir John of Gatesden.

Gilbert was eventually saved by the great baronial revolt against Henry III and his corrupt officials which began in 1258. Sueing for his inheritance, he lost the first case on a technicality but he claimed a second hearing at which he won. Both Gilbert and John claimed to have charters proving that they ought to have Carshalton. Gilbert was able to produce one from his grandfather (William de Coleville) saying he should have it. John of Gatesden said that he had a better document, but when he was asked to produce it he said he had had to send to Winchester for it and the messenger had lost it along the road on the way back. Naturally the jury decided that Gilbert had won the case. Wicked John of Gatesden saw that all was up, repented the error of his ways, became a monk (to be precise a Premonstratensian Canon) and died almost immediately afterwards.

As compensation King Henry III gave Gilbert the much desired and valuable right to hold a market in Carshalton every week, and a fair every year. The Carshalton Fair was established by royal charter on 14 March 1259 (and was presumably held for the first time in September 1259) although nobody seems to have thought of asking why this grant was made to Carshalton then. But 1258/59 were the very years when the great crisis between King and barons broke out, when the barons tried to establish that they controlled the King's government. It is not entirely fanciful to assume that both sides were buying support as hard as they could, and that Henry III wanted the help of the new lord of Stone Court and his people. And the people of Carshalton do seem to have been grateful for their Fair and did not join the anti-Government rising in which so many Surrey people participated. But in 1271 the Fiennes came back into the story. They said that the de Colevilles might be sub-tenants of the manor of Carshalton, but they were still the tenants in chief. So that after all this, the manor of Carshalton still really belonged to them all the time! – and it did.

The rights of the de Colevilles as lords of the manor are now held by the London Borough of Sutton. (The Carshalton Charter Fair was revived in 1983 to mark the 20th anniversary of the Carshalton Society and has become a regular annual event.)

Lydiard Tregoze passed first to the Beauchamp family, and then to the St Johns. Three-and-half centuries later, soon after 1500, Sir John St John (who was in fact a cousin of King Henry VIII) married a Carew heiress and acquired a title to the manor of Carshalton.

LIFE IN THE THIRTEENTH CENTURY: KING VERSUS BARONS

Most people know of Magna Carta, the Great Charter of 1215, which the barons forced King John to accept at Runnymede. These baronial demands for charters of liberties and for re-issues of Magna Carta itself went on throughout the century. There was in fact a more serious constitutional crisis in the middle of the century, between 1258 and 1264, when the barons under Simon de Montfort ended up by going to war against King Henry III and his son Prince Edward (I). It was a very important crisis. Not only was the King defeated and taken prisoner at the Battle of Lewes; but to some historians this crisis produced the first real English Parliament (Simon de Montfort is often regarded as the father of Parliament). It turned Carshalton High Street into a playground; and it made Carshalton Church into a stable – so we are told.

In the spring of 1264 Simon de Montfort and the baronial party had seized control of London, where the opposition to the King enjoyed considerable popular support, and there was a great deal of further support for the barons from the men of Surrey and Sussex. The King's chief supporter, the Earl of Surrey (John de Warenne), had in fact been chased out of the county altogether and had shut himself up in his castle at Lewes, and it was to Lewes that Henry III and the Royal army went to rescue him. Simon de Montfort and the baronial army followed on their heels, intent on catching the King and defeating him at the Battle of Lewes in May 1264. Victory would enable them to take over complete control of the Government for a short time.

The story goes that Simon de Montfort and the baronial army marched out of London and moved south on to the Downs and through the Weald, gathering men and supplies as they went. The inhabitants of Carshalton heard that Simon and his army were approaching Carshalton (which was always Royalist) and would seize all their cattle as army supplies. In the ensuing great panic, as the villagers debated what to do, somebody had a bright idea. As the first Christian church was in a manger, where the Three Kings worshipped the infant Jesus, it would surely therefore be alright to reverse the process and put all the cows and oxen and so on into the church for safety. And when the army arrived, it found that there were no supplies – all the cattle had taken sanctuary in the church.

It's a good story (and comes from Dr Peatling); the only trouble is that – like so much medieval history – it probably isn't true. As far as has been ascertained, Simon de Montfort did not come to Carshalton before the Battle of Lewes: Carshalton is not on the way to Lewes from London, and the Weald was pretty impassable anyway. In fact he seems to have gone well to the east – to Robertsbridge, Battle and Fletching, all in East Sussex, and he advanced on Lewes from the east. One suspects that if Simon de Montfort did come to Carshalton to take cattle, it was in fact the earl's son, Simon junr, who was made Warden of Surrey and Sussex after the victory of his father at Lewes. He

would have administered this area for the rest of 1264 until both the de Montforts went west and were killed fighting the royal army at Evesham in August 1265. But if anybody came after Carshalton's sacred cows, it was probably young Simon.

OLD LOCAL NAMES

The name Carshalton has been spelled in various ways through the ages – like Heinz, there are 57 varieties. As regards the second half, 'alton', there is no great difficulty because this is a direct descendant of the Anglo-Saxon name, Aewelton (the settlement by the well or spring). The changes of spelling were caused by differences of pronunciation – alton, olton, orton, oulton (ow or oo) and so on.

But by the twelfth century the full modern name had made its appearance, incorporating the 'car', of Carshalton. Quite obviously this was pronounced like a cough, Ker-sawlton, and for the next five or six centuries nobody quite knew how to spell it. Did it begin with a C or a K? On the whole the Middle Ages preferred a K, and it wasn't until Tudor times that the C became more usual. Even in the late-nineteenth century one can still find Kay-sawlton, and eighteenth-century maps exist with the name as two words Case Horton. And beyond this there are whole strings of Cas, Cers, Crass, Cress, Criss, Cross etc., all spelled with a C – and then all over again with a K. Quite obviously, for literally centuries, nobody knew what the name of Carshalton really was – and if the locals didn't know, visitors were constantly baffled and perplexed, and would use all sorts of spellings, often several different ones at once.

A major addition to our sources for the history of old Carshalton are the Court Rolls – the records of the Manor Court – for the sixteenth and seventeenth centuries, held by the London Borough of Sutton. (The medieval Court Rolls, from 1359 to 1506, were printed in 1916.) These documents are invaluable in linking the medieval and modern records together. Not only are they extremely difficult to read and decipher, but they are legal documents, and it is a well-known characteristic of legal documents that they are not meant to be understood. A difficulty is also posed by the fact that they contain a mass of unfamiliar personal and place names, nearly every item requiring considerable detective work to be done on it in order to identify where it might be on a modern map. When one sees this multitude of unknown names, it begins to look as if almost everywhere in Carshalton was renamed during the course of the eighteenth century.

The burden of dealing with this information is, fortunately, somewhat eased by the fact that with the Rolls comes a very helpful abstract, made in 1714 by William Lany, who was probably the steward of the manor. This gives a summary of each property and how it changed hands between the fifteenth century and 1700. There are many gaps in this, and some of the entries are very short, but at least it is fairly easy to read. It shows the manor divided up into about 70 different estates, properties and holdings; of which probably only about a dozen have the names by which we know them today.

One of the reasons why so many names are unfamiliar is that a property tended to take the name of its owner, and therefore changed its name whenever a different family took possession of it. Others, on the other hand, acquired a name from some owner in the remote and distant past, and kept it for centuries in a steadily more and more corrupt form until the original name had lost all significance. Some of the more picturesque names are personal ones. Thus Romesland is not some pre-Reformation property belonging to the Pope, but took its name from the simple fact that it was held by Isabella Rome. Similarly Pope's House (which was in West Street) had nothing to do with His Holiness, but was owned by the Pope family who feature repeatedly in Carshalton history during the seventeenth and eighteenth centuries; the house called Punchards, with seven acres of land in the common fields, derived its name from its owner Thomas Punchard, one of the village innkeepers, who was prosecuted in 1651 for cheating his customers by selling beer in smaller than standard-size tankards. It must have been a profitable occupation, since, when he died in 1671, he not only had the house and seven acres but three other houses as well, with three barns, three gardens, two stables and two orchards. Punchards was itself left to a certain Nicholas Horndon, although he sold it in 1682 – but it then kept the name Horndon. And since the clerk of the court could not spell very well, it finished up the century as Herndon.

A property with the interesting name in 1445 of Spykes and Purcers turns out to be just two houses owned by Maud Spykes, one called Spykes and the other Purcers, again probably a personal name. But when in 1552 Nicholas Burton was asked to explain how he came to be holding a house, garden and lands called Pyncasses, he was at a loss – and so are we. All he knew, he said, was that his grandfather had had it; and the same applied to 'a toft called Cathaw'. A toft is usually the place where a house had once stood, often marked by a clump of trees – a grove – and a cathaw would seem to mean a field created by an enclosure with a hedge round it. We of course are still familiar with the term haw, as in Bramblehaw, Greenshaw and Roundshaw. Cat would seem to be a local speciality; both Sutton and Carshalton had fields called Catsbrain. In our documents the name appears in 1488 as Catbrake, and in 1535 the same field is given as Crackbrain. It was owned in both years by the Tye family, who also had fields at a place called Bakers Cross in Carshalton, and at Carew's Elms, which seems to have been on the Sutton-Carshalton border.

The old name for Butter Hill is Taint Hill, which takes us straight back to the Anglo-Saxon period, and tells us that Butter Hill was specially noted for its trees. Another Carshalton name referring to trees is probably Nineholms – presumably holm means oak tree here rather than island, and is a name like Sevenoaks. John and Agnes Barnes were given land at Nineholms in 1542 on the condition that they built a house on it within two years: it seems that they did, and the entrance was sufficiently outstanding to become a local landmark, because the name of the area then becomes Nineholms' Gate. As it was demesne land it may have been near Carshalton Park, even perhaps one of the entrances to the manor itself. Similarly in the later-seventeenth century Briton's Gate was another local landmark, and again seems to have been near the Park.

Clearly the greatest importance was attached to the care of trees. Thus in 1560 the Manor Court was told that John Dove had cut down a walnut tree, and his lands were forfeit until he had given satisfaction. The lands in question were up Green Wrythe Lane for the most part, and earlier in the sixteenth century had belonged to Thomas Oscomb. Oscomb is of interest in that he is one of the few people mentioned of whom we can say that we know exactly where he lived. He had a cottage and garden at the corner of Mill Lane and North Street, where the present Stone Court Council offices are in the Grove. He died in 1535 and his son John refused to take the cottage over from him, saying it was too ruinous to be worth the trouble of taking. Whereupon the lord of the manor declared it forfeit and seized it, and three years later gave it to the Gainsfords to add to their estate of Stone Court. Had he not done so, then the present Stone Court would not have been part of the Grove – and would never have become Stone Court at all.

The lord of the manor who was so concerned about losing his walnut tree in 1560 would have been John St John. In the same year he was extremely vexed that a certain John Furman or Froman had squatted on a piece of waste pasture down by Little Woodcote called Pillory Down. He demanded to know what right Froman had to be there and to stop it being used for pasture. It seems to have taken him five years to decide that he had no right to be there, but he then accused Furman/Froman of cutting down his bushes to burn on his fire, and of using the land to pasture his own sheep – and he sued him for trespass. (Interestingly a John Fromond, Gent, was buried at Carshalton on 22 October 1580.)

An entry in 1676 refers to the chalk pit on the way to Barrow Hedges and Banstead, which is the site of Pit House in Park Hill. The Hogpit pond in the Park, on the other hand, is featured much earlier: it is mentioned in 1444 (Hoggpytte) and again in 1530 (Hogpyt). That is one name that has not changed. In 1530 there is mention of the highway to Reigate running south past the Hogpit, which is now marked only by the path across Carshalton Park; and running to the west of the village was the Boggway, whose name would presumably speak for itself (the boggy way). 'The West Street' follows shortly afterwards in 1539. At the same time Green Wrythe Lane appears as Sheephouse Lane, because the canons of Merton Priory came down it to their sheep pens in Carshalton, and the land alongside the lane is owned by the priory itself. Lastly there are two mystery roads mentioned. One is Church Lane, obviously somewhere near the church, in 1645, and the other is the curious Twysilds Way, which ran somewhere to the south of Sutton, mentioned in 1488 and 1535.

By far the longest entry, running from 1530 to 1700, is for the area of land on either side of Carshalton Park Road where it joins Pound Street. On one side is the Greyhound, which appears throughout under the name Calcockshaw or Cockershall and seems to have consisted of a close or meadow with an orchard. On the other side was the old house called The Pulpits which was owned during the reign of Henry VIII by a family with the delightful name of Christmas. There was Father Christmas (called Thomas), Mother Christmas and two daughter Christmasses. Again the name The

Pulpits had no ecclesiastical connotation, but was purely pagan. In the seventeenth century it was Pupletts, and this was itself a corruption of Popletoes – the owner in 1500 had been Adam Popletoe.

It is a pity that we have lost not only so many of our fine old buildings, but also so many of our old street names. Even 100 years ago (on the first Ordnance Survey of Carshalton) there were some unusual names, for example Private Street, which is now William Street just behind Wrythe Green, and No Man's Land, now Boundary Corner. It is interesting to see that Honeywood Walk was not the modern Festival Walk, as one might suppose, but the piece of the High Street which runs from Ann Boleyn's Well to the Greyhound. This is interesting, because it explains how Honeywood House got its name: it took it from the nearby road. Honeywood House was of course in existence 100 years ago, but it was then known as Spring House or Stream House.

We have kept the names of the main roads of the old village: High Street, Pound Street, North Street and West Street, but we have lost most of the names of the roads radiating out of the village into the fields and farms of the surrounding countryside. These

Mill Lane prior to development.

were hardly roads: as their old names state, they were lanes (such as Acre Lane and Park Lane). But we have lost Crooked Lane, mentioned as far back as 1530. This was the old main road from the church to the Windsor Castle, which wandered round the side of the Park from Church Hill, round behind the Greyhound, to Park Hill. One can still find sections of the actual lane on Orchard Hill and at the top of Wallace Crescent. We can still walk along Dark Lane, but we call it Shorts Road. There used to be a Waterhouse Lane, between Pound Street and the beginning of West Street, but this has now been absorbed into West Street itself, although the name continues with Waterhouse Cottage, No. 2 West Street. We still have West Street Lane and Mill Lane – although the latter is an abbreviation of the original Paper Mill Lane (since it went past the eighteenth-century paper mill) and this road was at one time known as Pall Mall.

But where was Spartelmy Green Lane? In 1781 one of the local landowners, Mr George Shepley, sued the Parish Council for not keeping Spartelmy Green Lane in good repair. The parish contested this, and hired a lawyer to oppose it. But Mr Shepley won his case two years later, and the road had to be repaired. The Parish Council put 6d. on the rates to pay for it, which can't have been very popular – perhaps that's why the name was changed. But it would be interesting to know where Spartelmy Green Lane was and why it was so named – perhaps it was the present Strawberry Lane.

MEDIEVAL TIMES: ROAD PATTERNS & BUILDINGS

Carshalton has no detailed map before the middle of the eighteenth century. The earliest map of Carshalton (in Arundel Castle) of about 1620 is a very partial and uninformative one. There is no map of Carshalton in the Middle Ages, nor the necessary information to enable us to draw one. By about 1350, at the time of the Black Death, when the village would have been at its largest, we are just beginning to get the Manor Court Rolls, so we have a great many names of places and people – and no idea where to locate them.

We know that medieval Carshalton was a much wetter place: in fact there were so many streams criss-crossing it that it was virtually a series of islands. There were three streams running from the Downs down to the village to feed into the River Wandle. One of them still exists in the form of the canal in Carshalton Place/Westcroft Canal; there was another down the west side of the Square; and there was a third one down Banstead Road and west of Cambridge Road and Shorts Road. Besides the stream along the High Street, and of course the river itself from the Ponds, there was also a stream which ran from the Carshalton House lake along Festival

Walk, which then ran across the Ecology Centre to Stone Court. Another stream, which in fact came from Sutton, ran across Wrythe Green and went into the river at Hackbridge. This was splendid country for water mills, and it is perhaps surprising that in 1350 there only seem to have been three of them: at Stone Court (the mill in the Grove), at Butter Hill Bridge, and at Hackbridge on the Bacons estate, better known later as Shepley House.

With so many rivers and streams it is a wonder there was any room for roads, but we know that medieval Carshalton had something of the same criss-cross pattern. The most important road was North Street, coming down from Merton across Wrythe Green, crossing the Ponds by a causeway to the church, and then continuing up the Square and across what is now the Park to Reigate. There was another very old road to the east of Cambridge Road, running up Shorts Road (Dark Lane) and then curving round by the football ground to cross Wrythe Lane before running east along Nightingale Road to the Hack Bridge.

But the village itself basically ran along two other east–west roads: indeed it was a double village, really two almost geographically separate villages. One road, which became known as the Horse Road because it was on flat ground and could take carts, ran from the mill at Stone Court along West Street Lane to a crossroads. It crossed West Street, which we know was there by 1300, and then carried on to Westmead Corner and so along the Lower Road to Sutton.

The other road, and the other Carshalton, ran from Westcroft Road along the High Street to a crossroads in the Square, and then along the south side of the church, zig-zagging its way towards the Windsor Castle and Sutton. No doubt you could ride it, but it was much more hilly, and was known as the foot road or Crooked Lane. The word 'lane' is a good indication of an extremely old road.

So there were two groups, two lines of houses, one in the West Street Lane area and one either side of the church. There are undoubtedly medieval sites both east and west of the church: both Queen's Well and The Pulpits were medieval in origin; but the only houses now existing which may have actually seen the Middle Ages are the Wine Bar and the Cottage in the churchyard (4 and 6 High Street).

In the other direction North Lodge appears to be medieval; and West Lodge in West Street Lane is on a medieval site – there are others at Nelson House and The Racehorse. We also know that there was a substantial house called Kinnersley's (Kenwardesleys) by 1350, which later became known as the Old Farm, then Carshalton House (and now St Philomena's), and which acted as a kind of manor house for West Carshalton. The corresponding manor house for East Carshalton was called Stone Court, but we do not know where the medieval Stone Court was, although one would guess it was on a kind of island before the 1500s – in effect a moated site – to the west of the present Leoni Bridge. The only absolutely authentic medieval building in Carshalton still standing where it undoubtedly was in 1350 is the southern part of the Parish Church. This contains the Lady Chapel, which was the original medieval chancel, and what remains of the nave, arcade and south aisle left after the Victorian rebuilding of the church.

In considering the layout of medieval Carshalton one might be allowed to ask the question of why the church is where it is. Generally speaking, the sites of most medieval churches had been chosen during the Anglo-Saxon period by one of two methods, or some-times a combination of both. Christianity was spread throughout England during the seventh and eighth centuries by the minster system, by which groups of priests gathered in regional centres, usually monas-teries, and went out from there as missionaries to the surrounding villages and hamlets to preach, to bap-tise, to help the sick and so on. It became customary for the place where the minster priest would regular-ly visit to be marked with a cross. The Downs were probably covered with a network of stone crosses – such as can still be seen in places like Dartmoor or the North Yorkshire moors – and there are still reports in the eighteenth and nineteenth centuries of local farm-ers getting rid of crosses up on the Downs. But of course they were also in the villages, and there is thought to have been one behind the wine bar where Crooked Lane came out into the Square. It is marked on the 1783 estate map as 'the obelisk', and the base of it was excavated in the 1980s. It was the place to which the priest came from the nearest minster, which was on the royal estate in Wallington. It has been sug-gested that the name Carshalton was originally Cross Alton – and although it is not easy to be persuaded of that, Carshalton almost certainly had a cross.

If you are going to build a church, then a cross site was a suitably holy place to choose. But there were other considerations. Churches had to be on raised ground to keep them out of the water (nothing is more damaging to a church fabric than damp); on the other hand one needed water nearby, if only for ritu-al purposes like baptism. The present church site is of course on raised ground, but with a stream on one side by the wine bar, and a holy well on the other side. And that was another factor. Following the famous instructions given by Pope Gregory I to Augustine in 602, the missionaries were ordered to have a deliberate policy of choosing pagan temples and shrines to convert into churches. We don't know a great deal about pagan sites because they have all been destroyed, but the experts tell us that they were usually marked by one of three natural features: a big rock, a grove of trees, or a stream or spring. Holy wells were used not only for therapeutic purposes, and for ritual cleansing, but there was also

divination, a belief that running water can be used to foretell the future – an idea of which the use of tea-leaves to tell your fortune is a remnant.

So it seems that we had a very early church in Carshalton. It would have been built like most early Anglo-Saxon churches of wood – the word 'timber' comes from the Anglo-Saxon word to build/building – and it would probably have been in a sort of enclosure or earthwork between the wine bar and Church Hill as a protective measure. When the so-called 'Great Rebuilding' of Anglo-Saxon churches (turning them from wooden buildings to stone structures) began in the eleventh century, one very common feature was to give them towers, places of refuge (as one still finds in Ireland today). And as refuges, they were equipped with alarm signals; they were given bells. It comes as some surprise to learn that the word 'belfry' does not come from bells, the place where you hung bells, but is in fact the other way round: the word 'bell' comes from belfry, and a belfry was a combination of two Saxon words (bergen and frithus) meaning security and peace, in other words a belfry was a secure place, like a tower.

At the time of the Norman Conquest in 1066 we probably had a little stone church with a tower at the back behind a combined nave and chancel – the subsequent Lady Chapel. After the Conquest the church was witness to successive waves of expan-sion: a nave was tacked onto the other side of the tower; aisles or 'wings' were added onto that; a cer-emonial door was put into the south side leading out onto the main road, Crooked Lane; and so on. But none of this provides us with much of a clue as to where the manor house was: church and manor house developed independently.

The alternative method of choosing where to put a church, which became commonplace from the eighth and ninth centuries onwards, was to put it as close as possible to the manor house. Thousands of churches are virtually next door to the manor house, so that they could be used as chapels by the lord and his family. They were called 'proprietary churches': the lord owned the land and the building – he could even sell them – and he appointed or dismissed the priest. These proprietary churches might remain quite small, because serving the needs of the parish was in a sense a secondary consideration. On the other hand lay lords often wanted to expand their churches for reasons of prestige or piety so that by 1350 the two types of church were probably indistin-guishable in appearance, and only their location gives a clue to their foundation. Of course Beddington is a very good example of a proprietary church, a church which nestles up against the manor house almost like a private chapel. But this only leads to the suggestion that Carshalton is a much older church than Beddington, a minster church which survived even though its mother church in Wallington has totally disappeared.

Far left: *The Public Hall with its Pre-Raphaelite Gothic windows, taken from a Tatton Winter painting, late-nineteenth century.*

Left: *Water on the south side of the High Street flowing out from Carshalton Park, opposite the bystander. Note the two-directional flow.* (S.L.S.L.)

Below: *View of High Street looking west in 1886, taken from a Tatton Winter painting.* (S.L.S.L.)

Below: *View of High Street looking east in 1890 showing the Fox and Hounds. This is taken from a Tatton Winter painting.* (S.L.S.L.)

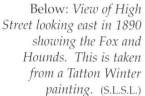

Chapter Two

ROADS & BUILDINGS

CARSHALTON HIGH STREET (NORTH SIDE) SINCE 1600

The medieval village of Carshalton was clustered around the east end of the church, the bottom of the Square, and entrance to the Park. But the north side of the High Street was all part of the manor of Stone Court, and consisted largely of a series of meadows stretching from the Ponds right across to Butter Hill. Parts of the manor had been sold off by 1600, and the High Street frontage was just beginning to be used: but there still wasn't very much to be seen. There was a house on the corner by the Ponds but, moving eastwards, the next house was on the site of the last shop before the present car park, which might be the original of Haydon's butchers shop. There were probably some cottages behind this, but they aren't marked on the 1620 map of Carshalton. Then came the fair ground, where the charter fair would have taken place: and part of this still survives in the form of the open space in front of the Park Lane Pharmacy. Then the map shows nothing but fields all the way to Westcroft Road and the Wallington boundary, except for a big house roughly on the site of the present shopping precinct, Beacon Grove.

Life for local historians would be much simpler if one could just say that this large house was the house belonging to the Hammond family, because the Hammonds are extensively documented between the 1650s and the 1750s. Best known amongst them was the immensely rich Sir William Hammond (1664–1741), who was a 'Turkey Merchant'. This does not mean that he was like the gentleman in Norfolk who produced 'bootiful' birds for Christmas dinners – but that he was a clothier, a member of the Drapers Company, which traded cloth and silk with the Levant, in Constantinople, Syria and North Africa. He was doing very nicely until, like his friend Sir John Fellowes of Carshalton House, he became a director of the South Sea Company, and was nearly ruined when the bubble burst. We have a room-by-room description of the three-storey house in Carshalton which he was forced to sell in 1722 to repay his debts, but it omits to say exactly where the

house was. We do know that the family owned Westcroft, and they went on living in Carshalton, and being buried in the churchyard. In 1741 Sir William stipulated: 'my body be buried in the most private manner, no person to be invited to my funeral... except my three sons' – and the last Carshalton burial seems to have been that of his grandson Cordwell, who was buried in 1760 after being drowned. All we can say for certain is that the area from the Pharmacy to the Fox and Hounds was called Hammond's Orchard, and this name went on being used well into the nineteenth century – and that there was still a substantial house here in the 1780s. In 1789 James Edwards describes:

A good brick house with gardens on the east (side), enclosed against the street with a high wall, (which) belongs to Mr Wallace the surgeon (who lived in Pound Street), but is occupied by Mr Morphew, who keeps a boarding school here for young gentlemen.

This suggests that the old house had been converted into a school for boys.

Half a century later, in the 1830s, the house became a rectory, and Hammond's Orchard is now The Glebe, the land being used to provide a living for a parish priest. The Reverend William Vernon certainly lived there between 1835 and 1845. There is one picture of it, again three stories with dormer windows, which could be a seventeeth-century building, now with iron railings along the front of it. It may well have been the old house. In any event, in the mid-1880s the rector, Lord Victor Seymour, declared that it was falling down, was inhabited only by rats, and he wasn't going to live in it. So in 1886 a new rectory was built, which apparently kept a piece of the south front of the old house, a staircase dated c.1700, and the old cellars. This building lasted right up to the 1960s when it was demolished to form the shopping precinct. The rebuilding was paid for in the usual fashion by leasing off part of the estate. The architect, a man called Crutchloe, built three houses along the High Street frontage to the east. The first, No. 33, he built for himself, and put the old rectory railings round it. This too has vanished under the

Above: *Parkfields, Westcroft Road, in the early-twentieth century.* (S.L.S.L.)

Top right: *Parkfields, Westcroft Road, showing detail of the front.* (S.L.S.L.)

Right: *Rear of Parkfields, Westcroft Road.* (S.L.S.L.)

Below: *At the end of High Street showing the junction with Westcroft Road (left), Acre Lane (centre) and Park Lane (to the right). The gateway is the entrance to Bramble Haw.* (S.L.S.L.)

precinct – but we still have No. 35 (Dr Peatling's house).

Then comes the Public Hall. By the 1870s there was a great public demand for a community centre of some kind – and this being the nineteenth century, self-help was the order of the day. The rector (Reverend W.A.B. Cator) donated that piece of the Glebe/Hammond's Orchard next to the Fox and Hounds, a public subscription was opened and a Public Hall Company formed at a meeting of local residents in 1872. The foundation stone was laid in June 1874 and the present building duly appeared. But it looked rather different because it did not have the present front extension: it looked much more like the old Sutton Public Hall, with pointed brick arches and 'Pre-Raphaelite Gothic' windows. It did not have the Small Hall alongside it: this was built in 1885 for local council (at that time Board) offices, and was the home of the Urban District Council until the beginning of the twentieth century, when new offices – now Carshalton Library – were built (1908). The Small Hall was now incorporated into the main building, and a wall constructed round the back of the site – which still bears the rather enigmatic statement carved on a stone, which reads: 'This wall belongs to these premises, 1893.'

At first the hall was used mainly for meetings and lectures, and in the later 1870s there was a small bank there as well. In the Edwardian period it became a roller-skating rink; then from 1912 to 1931 a cinema, called the Picture Palace, then the Palace Theatre. It was acquired by the local authority, and after the war it was reconstructed and re-opened for public use in 1949. (The Public Hall became the Charles Cryer Theatre in October 1991.)

WESTCROFT

One can hardly go further east in the old parish than Westcroft Road, part of which is in fact in Wallington. Westcroft means the west farm, and we are still fortunate enough to possess the old Westcroft farmhouse to prove it. But why West-croft? West of what? There must have been a point of reference somewhere in Wallington, although a medieval use of the name Westcroft has not been discovered.

A possibility is provided by the oldest map of Carshalton, the mid-seventeenth-century map now in Arundel Castle (because the Howard family had estates here in the seventeenth century). This map shows that adjacent to Westcroft Farm on the east – across the road now called Butter Hill – there was an estate with a large house clearly marked as 'The Berrie'. The map shows a small drawing of a typical two-storey Tudor manor house, with three large gable ends facing outwards along the front. We know that it was built of red brick and demolished in 1792. We know this because two Carshalton men,

Thomas Smith and Thomas Prior, aged 44 and 37 respectively, were buried in Carshalton churchyard, having been crushed by a ceiling falling in on them when knocking the house down. One should not demolish old Tudor houses.

In 1787 the house had been bought by Mr Francis Gregg, a solicitor and Clerk of the Skinners' Company, who became MP for Morpeth. He was a fanatical house builder and his new house was called Elm Grove House. This too has vanished, but you can still see the pond in the garden at the end of Manor Road North.

The last real owner of the Berrie was Mr Thomas Potts. He too is buried in Carshalton churchyard, because, after selling the house to Mr Gregg, he moved across the parish boundary and took a lease of Bramble Haw, the big stone house which had been recently built at the corner of Westcroft Road and Acre Lane. This was built with the stones originally intended for the new Carshalton Park House, which Thomas Scawen was supposed to build but never did. When the Scawens sold off their Carshalton estates during the early 1780s causing the biggest property upheaval that Carshalton has ever known, Bramble Haw passed into the ownership of the Beynon family. The Beynons now possessed most of the Westcroft area: as well as Bramble Haw, their main house was Parkfields (now 37 Westcroft Road), and they also owned Westcroft Farm. But there was one part of the Westcroft area which the Beynons never got, and this, curiously enough, was the house which bears the name, the house called Westcroft opposite Bramble Haw where Westcroft Road joins the High Street. It is still there.

The earliest use of the name Westcroft so far discovered is in 1766, when it is listed as one of the properties owned by Thomas Scawen. One is never quite sure with these early references to Westcroft whether the farm or the house is meant, but in this case the reference is probably to the house. It certainly dates back to the early-eighteenth century, but was much smaller originally than it is now. The old part is the front part at the west end, which was of timber frame and plaster construction. During the eighteenth century, when the Scawens owned it, it seems to have been leased to the Hammond family, whose own house was the other side of the Fox and Hounds. And when the Scawen estates were broken up in the 1780s, instead of being sold off with the Grove, as one might have expected, it remained with the Carshalton Park section of the estate, and so was acquired by the Taylor family who owned the Park throughout the nineteenth century. The Taylors did not use it themselves, but leased it out to other gentlemen.

The first actual occupant that we have been able to identify was a Mr Robert Burra. Robert Burra first appears in the Rate Books as the tenant of Bramble Haw in 1812 – he is called Burrows, and it took the

Left: *Bramble Haw mansion, demolished in 1927.*

Above: *Bramble Haw, south side.* (Both S.L.S.L.)

Westcroft Farmhouse. (S.L.S.L.)

Westcroft in October 1967 as the Youth Employment Office.

Westcroft showing the Victorian extensions. (S.L.S.L.)

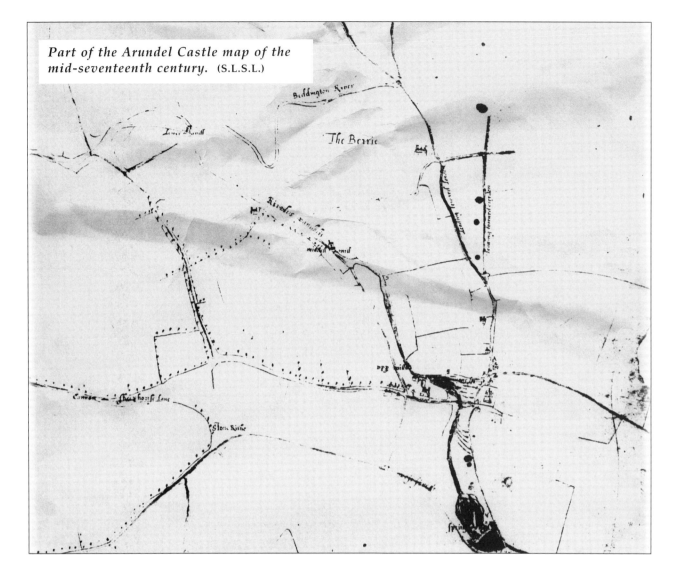

Part of the Arundel Castle map of the mid-seventeenth century. (S.L.S.L.)

rate collector a year to learn how to spell the name. He seems to have lived in Bramble Haw until the 1830s, but he then crossed the road to live in Westcroft, and left Bramble Haw to James Burra, whom we take to be his son.

Early in the twentieth century an old lady recorded how, when she was a girl, she used to walk home from church on Sundays along the High Street, and she always tried to walk behind the two gentlemen from Westcroft Road, Mr Burra from Bramble Haw and Mr Beynon from Parkfields, who used to walk along together. The reason for this small girl's fascination with the back view of the Westcroft gentry was that James Burra used to go to church wearing a wig with a long pigtail down his back, whilst Mr Beynon was even more splendid – he wore a swallow-tailed coat, and a wig with two pigtails.

We lose track of the Burras by about 1850, and the main item of interest about Westcroft during the nineteenth century is that it was made into a substantially larger building, by the addition of a large east wing with two projecting arms, and was at last incorporated into the Grove. When he married, the rector, the Reverend W.A.B. Cator, refused to go on living in the rectory, and moved instead into the Grove in 1856. He eventually bought both the Grove and Stone Court in 1872, and then five years later (1877) he bought Westcroft as well – although a Mr Page was the actual occupant during the remainder of the century.

There was a curious situation early in the 1900s, when a Miss Bentley was in residence, and allowed her gardener, Mr Goodwright, to live in part of the house – and he seems to have wrought so well that he eventually took over the whole house by 1910. Between the wars it was the home of a Mrs E. Malcolm-Wood but it had already been purchased by Carshalton UDC either in or just before 1923 when the Council bought the Grove. And so it has now become the property of the London Borough of Sutton.

So this house, Westcroft, has a history – not perhaps very exciting – but nevertheless extending back over at least two and a half centuries. It is a Grade-I listed building, and we were very glad that it should be included in the group of Westcroft Road buildings which form part of the village Conservation Area.

NORTH LODGE

Was this property called North Lodge simply because it is in North Street? Or was it once the northern lodge to a larger estate? If so, the estate was that known as Beechwood, a big house on the corner of West Street Lane and North Street. This is a possibility, because in the back garden of North Lodge the garden wall has the marks of an old archway in it, which shows that it once led through to the land on the other side, and there is a pillar which records that 'this wall... is built on the Beechwood estate'. So it could have once been attached to Beechwood, but they have always been separate properties as far as is known. It almost certainly was not attached to the Byne property, Bornhem House, on its north side, because there is a very thick old wall between them, of which one can see a section in North Street.

The owners were traced back to 1821, when the property was held by Philip Jones, whose occupation was given as tax collector in 1838. He appears to have died soon afterwards because in the Tithe records of 1847 the occupant was his widow, Mrs Philip Jones; and the next generation, Thomas Jones, coal merchant, claimed in 1870 that his business had been established since 1847 (presumably when his father died). But the buildings are more illuminating than their owners.

The most recent building appears to be the stable at the rear of the courtyard. It is not shown on the 1847 Tithe Map, and so was apparently built after 1850. The house itself is in three parts, of which the most recent is the cottage on the left of the archway: with its slate roof it might be late-eighteenth/early-nineteenth century. The archway or coach entrance looks like part of the original building, but is probably a later insertion, because traces of weather-boarding can be seen on the right-hand side of the archway passage, suggesting that it was once the exterior wall of the original north house. The main house might well be the oldest secular house in Carshalton. It is a timber-frame building, with massive beams running up all three storeys and meeting at the pitch (like a cruck house), with the top floor built right up to the pitch of the roof. At the back, in what was presumably once a wash-house but is now the kitchen, there are traces of flint and chalk block walling, remains of a copper and a bread oven, and in 1985 a well, with water still in it, was found in the floor. There seems to have been a pump installed above it.

Nobody knows how old all this is. The official 'listing' simply says seventeenth century or earlier. Dr Peatling gives a date of about 1550–80, but there is no evidence for this. It seems highly likely (besides the Parish Church and the wine bar) that this is one of the few medieval buildings left in Carshalton. We must remember that North Street and West Street Lane are two of the oldest roads in Carshalton. West Street Lane is the beginning of the old road leading to Sutton in one direction, and it led to the Town Mill at Stone Court on the other side (Mill Lane now). North Street was the road down which the Augustinian canons came to their church at Carshalton and their sheep-houses and sheep-runs up on the Downs behind. We remember that two of Carshalton's manor houses, Stone Court and what became known as Long's House, were built on to North Street – this was the old centre of the medieval village before the High Street was developed, and North Lodge was right at the middle of it. W.G. Hoskins, in many ways the founding father of English local history, had a sort of motto or maxim: 'Everything is older than you think.' This is probably a case in point.

North Lodge, North Street, October 1967.

North Lodge showing the north side, October 1967.

THE SAVING OF WOODCOTE HOUSE

From 1965–75 the Carshalton Society fought and finally won an ongoing battle to save Woodcote House (or Bedford Cottage as it used to be called) from demolition. There was a very strong local tradition that it had once been a toll-house at Rosehill. It had somehow been moved down Wrythe Lane to Wrythe Green – although the owner at the time of writing strenuously denied anything of the sort, because he wanted to demolish it. After about five years of sporadic research – with some help from the GLC – we reached the point where we could say definitely that:

1. There was a toll-house at Rosehill in the first half of the nineteenth century. The Sutton–Tooting road was a turnpike from 1718 onwards (and Woodcote House had a weathervane dated 1758). It is thought that it is shown on the 1816 Ordnance Survey, just round the corner from Wrythe Lane on the road towards Sutton.

Woodcote House at Wrythe Green, showing the weathervane given to the Victoria and Albert Museum by a previous owner.
(S.L.S.L.)

2. That it was not a Sutton toll-house, because the Sutton toll-houses were operated by the Croydon and Reigate Turnpike Trust, whereas Rosehill toll-house belonged to the Surrey and Sussex Trust. So Rosehill was the boundary between the two turnpikes.

3. That if the toll-house was sold off and carted away to Wrythe Green, then this must have happened about 1866. We know that Woodcote House first appeared at Wrythe Green at about this time, and that the person who moved it must have been the rich, eccentric land speculator, Jonah Cressingham, who lived at Stone Court. He owned both the Rosehill and Wrythe Green sites and so could have moved the toll-house from one piece of his land to another.

What is not certain is whether or not he did this. How to prove that Woodcote House was once the Rosehill toll-house? We were stuck until Michael Coleman got to work. He found out not only that Woodcote House had originally been all one house (which is what we thought, but it had been the source of much argument), but that it had also originally been much smaller: most of the back parts, the wings of the building, are of later date. But the really exciting discovery came when it was stripped down to the timber frame, and it was discovered that the roof timbers fitted on to the top of the timbers of the ground floor. In other words, at some point (presumably during the reconstruction at Wrythe Green), the roof had been taken off, the whole of the upper storey, an extra floor, had been inserted, and the roof put back on top of that. And then the whole building had been sheathed in a herringbone weatherboarding (which seems to have been an 1860s speciality) so that the join was covered up.

So the original Woodcote House was a much narrower, flatter, one-storey building – much more like the usual pattern of toll-houses – and if we wanted to find another similar building this was the sort of thing to look for. And knowing now what to look for, Michael Coleman found an almost identical building – the same half-octagonal bay, the diamond-pane windows, slate roof and weatherboarding (but horizontal weatherboarding, of course): a complete one-storey Woodcote House – south of Purley on the Godstone Road (the A22). This was just the place where one would expect to find it, because this piece of road was also a turnpike administered by the same turnpike trust, the Surrey and Sussex, which owned the road at Rosehill. Now that we know what to look for, perhaps others are still surviving elsewhere.

Well, of course, it is one thing to stop demolition of an historic building: it is another thing to get it repaired. By the grace of enormous good fortune two of our most public-spirited members, Michael and Susan Coleman, decided to have a go. They bought the house, obtained grants, and did the work between 1975–77 and one can now go up to Wrythe Green and see what a splendid job they made of it.

ALTON LODGE & COLSTONFIELDS

West Street is well worth a visit at any time. It has the largest concentration of listed buildings in Carshalton: there are no less than nine of them (as well as a further eight, which are specified as being architecturally interesting). This is in fact the oldest road in Carshalton after the High Street, and there are a number of references to 'the west street' during the seventeenth century. The title of the oldest house in West Street belongs to number 70, better known as Alton Lodge, which is to the left of the entrance to Carshalton Laundry. (Sycamore Close flats now occupy the site of the former laundry.) This goes back to the Jacobean period, i.e. the early 1600s, but we don't know much about it until a century later when it was owned by a wealthy gentleman named Richard Garrard who lived there with his only daughter Mary.

It so happened that the rector of Carshalton was one of their neighbours. In 1738 the Reverend Edmund Lodge bought a house in West Street from the Parkhurst family of Epsom, and, since he came from Bristol, he renamed the house Colstonfields after the district of that name in Bristol. The house was later numbered 44 West Street, but it no longer exists, although the name is preserved in the Colstonfields ditch on the opposite side of the road, which runs along the footpath by the convent wall. But from Mary Garrard's point of view, the most interesting thing about the Reverend Edmund Lodge was not that he was a near neighbour, but that he was unmarried. No doubt in spite of fierce opposition from all the spinsters of Carshalton, she succeeded in marrying the rector, and moved along the road to live at Colstonfields. But her father does not seem to have relished being left alone in Alton Lodge and died soon after the wedding.

Alton Lodge now passed to Mary and, since a wife's property became her husband's, in effect it went to the Reverend Lodge. With two substantial houses in West Street he was now a wealthy man by local standards. But he did not stay long. In 1759 he was appointed Archdeacon, gave up his rectorship and left Carshalton. But the property remained in the hands of the Lodge family: there was a son and a daughter, another Edmund and Mary, neither of whom married, but who lived together to a ripe old age. When Edmund died in 1839 aged 85 he was the oldest member of the Society of Antiquaries. He was a noted historian, who published several books on historical subjects, and his wealth enabled him to buy a position as one of the Heralds of the College of Arms. He must therefore have officiated at the Coronation of George IV, William IV and Queen Victoria, and he had to be consulted by newly-created peers about their coats of arms. Amongst these was Admiral Lord Nelson, and it was probably to commemorate Nelson's visits to West Street to see Edmund Lodge that number 19 West Street was called Nelson House. There is a story that Lady Hamilton lived in number 19 and that Nelson really came to West Street to see her – but this is probably just a local legend. Of the two Lodge houses, Colstonfields and Alton Lodge, we lost Colstonfields when it was demolished in 1948. The site has remained vacant ever since, and is used as a car park for the Hope public house – a sad end to a fine building. Alton Lodge was threatened but fortunately has survived.

Alton Lodge, West Street, in 1967 showing the entrance to the former Carshalton Laundry.

Colstonfields was in the gap between the Hope public house (left) and London House. See also p.119.

SOME ROAD NAMES & BEATING THE BOUNDS

Most people simply have no idea of how much local history can be learnt merely by standing in a road and looking at it. Why does it go where it does? Why does it run between this point and that point? Why does it turn here, bend there, stop at this or that spot? Of course the great danger of road widening and straightening is that it destroys this sort of unobtrusive but vital historical evidence.

Now we tend to think of roads as being something like rivers: they go on flowing along fairly straight until they meet an obstacle and have to bend round it, so that they become bent and winding. Old roads, we say blithely, are twisting roads. Wasn't it Hillaire Belloc who said something about the rolling English drunkard who made the rolling English road?

That may be true for Sussex, but on the whole Surrey people had quite enough walking to do as it was, and they really preferred to go in straight lines – a straight road is shorter and quicker. If there is a distinct bend in a local road it may be there to avoid an obstacle, but it's much more likely to be due to a relatively modern road 'improvement'. Most of our very bad local road junctions are the result of the old route being altered to divert it along a new line – and when this happens, the old road often gets lost after a time. So that in Carshalton we have a whole network of lost roads: the more you look, the more you can find. You can often pick them out on a modern map, noticing how two quite separate roads often line up with each other, to suggest that in the gap between them there is a lost road. Let us examine four of our lost Carshalton roads:

Old North Street As Mr Jones says in his history, North Street is one of the oldest roads in Carshalton – but this is only true up to a point, and that point is the Catholic Church. It used to run straight on, across what is now Carshalton College of Further Education, to meet Nightingale Road/'Hagbridgewaye' about 50 yards east of the present junction with Wrythe Green Road. There was probably a straight crossroads with Green Wrythe Lane/'Canons Sheephouse Lane' – and it was only when the parish poorhouse (Leicester House) was built on Wrythe Green that Green Wrythe Lane was moved westwards across the Green itself to the other side of the poorhouse. But the Wrythe Green parade of shops and the garage on the corner are built on what was originally the Green. This is why North Street is called New Road on the 1868 Ordnance Survey – because the present road is no longer in its original position. We don't know when the change was made, but it was probably about 1790 and this at the hands of a Mr Shepley of Shepley House.

West Street Lane Almost certainly this road ran to the manor house of Stone Court, which we know was in the middle of the lawn in front of the present Stone Court building, and to the corn mill by the present millwheel. It therefore ran in to this estate through what is now the gateway on the corner of Stone Court – so that the road was on the other side of our Stone Court House, and there was no Mill Lane behind the house, as is the case now. We know that Mill Lane was moved: Mr Jones' book quotes a deed of 1717 to this effect. But he suggests that Mill Lane/'Pall Mall' originally came out further north up North Street. On the contrary it would now seem that it ran south of its present line – although the change probably took place long before 1717.

If we follow the line of West Street Lane across West Street and the grounds of Carshalton House, it runs directly into the Lower Road from Sutton at Westmead corner. In other words there was a crossroads in West Street (which can just be detected on the Arundel map of c.1620). This is probably the road through 'Hillclose' stopped up by Dixey Long in 1656 – and instead we now have the Colstonfields footpath from West Street to Shorts Road. We know that West Street itself originally ran on the other side of the lake in the grounds of Carshalton House to come out at the Windsor Castle. That corner in West Street once bent the other way.

There is the continuation of **Banstead Road** which came out directly opposite Shorts Road/'Dark Lane' – another crossroads over the present Carshalton Road – and when Shorts Road reached Westmead Corner it didn't stop there as it does now, but went straight on, yet another crossroad. We can trace it through the curve of Colston Avenue, across the football ground, to the footpath by Carshalton High School for Girls, and so out to Wrythe Green at the bottom of Wrythe Lane. You can just see this crossroads on the Rocque Map of the 1760s.

When **Carshalton Road** (from Sutton to Carshalton) got to the Windsor Castle, it did go straight on. We can then trace its path along the wall of Carshalton Park (the wall at Wallace Crescent), round the south and east of Wallace Crescent, slanting down across Carshalton Park Road, through the gardens of the houses on Orchard Hill, to the top of Church Hill. This was Crooked Lane, which was closed down in 1826 when the present High Street past the Ponds was built. Before this the road had run on the south side of the church, so that the cottage in the churchyard was on the High Street, past the village cross at the east end of the church, and out into the Square by the lane beside the present Library. Where else would one expect a high street to run but into the Square, which was also the crossroads for the road which ran across Carshalton Park, the hollow-street, before the park was made.

North Street, Carshalton.

Top: *North Street looking north, early-twentieth century.*

Above: *Carshalton Road from the top of the hill, looking east, c.1900.*

Left: *West Street Lane c.1885, from a Tatton Winter painting.*

(S.L.S.L.)

The Hack Bridge in the early-twentieth century and (inset) *in 1981.*

Boundary Stones

In 1792 the Parish Council ordered a set of boundary stones to be erected all round the edges of the parish. As far as is known, only one of these original stones survives. You can see it mounted on a wall at the Wallington end of Westcroft Road, on the right-hand side, marked C.P. (Carshalton Parish) 1792. These square-topped stones seem to have lasted about a century. In the 1890s the Carshalton Urban District Council erected a new set of stones, with rounded tops. These were placed at various places round the boundaries of the urban district – along Woodmansterne Road, at the top of Wrythe Lane, and around Love Lane and Green Lane, and by the river at Beddington Corner – but there must have been many more in other places.

Carshalton parish boundary stone at the end of Westcroft Road dated 1792.

Carshalton Urban District Council boundary marker dated 1898.

Beating the Bounds

Until maps became common during the nineteenth century the only way to make sure that the villagers knew where the parish boundaries were was to make a perambulation of the parish borders, a beating of the bounds. And to make sure that the young were sufficiently impressed with the memory of where the boundaries were, one of the boys of the parish was traditionally beaten at each important landmark. This was a very old custom going back to medieval times, when it was associated with the religious procession into the fields at Rogationtide to pray for good crops. It was therefore usual to make the parish perambulation before Ascension Day, not annually, but every few years. Since the expenses could be charged to the parish, it was laid down by law that it could not take place more frequently than one year in three.

Carshalton churchwardens' accounts record a perambulation which was made in the middle of May 1833 – an important social event for all classes in the village. There was the new young squire, John Taylor, who had inherited Carshalton Park the previous year and the rector, the Reverend Charles Cator, with the churchwardens, including Benjamin Brightling (the father or grandfather of the Carshalton historian). There were the parish officers, the overseers of the poor who looked after the workhouse and the parish charities, the surveyors of the highways, and various farmers, tradespeople and labourers. There was also a crowd of small boys – but apparently no ladies.

Above: *Catsbrain Shot, March 1917, looking north-east.* (S.L.S.L.)

Above: *Culvers estate, 1920s.* (S.L.S.L.)

Above right: *All Saints Rogation procession in Wrythe Lane, 1919.* (S.L.S.L.)

Right: *Catsbrain Shot, showing Boundary Road, March 1917.* (S.L.S.L.)

All participants assembled after breakfast on the boundary by Wallington Green, and then set off, walking round Irongate Field to the famous gates of Carshalton Park, then up Park Lane, past Woodcote, until they reached the southern edge of the parish not far from Woodmansterne Church. At each boundary stone one of the party was ceremoniously bumped on it – not just the small boys: everybody had to take a turn at being bumped, even the rector and the lord of the manor. Of course this caused a great deal of merriment, and was no doubt a very salutory experience for local worthies: perhaps we should revive the custom.

In 1833 there were virtually no houses in the southern part of the parish. Instead there were the great open fields which had existed from medieval times – like the Southfield or the Westmead, the west meadow – the common fields were still divided up into narrow strips for cultivation, although an increasing amount was becoming enclosed land. Each part had its own name, and very curious and romantic names some of them were. Our perambulation party has already walked by Catsbrain Shot, Trotting Way, Maple Piece, Mulberry Plain, and is now on Cotton Downs. There was also the less attractively named field called Snailes Pit. From here the group turned north again up Woodmansterne Road, by Willowy Downs and Maidens Grove to Beech Furlong, round the edge of the Oaks Park (which was not then part of Carshalton) and up the old racecourse, the Long Gallop, to Carshalton Downs, at the end of what is now Banstead Road South. Here lunch was taken by the roadside at 11 o'clock. The churchwardens, in true Biblical fashion, brought baskets full of bread rolls. The local grocer, Benjamin Marfleet, who lived at Honeywood, sent 12lb of Double Gloucester cheese; and the Greyhound and the Kings Arms provided 24 gallons of beer to wash it down.

The party, no doubt greatly refreshed, now faced the long afternoon of tramping beside the Sutton border, along the Ridgeway, past Westmead, through the fields named the Averys, right up to Rose Hill, until they were nearly at Morden. Then east along the turnpike road to within sight of Mitcham Church, and then down to the river at a place called Bennett's Hole, where the three parishes of Morden, Mitcham and Carshalton met at a point marked by three boundary stones. From here the boundary usually ran down the middle of the River Wandle, and here the fun became fast and furious because it was necessary to wade into the middle of the river – and those who wouldn't go in voluntarily were thrown in. Nets were cast into the water and pulled in to the Carshalton bank to symbolise the claiming of the villagers' fishing rights. And so they made their way. They passed the numerous watermills and the great fields full of bleaching linen on the Culvers estate – Cookson's Meadow, Skinning Mill Mead,

Rushymeadow and Mount Pleasant – past the Hack Bridge and the West Croft, until a very tired but happy party once more reached Wallington Green and dispersed.

But that was not the end of the day, at least not for the more senior members. That evening at 6 o'clock 15 people went to dinner at the Kings Arms and another 15 at the Greyhound, and dined at the parish's expense. We still have the bill: the total cost was £18, although the parson and the squire contributed five guineas each, so that the parish would not be too heavily in debt. This may not sound very much but it was a good deal in those days, and it is interesting to compare this with the menu for a similar perambulation a quarter of a century earlier in March 1806. This only cost £8 – but that was 30 times the cost of the lunch which was a mere five shillings. Half of the £8 went on drink: wine, sherry, brandy and punch, not to mention beer; another £2 was spent on meat: beef and lamb; and the rest on various sundries – puddings, 'sallad', cheese, biscuits and tobacco. So we can be sure that they did themselves well: and I expect they thought they had earned it. If anybody would like to try it nowadays, the distance is about 14 miles.

WRYTHE GREEN

The Wrythe used to be very much bigger than the present Green and stretched a quarter of a mile further up Green Wrythe Lane. There have been two explanations for the name Wrythe. It often used to be called Carshalton Rye, and since rye was grown in this area, and the Wrythe is close to the part where the common fields were situated, it may refer to fields of rye. But there is another possible derivation, which seems the more likely one, and would make the Wrythe another of the oldest places in Carshalton. There is an Anglo-Saxon word rithe meaning a small running stream. A stream is the sort of place to find gravel, and we know that there was gravel being dug from the Wrythe in the first half of the nineteenth century – the gravel pits were on the west side of Green Wrythe Lane. But gravel was certainly being dug here long before this, and a document of 1591 speaks of the Wrythe as the 'Stony Rye'. So it looks as if the Wrythe is the gravel-bearing stream which the Anglo-Saxons found here.

A pond used to stand on the west side of the Wrythe, from which a stream ran down West Street, and then along a ditch at the foot of the wall at the back of the convent to Westmeads Farm. So there was a stream – and it was always overflowing and flooding the neighbourhood: which probably explains why houses weren't built on the Wrythe until quite a late date. At the beginning of the nineteenth century the only house on the Wrythe was the workhouse – later known as Leicester House or

THE BOOK OF CARSHALTON

The Wrythe in the 1930s.

House at the Wrythe on the corner of William Street and Green Wrythe Lane, c.1920. (S.L.S.L.)

Baines School – and that wasn't built until 1791–2. Half a century later we hear of 24 houses on the Wrythe, and a committee appointed in 1854 to examine the drains of Carshalton reported to the Parish Council that none of these houses could use their privies because they were all full of flood water from the springs. And in this unfortunate predicament the residents were having to use a ditch in front of their houses.

The Parish Council took vigorous action, and appointed another committee which reported ten years later in 1865 that the position at the Wrythe was as bad as ever. And the following year the parish had to resort to a rather quaintly named official, the Inspector of Nuisances, to ask him to see that the place was properly drained. Life was not always idyllic in rural Carshalton.

We have quoted Brightling's *History of Carshalton* to make the point that there were no houses at Wrythe Green in 1800, with the exception of the workhouse, presumably put there because it was a suitably remote and empty spot, appropriately segregated from the more respectable parts of the village. There is no very obvious way of checking Brightling's statement about the absence of houses. Our earliest detailed map of the area dates from the 1830s. Although the rate books can take us back another century to the 1740s, their information is given under names of owners and occupiers which is not much help if you don't know the name of the person who lived there first.

Until recently it seemed clear that the workhouse was the first building to have appeared at Wrythe Green but recent research has revealed that in October 1646 the lord of the manor of Carshalton granted Adam Etherton life tenancy of 'a cottage built on the wast[e] called Stone Rye'; and in July 1682 it is recorded that an Adam Etherton had died, and the lord of the manor ordered his cottage to be seized forthwith. No more is heard of the property, and this seems to have been the exception which proved the rule: there were to be no houses on the Wrythe for another century, and it remained as wasteland.

Herb farm at the Wrythe which was perhaps part of Short's Farm at Westmead. This picture shows flowering camomile in Draper's Field around 1920. Bill Draper is thought to be one of the workers. (S.L.S.L.)

Wrythe Pond in 1913. The view is looking along West Street with West Street Chapel on the left of the tree and Camden Road School and the station to the right.
(S.L.S.L.)

HONEYWOOD

Mr and Mrs John Burke of Carshalton and their family lived at the house we know as Honeywood during the eighteenth century and feature in a portrait attributed to the German artist Zoffany. This claim was unsubstantiated and the picture is now in private ownership. The John Burke of the picture was an eminent lawyer: he came from an Irish family – so he usually pronounced and spelled his name as Bourke – and he was a relation of the famous Tory politician Edmund Burke. We know that he was living in Carshalton by 1780, and that he lived in the house which we know as Honeywood. According to local legend it was John Bourke who realised that his dining room was built over the stream from Margaret's Pool. He cut the trap door in the floor (which is still there), either so that he could do his fishing at home, or so that when he had a dinner party he could pull up the bottles of wine which had been cooling in the water below.

But John Bourke was not the owner, only the tenant. Old photographs of the Upper Pond show that there were originally two houses here – there was another between Honeywood and the Greyhound. In 1780 both houses were owned by the Otway family; and subsequently by the occupant of the other house, a London timber merchant who rejoiced in the name of Morphew Yerraway. After John Bourke died in 1805/6, his wife Mary went on living in Honeywood until 1812, by which time Morphew Yerraway's son James, a coal merchant in London, lived next door and was the proud owner of both houses.

There is evidence that the building started life as a medieval water mill, and there is some indication that it was still there in this capacity in the sixteenth century. It was not until the middle of the nineteenth century that we start getting names for it: Spring House, Stream House, Wandle Cottage in the 1860s/'70s, and a list of names of well-known occupants. William Hale White was there in 1864/5 and hated it (see page 54). The new resident was only temporary: Richard Gunter, a rich tea merchant, lived there for just a year whilst he rebuilt the house called The Lodge.

But it was another London merchant, John Kirk, who plays a more important part in the fascinating history of the house. He bought the remainder of the lease in 1878, and then five years later in 1883 he purchased the freehold of both houses. Almost immediately he knocked down the one nearest the Greyhound, which was called Honeywood (Honeywood I), and kept the name for his own house (Honeywood II) – to which he added sizeable extensions in 1898 and 1902. So the Honeywood we see today (now the Heritage Centre) is as it was in the Edwardian period, and there is in fact a very good Edwardian billiard room in it.

From top: *Looking across the Upper Pond before 1883 towards Honeywood (I) (left) and Honeywood (II) (right); View of Honeywood (I) across the Upper Pond, 1880s; Honeywood before the southern extension of 1902; Honeywood after the Edwardian enlargement.*

THE SCAWENS & THEIR PROPERTY

The wall round Carshalton Park was built in about 1700 to replace the wooden palisade which, during the sixteenth and seventeenth centuries, had fenced off the park from the common fields surrounding it on three sides. During the first two decades of the eighteenth century Sir William Scawen was planning the great improvement scheme for the Carshalton Park estate. He employed the famous Venetian architect, James Leoni, to design a splendid new mansion to replace the old medieval manor house, and to lay out and landscape the grounds of the park. When Sir William died in 1722 he entrusted the task to his heir and nephew Thomas Scawen. The designs were subsequently published, so we know what the palace (as Leoni called it) was to have looked like, and also where it was to stand – just east of the Square, running up from Brookside to Ruskin Road. The only part of the proposed mansion which was actually built, around 1727–8, was an outbuilding, which was to form one side of the courtyard adjacent to the house. This building, which Leoni calls 'the Greenhouse', was in classical style with columns and a portico. It was apparently intended to serve a dual purpose: partly to grow plants and fruit – it is sometimes called an orangery, presumably in imitation of Beddington – and partly to be a sort of covered bath house or bathing place. This is the building at the corner of the Square and Brookside. During the nineteenth century it was turned into stables and a coach house. In the early part of this century it was converted into a chapel or 'temple'. And when the estate was finally disposed of in about 1928 it was bought by the local electricity board and has been used by them to store equipment. (The building was rescued from demolition and now houses a private firm.)

But although Sir William Scawen had the lordship of the manor of Carshalton, this did not mean that he owned all the various estates in Carshalton. When his nephew and heir Thomas Scawen decided in the later 1720s not to continue with the great project for a new mansion house in the Park, Thomas had to buy one of these estates for himself. In December 1729 he bought the **Stone Court** estate (still known locally as 'Gainsfords Place'), although the Tudor house had been either rebuilt or replaced by a new mansion in about 1710 by the Cator family who owned Stone Court from the 1690s to the 1720s.

But buying one of the great estates of Carshalton, especially a heavily mortgaged one, was an expensive business, and it appears that Thomas Scawen had to borrow extensively to pay for his new acquisitions. So the next problem was how to pay back the money he'd borrowed and get himself out of debt. He thought he could solve this by selling the Irish estates he had inherited from Sir William in Galway and use the money from that to pay for Stone Court.

There was, however, the difficulty that the Scawen estates in Ireland were inherited family property. To sell them he would need to break the entail, and that required permission from the king, in practice, Parliament. So in 1733 a private bill was prepared, and was read in the House of Lords and approved on 19 February 1734. Local historian Andrew Skelton, who has been working on the Scawens, has had the sense to actually go and read this Act of Parliament, and very kindly provided a copy. Since Thomas Scawen was purchasing the Stone Court estate to replace the Irish estate in the family inheritance, the Act gives a substantial description of the Stone Court estate in Carshalton in the early 1730s. It is a very long document, full of names of tenants and subtenants and previous owners and occupants. Any description of Carshalton years ago such as this is of great historical value and solves a number of problems or confirms our guesses; it also raises fresh questions to which it does not provide the answers.

There is no known picture of the eighteenth century Stone Court house, although we know that it was square and built of red brick with a long gallery upstairs. Our document calls it a 'new brick capital messuage or mansion house', together with a dovehouse, barns, stables, outhouses, yards, gardens, groves, sandpits, ponds, moats, streams and 'peculiar piscaries', i.e. fisheries. We are told that this all lies along the water from the churchyard, running under Stone Bridge to Pope's Mill. This was the Upper or Town Mill, whose wheel is still in the Grove and had nothing to do with the Church of Rome, but is explained by the fact that at this time the Popes were several generations of millers who had the Stone Court mill between 1707 and 1779.

In 1734 the mill is said to have been run by Widow Pope who carried on until the son Christopher took over four years later. The Stone Bridge mentioned must be the Stone Court Bridge, to which references go back to the Middle Ages, which crossed the river lower down, more as an extension of West Street Lane through the archway. Stone Court also gave him the Herbert paper mill along Mill Lane (the former BP site).

Other properties which Thomas Scawen bought to increase the Scawen domain were:

Culvers Mill, the corn mill known then as Carshalton Mill. He bought a leather or skinning mill at Goat Bridge, which he let out to a Huguenot family, a French family called Savignac – and there were to be four generations of Paul Peter Savignacs there. And he bought 'that mill, formerly a water grist mill (i.e. corn mill) called Burton's Mill, the old medieval Middle Mill of Carshalton, now used... for a copper mill' which Scawen had purchased from the Fellowes family in May 1732 together with a millhouse, ten acres of riverside meadow and fishing rights.

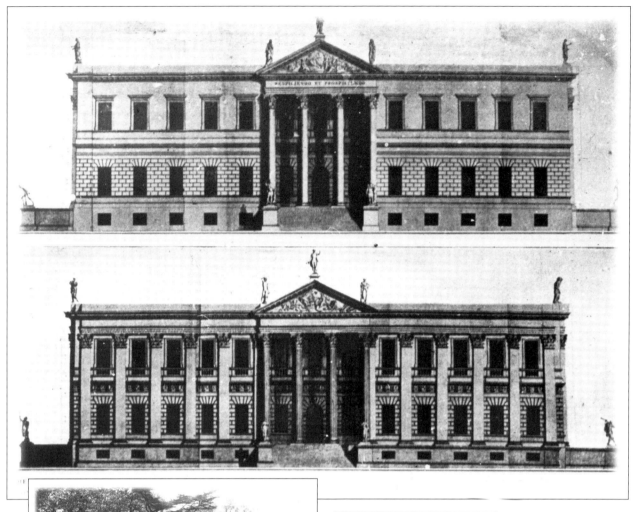

Old cedar tree and Scawen Bridge, the Grove.

Above: *Leoni's design for Carshalton Park House.* (S.L.S.L.)

Left: *The Orangery when it was used as a chapel in the early-twentieth century.* (S.L.S.L.)

Parsonage House (presumably the Old Rectory) he bought from the Carleton family – and it is interesting that one of the small fields or closes attached to it is called 'Little Boulogne'. This takes us right back to the eleventh or twelfth century when Carshalton was held by the family of the Counts of Boulogne.

Lastly, amongst the various fields purchased by Scawen are several in the area called **Pillory Downs** (the name is still in use today), but this item has a double interest. It is described as lying between the road to Woodmansterne and Lamberts Downs – in other words The Oaks – on the west, and on the east

side the road to Reigate. And at once we may recall that the seventeenth-century map of Carshalton in Arundel Castle shows a road to Reigate which began at the Square and ran across Carshalton Park and the great South Field, but which has today almost totally disappeared. The other point of interest about this particular purchase is that Thomas Scawen bought Pillory Downs in 1729 from the trustees of the South Sea Company who were selling up the property confiscated from the Directors of the South Sea Company after the famous bubble had burst. Two Carshalton landowners were ruined in this fiasco – Sir William Hammond of Carshalton High Street and Sir John Fellowes of Carshalton House.

Chapter Three

FAMOUS NAMES

CHARLES BRIDGEMAN & CARSHALTON HOUSE

It is a truism that the eighteenth century was the great age of the landscape garden. The leading landscape gardeners were celebrated public figures, arbiters of taste and fashion and design – men like Capability Brown, William Kent, Humphry Repton – who could change the whole appearance of a great estate, and whose principles were copied in a thousand smaller places. But in many ways one of the most interesting, original, and influential, was Charles Bridgeman, the King's Gardener during the reigns of the first two Hanoverians, George I and George II.

Bridgeman was to die of dropsy in 1738, and since he must have been in his fifties by that time, we may guess that he was born in the 1680s. But we know almost nothing about his early life, except that his father was a gardener at Wimpole near Cambridge, and the young Charles Bridgeman was born and presumably brought up there to follow in the same trade as his father. The first known fact is that in 1717 he married a London girl called Sarah Mist, whose father and brother (both called John Mist) were royal paviours – they supplied paving stones and building supplies to the royal palaces and gardens. A year later Sarah's sister Elizabeth married a George Devall (or Duvall), described as a plumber, someone who organised the waterworks for great houses and gardens. They formed a team, a family firm, offering parks and gardens, layouts, stonework and waterworks for royal palaces and other great houses. Within a year or two they were working for Sir John Fellowes at Carshalton House.

Some of the Bridgeman parks and gardens include Windsor, Kensington Palace, Richmond, Hampton Court, St James' Park, Hyde Park,

Panel from the Painted Room, early 1700s, Carshalton House.

Twickenham and Marble Hill. Away from London there are the great estates at Blenheim, Castle Howard, Claremont and Stowe (regarded as the most superb garden of the age). Apart from royal patronage, Bridgeman had the support of the three most influential patrons of the early-eighteenth century.

Wimpole was the home of the Harleys: Robert Harley, Earl of Oxford, leader of the Tory administration under Queen Anne, and Edward Harley, 2nd earl, the acknowledged leader of taste and learning, patron of poets and artists. This is probably the reason for Bridgeman's connection with the Duke and Duchess of Marlborough: he worked for the Duke at Blenheim and the Duchess at Wimbledon. Bridgeman also worked for Lord Burlington, the leader of the Palladian movement in architecture, at Chiswick and Stowe, and through him was connected with Alexander Pope. Bridgeman and Pope worked together at Twickenham. The third patron was the eminent architect Sir John Vanbrugh, with whom he worked at Blenheim and Castle Howard, and also at Kensington Palace, where he met Henry Joynes, the royal surveyor. Vanbrugh and Henry Joynes have been suggested as the designers of the Water Tower at Carshalton House. But Vanbrugh was also immensely useful to Bridgeman politically, since he was connected with most of the leading Whigs (notably through the famous Kit-Kat Club), and it was in this way that Bridgeman gained the support of Sir Robert Walpole, the effective Prime Minister during the 1720s and '30s.

But Bridgeman was always well connected, and worked with many distinguished architects. He acted for the South Sea Company, the great corporation of the day, of which Fellowes was himself Director and a governor, and so collaborated with architects like James Gibbs (King's, Cambridge) and

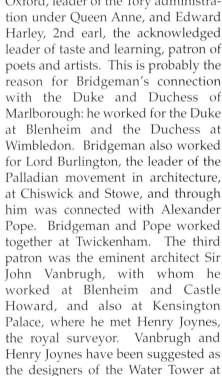

Colin Campbell (Beddington). During the 1720s he worked together with Leoni, the architect of Carshalton Park, at Wrest Park, Moor Park, and probably Carshalton itself. There are connections and inter-relationships in all directions – and one sometimes wonders whether it really was coincidence that the next owner of Carshalton House after the Fellowes, Philip Yorke, Earl of Hardwick, decided to move from Carshalton and bought instead the house at Wimpole, from which Bridgeman himself had come.

As far as one can detect specific Bridgeman work there appear to be four things to look for:

1. Extensive tree planting, for example the formation of avenues of elms, or clumps of trees such as oaks to set off a building, although he was also quite ruthless about cutting down trees which were not growing in what he regarded as the right place.

2. He liked large bowling-green lawns, ending abruptly with a ha-ha, ditch or grassy bank.

3. He was keen to create large, sometimes very large, lakes and ponds (with little thought, said his critics, for all the good land going wasted underneath).

4. He liked to set off his gardens with classical style stonework, whether it was the use of statues or the construction of summerhouses, hermitages, grottoes and caves.

The grounds of Carshalton House display all these features – although all we know for certain is that in 1720/1 Bridgeman was supplying trees, Mist was supplying stone, and Devall was 'plumbing'. They may have been planting the avenue of trees which now leads from the entrance gates round to the mansion, building the Hermitage and cave at the south end of the lake, the grotto at the north end and may have put the lake itself there. (Work on clearing out the lake by the Manpower Services Commission in 1984 showed that there was not a lake in the grounds originally.)

THE HOWARDS & CARSHALTON

During the reign of James I, around about 1614, the two great families, the Howards and the Cecils, decided that it would be advantageous to form a political alliance, and to cement it in the usual dynastic manner by marrying their children together. Sir Robert's aunt, Catherine Howard, married one Cecil and eventually became Countess of Salisbury and mistress of Hatfield House. His father, Thomas Howard, had married the daughter of another Cecil: so our Sir Robert was on one side a Howard through his father, and on the other side a Cecil through his mother – a powerful combination. Sir Robert himself, who was born in 1626, was only the sixth son and could not expect to inherit the main family estates. There were in fact at least 14 children of the marriage, and it is interesting that two of his brothers (Edward and James) also made a name like him later on by writing plays. Thomas Howard, Sir Robert's father, who became Earl of Berkshire also in 1626, was high in royal favour until the Stuart monarchy was overthrown. The Civil War, the defeat of King Charles I, and the establishment of the Parliamentary Commonwealth almost ruined him.

The Howards must have acquired property in Carshalton, if they had not got some already, by the marriage in Carshalton Church on 7 June 1576 of Thomas Howard, son of the 3rd Duke of Norfolk (our Sir Robert's great-great-great-uncle) to Mabel Burton. The Burtons owned a great deal of Carshalton at this time, including Stone Court and the Park, and they must have given Mabel a suitable dowry for marrying a Duke's son, especially a Howard.

The next reference is to a cousin, Charles Howard (Lord Admiral Howard of Effingham) who commanded the English fleet against the Armada, and who with Sir Robert Cecil governed England in the last years of Queen Elizabeth and ensured the peaceful succession of James I and the Stuart house. Charles Howard (Earl of Nottingham since 1597) owned Merton Priory and Haling House at Croydon,

Above and above right: *Carshalton House in 1783 and again in c.1870.*

and in 1603 we hear of him having a house at Carshalton. A year later he was appointed to take charge of the upbringing of the young Prince of Wales, Henry (d.1612), and in June 1606 Charles Howard wrote to Sir Robert Cecil that he was fed up with looking after the young prince. 'I am weary with waiting on the Prince,' he writes, 'who has been fishing at my house at Carshalton, and then afterwards goes hunting in Beddington Park'. The Howards, for obvious reasons, specialised in looking after the heir to the throne. Sir Robert's father looked after both Charles I and then Charles II when they were Princes of Wales. But amongst the Howards who gathered round the young Prince Henry, in the years before his death in 1612 there was yet another Howard – Thomas, our Sir Robert's uncle, 14th Earl of Arundel, and the great friend and patron of the famous architect Inigo Jones. His son was Henry, the 15th Earl of Arundel. Thomas and Henry are particularly important for local history because they were in fact lords of the manor of Carshalton: Sir Robert's uncle and cousin respectively.

In 1620 the manor was divided into two halves or moieties: the Burtons had one part, and the Howards bought the other – one gathers that the Burtons were none too pleased – but the Howards, Earls of Arundel, kept it until 1655 or 1656. And this probably explains why a number of old Carshalton records have been discovered in Arundel Castle, including our oldest map of Carshalton, a Howard estate map. Unfortunately it does not make clear what part of Carshalton the Howards had, or where their house was. But we know the Burtons had Stone Court and the Park – and one would surmise that the Howards had the piece from West Street to the Sutton boundary, and the north side of the High Street from the Grove across into Wallington.

Sir Robert (born in 1626) had a good war but a bad peace. In 1644 he was knighted on the field of battle near Newbury for his bravery in rescuing a Royalist general from capture by the Parliamentary forces. It was Sir Robert's elder brother Thomas who in 1648 was one of the ringleaders in the abortive Royalist uprising against Parliament, which planned to assemble an army on Banstead Downs on the pretext that they were all going to have a horse race. Unfortunately the main body, coming from Kingston, were being harried by a Roundhead regiment, and they went so fast in their anxiety to get away that they missed the Banstead Downs rendezvous altogether and were down at Reigate before they could be stopped. They were then chased back towards Kingston, and after a small skirmish at Ewell, the Cavaliers were soundly defeated on Surbiton Common. Parliament immediately garrisoned troops in places like Carshalton – said to be very malignant and tumultuous – to stop the like happening again. After the war Cromwell considered that Sir Robert was politically

dangerous, and he was imprisoned in Windsor Castle.

But the Howards were not going to be frightened away: they built a new house in Carshalton instead. In 1651 the manor court heard a complaint that the Earl of Arundel had built a house which had blocked the highway from Mr Best's house to the Parsonage Barn. This is proof that, even if they had now relinquished the manor, the Howards had at least one house in Carshalton in 1660. We should not then be too surprised that Sir Robert Howard himself (at last) became a local resident. Both he and his father anxiously awaited the restoration of the monarchy under Charles II in 1660 to revive the family fortunes. In 1660 Charles did in fact make grants to various members of the Howard family. Sir Robert got a couple of minor posts, although it was not as much as the Howards wanted, and they had to sell the family town house, Berkshire House in London (which was bought by the King, who used it for one of his mistresses). But Sir Robert seems to have been doing well enough. In 1666 Pepys noted in his diary that Sir Robert had already made himself a fortune of £20,000; he was making a name for himself in Parliament; was well-known to the King; and his political future looked very promising. But Sir Robert's real claim to fame at this period derives from his writings, and the intensely busy literary partnership which he formed in 1660 with a young poet named John Dryden, and the man who acted as publisher for both of them, Henry Herringman. (See *Sir Robert Howard and The Country Gentleman*.)

Sir Robert seems to have been rather unpleasant. It is difficult to know how far to trust the rude remarks of his political opponents, but he seems to have been proud and domineering, obstinate, pretentious and self-opinionated – and to have got worse as he grew older. He was caricatured on the stage. He was, however, a promising politician. He was married four times. His career prospered enormously during the 1670s. He became Secretary to the Treasury, and then Auditor of the Exchequer, positions of great wealth and power – and he kept this position for the rest of his life. Unlike so many of the Howards, he was firmly opposed to Roman Catholics, and welcomed the Revolution of 1689 and the take-over by William of Orange and Mary. In 1690 he was rewarded by being made one of the Commissioners of the Fleet, and was made commander of all the militia cavalry in England and Wales. He held a great parade of all the militia for the London region, which was inspected and reviewed by the Queen, who thanked him for his good service; and in 1692 Queen Mary dined with him in his house at Carshalton. Sir Robert was now 66, but he was far from being past it – and the next year he got married again to one of Queen Mary's maids of honour, an 18-year-old girl named Annabelle Dives. But it was his last effort in this direction. He died of gout in the stomach in September 1698, and is buried in Westminster Abbey.

Literary Connections, The Country Gentleman & The Exchequer

Sir Robert Howard was the most eminent court playwright of the 1660s; and from then until the end of the century (he died in 1698) he was a top Treasury official and a leading member of the governments of Charles II and William and Mary. His publisher Henry Herringman had his publishing house at the Blue Anchor in the Strand, and it seems likely that Howard and Dryden met at his house, which was a meeting place, almost a club, for gossip and literary talk by the Restoration wits. Dryden may have had a job as a Parliamentary Government official – and so was out of work with the Restoration of Charles II – and may have been taken on by Herringman and employed by him to do odd writing work. At any rate, when Herringman published Sir Robert Howard's first collection of (rather mediocre) poems in 1660, it was Dryden who wrote a preface, in verse, for them, in which he speaks of Sir Robert as his friend. He seems to have been living with Herringman, but now he moved into Sir Robert's house in Lincoln's Inn Fields. Two years later, in 1663, he married Sir Robert's youngest sister, Elizabeth.

By this time the main business of the partnership had become the production of plays for the King's players to perform. In 1660 the King had promised to revive the theatre, which had been banned during the Commonwealth, and established two rival companies, Davenant's and Killigrew's, who built their own theatres. Howard and Dryden began to write plays for Killigrew's company of actors, and when Killigrew built the Theatre Royal for them to be performed in, Howard was the major shareholder. Herringman, however, published for both companies.

Howard wrote, or partly wrote, about eight plays during the 1660s, two of them in co-operation with Dryden; only three were real successes. The best is certainly the comedy called *The Committee*, of 1662, which made fun of the Puritans, and was a standard work for the London stage for over a century – it has a comic Irishman as its main character. To summarise, Howard and Dryden wrote the plays, Herringman published them, and the Theatre Royal put them on – and things went well enough at first.

But gradually the relationship between the two brothers-in-law grew cooler. They engaged in a celebrated literary debate with each other about the use of verse in the drama, and what started as a technical argument became a personal dispute with bitter recriminations. Dryden's marriage was not going well. Howard's sister Elizabeth was said to be ill-tempered and not over-burdened with brains; and Dryden was unfaithful to her. In any case the poet resented any suggestion that he was dependent on Howard patronage. He was now just as successful a playwright as Sir Robert, and a much better poet: in 1668 the King made him Poet Laureate. He could now stand on his own feet as an author – something he accused Sir Robert of being unable to do. When Sir Robert's next, and last successful, play (*The Duke of Lerma*) appeared in 1668, Dryden suggested that most of it was plagiarised from another author.

Dryden also opposed Sir Robert's increasing political alliance with the Duke of Buckingham. And when Sir Robert wrote his last play, *The Country Gentleman*, in 1669, part of it was by the Duke, and they used it to satirise their political opponents. This caused a major political scandal, which ended with several members of the Government being imprisoned, and the King banning the play.

The work was discovered in 1973 in a manuscript, now in the Folger Library in Washington, and was published, for the first time ever, by Dent in the Everyman Library series, 1976. Those of you who enjoy Restoration comedies may like to have a look at it – although it is rather less bawdy than some of them, and not very easy reading in the original spelling. The basic theme of the play is town versus country, and, unusually, it is the country which comes out on top – whereas most contemporaries found country life just too boring for words.

But the country gentleman of the title, Sir Richard Plainbred, is the hero of the piece, and he spends most of his time approving of his beautiful daughters as they repeatedly make fools of the fops and gallants whom they meet on a visit to London. On one side he condemns the foolish aping of French fashions, particularly by one of the other characters, a London landlady trying to be genteel and overdoing it, called Mistress Finical Fart. When she offers him French cooking and French wines, he roars heartily that what he wants is good old English roast beef and English ale. On the other hand he praises the countryside as a place of peace and quiet, with unpolluted air, where the gentlemen look after the tenants on their estates, and are free of the dishonest lawyers who batten upon the gentry in town.

It becomes clear at the end of the play that all this has an underlying political purpose. Those who love the country, in the sense of the countryside, are also those who love their Country – 'we'll love our King and be true to our Country', declares Sir Richard. The country gentlemen of the play's title are the so-called Country Party in the House of Commons, whereas the townsmen represent the opposing Court Party. Sir Robert Howard is arguing that the Country party politicians are more patriotic than their opponents, and the King (Charles II) should listen to them and let them form his governments.

Nevertheless this is an interesting, and, for the period, unusual defence of the values of country life and the merits of being a country gentleman – usually derided as a bumpkin (cf. Goldsmith). It would be nice to think that it was Sir Robert's own experiences as a country gentleman at Carshalton which encouraged him to adopt this line.

That the play is a political satire, at least to some extent, is made apparent by the cast list of villains. The main plot concerns the question of whether Sir Richard's two beautiful daughters (Isabella and Philadelphia) will marry the two exemplary young country gentlemen, called Worthy and Lovetruth, who are courting them. Or whether they will be seduced by one of two pairs of town villains: the young fops, described as lying, scheming cowards, called Vapor and Slander; or two elderly gentlemen, who would relish having young wives, and are very much figures of fun. They are named as Sir Cautious Trouble-all and Sir Gravity Empty. They are described as 'men of business', politicians concerned with affairs of state, and they are very full of their own self-importance, are very stupid, and are constantly being deluded. They are in the business for the money, just like Vapor and Slander, but are much more self-righteous.

This sort of thing was commonplace enough; but what made this particular play notorious was that Sir Cautious Trouble-all and Sir Gravity Empty were openly identified with two contemporary politicians. This was done by inserting a scene into the play which left no doubt about the identity of the characters. They were both Treasury Commissioners – and therefore colleagues of Sir Robert Howard himself. One was Sir William Coventry, a former Commissioner of the Navy (and it is probably his copy of the play which is the one which we now possess); the other was Sir John Duncombe, who subsequently became Chancellor of the Exchequer three years later in 1672. Howard seems to have been trying to drive these Treasury officials out of office; although the scene in question was apparently written by the Duke of Buckingham, who wished to be the King's chief adviser, and was annoyed with Coventry and Duncombe for failing to support him. Our Sir Robert Howard obviously thought that he could advance himself by backing Buckingham rather than his colleagues at the Exchequer, as in fact he did.

Everybody knew that Sir William Coventry had designed for himself a round table for use in his office. He sat in the middle of it, and had all his papers spread out round him. He was very proud of it, and liked to show it off to visitors. When Pepys went to visit him in 1668 he subsequently wrote an account of it in his diary. In the play both Sir Cautious Trouble-all and Sir Gravity Empty have these round tables, one being the Secretary for Foreign Affairs, the other for Home Affairs. They get into the middle of these tables through a little tunnel, and sit on revolving stools, so that they can swing round to reach whatever pile of papers is appropriate.

They decide to have a competition to see who can swing round more quickly to get their documents. Sir Cautious shouted out the names of places at home, so that Sir Gravity could spin round and pick up the appropriate file; Sir Gravity called out the names of places abroad, and Sir Cautious would whizz round to get the file for that place. They start calling out names, getting faster and faster, so that soon both gentlemen are spinning madly round, getting thoroughly dizzy and carried away with themselves and making more and more noise. When Sir Gravity tries to stop and get out, he becomes stuck, trapped in the middle of his table. At the height of the commotion Sir Richard Plainbred comes to call. He sees these two mountebanks roaring and whizzing, and naturally decides that they are not appropriate suitors for his daughters.

It seems that Sir William Coventry got hold of an advance copy of the play – and he challenged the Duke of Buckingham to a duel, which was highly illegal, because Buckingham was a privy councillor and was protected like the royal family. Sir William Coventry promptly earned the King's displeasure and was imprisoned in the Tower (where he was visited by Pepys) and although he was soon released, it was clear that he was very much the provoked victim, his political life was ruined and he retired. The Duke of Buckingham's plot was successful – he destroyed Sir William Coventry. The King forbade the production of Sir Robert Howard's play on the stage so it has never been performed.

Sir Robert Howard seemed unmarked by the scandal, and indeed was singled out for promotion. In October 1671 he was made Secretary of the Treasury, and then in March 1673, he was designated the next occupant of the plum posts of Auditor of the Receipt and Writer of Tallies. These were very lucrative positions, but held at the time by Sir Robert Long, who for the previous ten years had been regarded as unquestionably the outstanding figure at the Exchequer. It was a top job, and when Sir Robert Long died in July of the same year, 1673, Sir Robert Howard took over for life, for the next 25 years.

Sir Robert Howard never wrote another play; he never worked with Dryden again; and Henry Herringman – although still only 42 – decided to retire from London into the country. The partnership was finished.

We know that Herringman retired from London in about 1670 because Henry Herringman and his wife Alice are buried in Carshalton Church. The tablet on the wall of the Lady Chapel says that having acquired 'a competent estate in the space of 20 years' from their marriage in 1650, they then 'came and settled in this parish', where 'they lived handsomely and hospitably'. They both died in 1703. Their house was probably at the eastern end of the High Street, but on the north side of the road. In 1672 the manor court allowed him to enclose a piece of waste land in front of his house – between the highway and Hammond's – and add it into his grounds.

But why should Herringman choose to come to Carshalton? It was (and is of course) an attractive place, and it was near enough to London for Herringman to keep his publishing house there going, at least into the mid-1680s. But it is also possible that Herringman was born here: it was a good old Carshalton name. There are some 20 Herringmans listed in the Parish Registers for the century between 1550 and 1650 – mainly because they had an incurable propensity for dying of the plague. Three Herringwomen in 1626 died 'not of the plague, but of a disease somewhat akin to it'; and in 1641 four of the six people who died of smallpox in the parish in that year were from the same family.

But there is no definite evidence that Henry Herringman was a native by origin, and it is perhaps surprising that his church memorial would not mention this if it had been the case. One could hazard a guess, however, that he came here because of his connection with Sir Robert Howard – possibly they even met in the first place because of Carshalton. Throughout the seventeenth century the Howards had at least one house in Carshalton.

During the final period from 1673, the same sort of pattern seemed to repeat itself. There were periodic scandals in which Sir Robert was implicated; but he always seemed to emerge unscathed with his political influence undiminished. It seems fairly clear that he was dipping his hand into the till, but then so was everybody else and he was not the sort of man to try to stop others doing it. It was all part of the system of patronage, bribery and corruption which was felt to be necessary to maintain the King's administration – and there were only two occasions when he almost got caught.

One was in 1676/77 when Howard's political enemy, the Earl of Danby, tried to get him dismissed by accusing him of blackmailing the tellers, the Treasury officials who administered different funds, taking money out of one fund, paying it back with money from another fund, and so on indefinitely. So the Earl demanded a spot check of all the money bags. To his surprise they were all full; so he demanded another check the following year – and this time one set of moneybags was short of £12,000. These bags were in the care of Sir William D'Oyly; and the story went about that D'Oyly and Howard had avoided detection the previous year by calling in the plumbers to cut out pieces of lead the size of half-crowns, which were used to fill the money-bags, with a few genuine coins sprinkled on top in case anybody looked. It was a dirty tricks department with genuine plumbers. But the fraud was found out, and Sir William D'Oyly was dismissed and ordered to pay back the missing money. There is a curious twist to the end of the story. In order to pay back the money,

Sir William gave the Crown a number of estates in Suffolk, which he said were his, and he produced title deeds showing that he had got them from his father. The Crown preferred to have the money, so it looked around for someone to buy the estates. It just so happened that the Secretary of State, Henry Coventry, the brother of the Sir William Coventry we've already met, wanted to finish his working life, and so he bought these estates as somewhere to retire to (paying £7000 for them). Too late, he discovered to his horror that there was another deed, which had been kept secret, in which it was stated that the properties were entailed and were to remain in the ownership of the D'Oyly family. So Sir William D'Oyly had paid off his debt with a property which he couldn't sell; and Henry Coventry had paid out £7000 for nothing. Once again the Coventry family had been worsted in their dealings with Howard, whilst Howard himself escaped without censure. He thought up a very long-winded cover story, and started telling it to the King, who was itching to get off to Newmarket for the racing, and after a while Charles II declared impatiently that he'd heard enough, and the affair was closed.

The second narrow escape was more dangerous. Two decades later in 1696/7 there was another major scandal in the Treasury, when it became clear that one of the clerks, called John Peters, was repeatedly defrauding the Exchequer. The total mentioned was £27,000 and the fraud involved the substitution of good coinage for clipped coins which had been handed in for melting down. Sir Robert Howard was in trouble because, as Auditor, he was supposed to check that this didn't happen – and the affair became a political attack on Howard himself. Once it became a party political issue of course, the rights and wrongs of the case ceased to matter.

In the event Howard was successful (although it didn't do him much good, since he died in the following year, 1698). Peters was allowed to fade away gently, although incredibly he even claimed compensation for loss of office and for having to pay back the money he had taken – and even during 1699 and 1700 there were attempts to get him reinstated at the Treasury. In 1699 there was even a petition got up by a gentleman appropriately named Mr Twitty, who declared that Peters was blameless, and got 167 members of the House of Commons to sign it. One of the signatures is that of Sir William Scawen, a merchant, who had been lending vast sums of money to the Government, and had been rewarded by a knighthood and governorship of the Bank of England in 1695. In the following year he was rich enough to purchase the manor of Carshalton.

Howard and Scawen were connected – a double connection both from financial dealings in London and property in the manor of Carshalton. But Duncombe, the two Coventry brothers, D'Oyly and

Sir Robert Long are all names which have local connotations. Despite being ridiculed in the play, Sir John Duncombe was to become a firm friend of Howard's in the 1670s, and the Duncombes were closely related to the Howards. It was George Duncombe, his father, who in 1620 had purchased the manor of Carshalton as a trustee on behalf of Anne Howard, the dowager countess of Arundel. Our Sir Robert subsequently married his sister-in-law off to William Duncombe and gave him the living of the church of Ashtead, when Sir Robert built himself a new house there in 1680.

The two Coventry brothers, Sir William and Henry, had a Carshalton relative called Francis, who had a half share in the lordship of Carshalton manor.

We know very little about Francis Coventry, except that he owned that half of the manor which had previously been the Howard half, and had passed in 1654 to Sir Edmund Hoskins – Coventry being himself the heir by marriage. Francis Coventry certainly lived in Carshalton because his name appears on the hearth-tax returns from 1664 onwards, and he seems to have lived here for over 20 years. He must have lived in the biggest house in Carshalton, because he had to pay for more chimneys than anybody else. It was the house which Hoskins had before him, and this would seem to indicate that he had Carshalton Park, and the old house, Mascalls, which later passed to Sir William Scawen.

The D'Oylys were not a Carshalton family, but they were closely connected with the Longs, and the Longs had very definite local ties. When Samuel Long went on the expedition to conquer Jamaica in 1654/5 he went as a lieutenant in the elder D'Oyly's regiment. His grandson Beeston Long returned to Carshalton after the family had made a fortune in Jamaica, to occupy the great house of the Scawens in North Street, the Longs' house at Rochester Road. But already there were other Longs in Carshalton. Dixie and George Long had the other half, the non-Howard half, of the Carshalton manor between the 1640s and 1660s. They probably lived at the Old Farm, the building which preceded Carshalton House (St Philomena's). Not far away at Cheam in the 1660s, in the palace of Nonsuch, could be found Sir Robert Long, Sir Robert Howard's predecessor as Auditor of the Exchequer.

Sir Robert Long was an old royal servant, who acted for Charles I's Queen (Henrietta Maria). When the Great Plague broke out in London in 1665, and then the Great Fire in 1666, on both occasions the Exchequer was saved by being taken by Sir Robert Long down to Nonsuch Palace, from where he ran the finances of the nation.

There must have been times when it almost seemed as if Treasury business was local business at Carshalton. The great affairs of state in London must have seemed like domestic issues to the country gentlemen of Carshalton because it was their families, closely interwoven and interlocked, who managed the Exchequer at the same time as they administered the manor. Carshalton and Whitehall were in a sense reflections of each other. As Sir Robert Howard put it, 'the country gentlemen are the men who run the Country.'

The Grotto, Carshalton House, c.1870.

MARK RUTHERFORD & HIS HOMES

There is a house in Park Hill, Carshalton, which is of considerable architectural importance and historical interest. It was once the home of the famous Victorian novelist Mark Rutherford, whose real name was William Hale White. In 1865 he had lived for a few months in Spring or Stream House (now known as Honeywood, or the Heritage Centre by the Ponds).

But William Hale White didn't like Honeywood: it was too damp for him, with the water running underneath the house itself, and he was too near the rector. White had a horror of noise; all his life he was tormented by wakeful nights whilst he listened to clocks striking, dogs barking, cocks crowing and trains shunting. But the worst thing was the bells, and he complained that the rector played with his bells like a child with a rattle. Not even double windows and cotton wool, he wrote, could keep out the din of the curate's plaything at the corner of the garden. He had already tried living in West Street, in a house later demolished to provide the station approach. But he was infuriated to find that none of the windows fitted, the draughts made all the fires smoke, and that the floors and walls were so thin that he could hear noises from kitchen to garret.

Having moved from house to house in greater and greater misery, he decided that something was radically wrong with English domestic building. He wrote to the papers about it. This led to contacts with Ruskin, architects like Philip Webb, artists like William Morris and the other members of the Pre-Raphaelite movement. The result was that he had a specially-built house which embodied a complete change in house design. The walls were 14 inches thick; there were specially designed fireplaces, decorations by William Morris himself, plenty of wood, brick and tiles as opposed to marble, lath and plaster – all built for solidity, and with tight-fitting shutters on the windows. It started a new trend in house design. This house was 19 Park Hill where he lived happily from 1868–88. He inspired his brother-in-law to build a similar house at No. 11; and his father retired to live at No. 5.

This 'Park Hill Circle' became the meeting place for many of the leaders of the Pre-Raphaelite movement – so that Carshalton became one of the centres of the advanced cultural and artistic movements of the nineteenth century.

William Hale White is commemorated by a Blue Plaque on the wall of his house which was unveiled on 21 October 1979 by Mark White, his grandson.

William Hale White's house in Park Hill. (S.N.)

Ruskin, Shepley & Margaret's Pool

More than anybody else, John Ruskin deserves the title 'the patron saint of Carshalton'. He gave its beauty wide publicity. He was the first person to take effective steps against its despoliation by an expanding, philistine society. Although not a local resident, he had spent part of his childhood in Croydon, and recalled the surrounding countryside with great affection. Ruskin may have been to Carshalton as a child, but his interest in the village – which he described in 1866 as the loveliest piece of lowland scenery in southern England – was stimulated by a series of visits to Carshalton between 1865 and 1871. During this time he sometimes stayed with the Tylor family at Shepley House which stood on the north-east side of Strawberry Lane. The entrance was almost opposite Strawberry Lodge, but the estate stretched all the way along Nightingale Road to the Hack Bridge itself. It was noted for its fruit gardens and many fine trees, especially an enormous cedar tree said to be 300 years old.

The house was a pleasant red-brick edifice, not particularly outstanding perhaps, but of considerable antiquity. We first hear of it being rebuilt by a Mr Parker in the middle of the eighteenth century. This indicates that there was a much older house there, and in a book published in 1789 it is stated that the original house was built on the site of a monastery, a Cluniac priory attached to the abbey of Bermondsey – but this has not so far been verified. The name of the house derives from its occupation by Mr George Shepley from some time before 1780, and then by his son Michael Shepley who died in 1837, and whose monument is in the Parish Church. Michael Shepley helped to build the original Hack Bridge, one of the early iron bridges erected in 1807, but now replaced by a much less distinguished concrete one. The family came from Southwark, and their interest in Carshalton revolved around milling. They had a big leather and oil mill on the Wandle where it ran along the eastern boundary of their land. Linseed was ground to extract the oil, which was worked into the leather, the linseed husks being made into cattle cake. It must have been a profitable business. Like so many wooden watermills, the mill burned down in 1785, and the damage was estimated at £1000, but it was very soon rebuilt and in operation again.

After the Shepleys the house was bought by Alfred Tylor, who had become one of this country's leading geologists by the time that he died in 1884. Tylor was one of Carshalton's benefactors: he left the Council £1000 to purchase the Wrythe Recreation Ground. But, more importantly for our present purpose, he was a close friend of Ruskin. On his way up to the City he would often call in to see Ruskin at Herne Hill; and Ruskin would often visit and stay with the Tylors at Shepley House. It was Tylor who helped to find the workmen who restored

Margaret's Pool under Ruskin's direction. But Carshalton also had attractions of another kind for Ruskin: Tylor had three very beautiful daughters. Ruskin was one of the most eminent of eminent Victorians, a man of many-sided genius. But like some other men of genius, his personal life was unconventional. His unconsummated marriage and divorce was one of the celebrated scandals of mid-Victorian England. In later life he was obsessed by a series of young women. When he was about 50 he had fallen in love with a girl of 12, and tried to marry her when she was 17: this was prevented – the unfortunate girl became distraught and died; and Ruskin himself suffered from periods of insanity.

In the week that she died, Ruskin was seeking consolation at Shepley House. The relevant page has been cut out of his diary, but he later recorded that he spent his visit trying to screw up his courage to propose to one of the Tylor girls, and wishing he could kidnap all three and live with them in an Arabian Nights palace. This was in 1875, but the episode made such a powerful impression that he was still talking about it two years later, and dreaming that he had married them all. Even in 1883 he wrote that he lamented 'the present order in society in that I cannot make a raid on my neighbour's house and carry off three graceful captives at the same time.' In fact by 1883 one of the daughters, Isabella, was safely married to a son of the famous statesman John Bright – an event which gave Carshalton its biggest society wedding of the century. Another daughter married six years later. But it was one of the Tylor daughters, Juliet, who was the only girl Ruskin ever invited to join his Guild for the Preservation of Rural England: he made her one of the trustees in 1876. He told her that if she ever married, she must only marry a preservationist. He was probably thinking of himself.

We need not dwell upon this more colourful episode in the history of an old Carshalton house. In any case Shepley House was nearing the end of its career. It had two more private owners. The last, Mr Dingwall, another celebrated Carshalton name, was a keen fisherman. On 1 April, 1899, he caught 60 trout in the river between his gate and Butter Hill Bridge and reckoned to take 500 a year from his stretch of water. But in 1914 he sadly recorded that the last of the trout had died, killed by the tar put down on the roads. It is ironical that it was his predecessor, George Shepley, who was so keen to get the roads made up. In 1916 the process of selling the estate began.

For nearly a century there have been doubts about the authenticity of the so-called Ruskin Stone, which stands beside Margaret's Pool at the corner of West Street and Pound Street, and records that this little spring or well was 'beautified and endowed by John Ruskin' and given the name of Margaret's Well in memory of his mother. The story of the stone's sudden appearances and disappearances is fairly familiar, but the existence of a copy of a correspondence between Ruskin and George Brightling during the 1870s enables us to be much more precise about the details of a celebrated controversy. George Brightling was the only person who has managed to write a history of Carshalton and it is a great pity that we do not have the original letters which passed between them. They were last heard of in the possession of Brightling's son: but he did allow some of them to be copied, and these copies are amongst the records in the London Borough of Sutton library.

On his visits Ruskin seems to have paid special attention to what is described as a 'dirty little pond' at the back of the Pound Street Police Station. It appears to have been in a filthy condition, full of mud and rubbish, with several sewers and drains emptying into it. One of the famous Wandle springs of very pure, clear water bubbled up here in a sort of fountain – and we still have the old pump which brought people from as far away as Wrythe Green to use it. This discharged into the pool through a moss-covered brick arch, now damaged and broken. There was a good deal of builders' waste, presumably left over from building the Police Station in 1846, and Mr Duncan, who used to let out horses and carriages from across the other side of Pound Street, used the pond to wash them in. Ruskin talks about a 'festering scum… of black slime' and in the well-known preface to *The Crown of Wild Olives* of 1866 he lashed 'the human wretches of the place' who insisted on throwing all their refuse into the water. He thought that half a dozen men could put it right in a day, but he despaired of anybody caring enough about it to do anything. Nevertheless, the idea of restoring the pond remained with him, and after visiting the pool on Christmas Eve, 1871, with Mr Tylor, he wrote to Tylor in the following January asking him to employ workmen to keep the pool clean and to plant the banks with flowers. Ruskin himself would re-design the spring, and pay all the expenses.

The Tylors decided that the obvious person to approach would be George Brightling. Brightling not only lived near the pool at Church Hill (Madeley Cottage), but was about to publish his history of Carshalton, although he was still not 30 years old. Brightling pointed out that the land belonged to the manor of Carshalton, and it would be necessary to seek the permission of the manorial court. This feudal relic was summoned to meet in April 1872, and the eminent architect, Gilbert Scott, was commissioned to prepare plans under Ruskin's direction. The central feature was to be a Gothic arch, made of marble, with a suitable inscription on it, placed over the spring against the back wall of the Police Station. Ruskin promised that all would be ready in time for April. At this point the first strains developed in the relationship between Ruskin and Brightling. Despite repeated promises, Ruskin continued to dither about the exact design of the arch. A week before the court was to meet, he suddenly went off to Italy, and from

the safe distance of Paris wrote to Brightling that he was too busy to bother with details. Scott could not produce the plans; and in the end it was Brightling who had to produce the scheme which was submitted to the court, and was duly approved and given 'planning permission'.

Ruskin spent the next six months touring Italy: he was suffering from a mental breakdown. Both points made him a difficult correspondent. When Brightling suggested in June that the pool should be fenced off from the road by wire, Ruskin agreed. In November he absolutely forbade it. Wire, he said, was made of iron: and he hated iron because it seemed to him that it was made of dead men's bones. Let the fence be made of wood: 'If the boys cut the fence into matches every night, I'll put it up again next day – but wooden it must be.' In June 1873 Brightling was no doubt somewhat shaken at being informed that seven tons of Cumberland rock was on its way to him, and would he please put it round the edge of the pond. He must have managed because large chunks of it are lying about the place today.

Brightling laboured on and gradually the pool was transformed. A neighbouring workman, George Manley of Church Hill, was paid 30 shillings a week to look after it. Ruskin's gardener gave advice on the flowers and shrubs to be planted (they had to be the sort that the children would leave alone – the problem of vandalism in Carshalton is clearly a very old one). Later, a rustic bridge was put up and a garden seat installed. Ruskin inspected the pond in the summer of 1873 and was satisfied with its progress. Brightling, who was, amongst other things, an insurance agent, profited by selling Ruskin an insurance policy on his pictures. But the much-discussed marble arch did not materialise. Ruskin in fact gave up the idea of marble, and suggested using porcelain. But Brightling seems to have got tired of waiting for Ruskin to make up his mind: after the latter's inspection in 1873, the local paper printed the text of an inscription which was to be engraved on stone and placed over the well. The report makes it seem that Ruskin was responsible for this, but clearly he knew nothing about it, and the source can only have been George Brightling.

The stone was eventually put up on the Police Station wall three years later with a rather shorter version of this inscription. Although Brightling was later accused of perpetrating an elaborate hoax, it seems unlikely that he was responsible for the wording. The inhabitants thought it was rather peculiar, but typical of Ruskin's high-flown phraseology. Indeed, Ruskin never accused Brightling of forgery; simply of putting up and publishing the inscription without authority. Tired of waiting for a definite decision, Brightling probably just used a draft version of the dedication which Ruskin had been discussing with him, and thought that he was carrying out Ruskin's intentions so far as these were discoverable.

But he did not tell Ruskin that he had done so.

Ruskin, meanwhile, was more concerned with other problems. There was the difficulty that mud and dust from Pound Street was continually being washed off the road into the pond, and the Parish Council ignored his complaints that something should be done about it. Moreover, the springs themselves did not react well to being tampered with, and ran about all over the place – like a child, mused Ruskin, continually getting into a mess. Sometimes they overflowed and flooded the neighbouring houses: an irate resident (probably from Honeywood) complained that the chairs were floating about his drawing room. The solution to this problem was to put in a sluice-gate (the remains of which can still be seen) at the point where the water from the pool ran into the pond behind Wandle Lodge, the wooden house next to the Police Station owned by two maiden ladies, the Misses Hetherington. The Hetheringtons were agreeable, provided that they had a right of way out of their garden across the sluice. Ruskin thought the matter was settled, and in January 1876 established a trust fund of £110, with Brightling as trustee, to be used for the continued care of the pool.

A year later, in June 1877, Brightling decided that he had better make another attempt to clear the mud out of the pond. He accomplished this by the simple expedient of opening the sluice-gate – with the result that all the mud was washed down in a tidal wave into the Misses Hetherington's pond. They had just spent the previous week cleaning out their own pond and were, understandably, very annoyed. They complained to the Tylors and said it was their fault for having made the arrangements between Ruskin and Brightling in the first place. The Tylors complained to Ruskin, and Ruskin, in a letter with a marked change of tone, accused Brightling of causing a disturbance with his sluice-gate, and deposed him as trustee and manager of the pond. Brightling's reaction was to tear out the offending sluice-gate and replace it with a fence – thereby causing even greater annoyance to the Misses Hetherington, who were now barricaded into their back garden and could not get out over the stream. There were more complaints, and it was at this stage that Ruskin learned about the stone dedicating the pool to his mother.

Nobody afterwards admitted to telling Ruskin about it: one story was that a party of students had come down from Oxford, and had mentioned it to Ruskin on their return; in another it was that the police objected to their wall being used; and in a third story it was maintained that the parish authorities disliked it for fear that Ruskin's heirs might take it as evidence for a claim to ownership of the pond. In fact it seems almost certain that the Tylors and Hetheringtons took their revenge on Brightling by telling Ruskin about it. They certainly told him how very upset and angry Mr Ruskin was with his behaviour. On 5 August 1877 Ruskin wrote to Brightling ordering him to arrange for the removal of the offending stone. Eventually there was a reconciliation, and Ruskin forgave Brightling. But Brightling refused to carry on with the management of the pool, and the trust was handed over to another friend of Ruskin's, William Hale White ('Mark Rutherford') of Park Hill. More mud ran off the roads into the pool, and in December Ruskin confessed that he was beaten. A year later he drafted another dedicatory inscription, but he only wrote it in his diary, and it remained unpublished. His part in the affair had come to an end. We shall never know exactly what he wanted: but then he never quite knew himself.

The rest of the story is soon told. William Hale White administered the pool until 1888, when the trust was handed over to the local authority, which eventually bought the pool from the manor and enlarged it when the Police Station was demolished in 1920. The 'Ruskin stone' itself went to a stonemason's yard in Pound Street, and it was sold in about 1880 for 30 shillings to Mr Jackson of Beechwood Lodge (in West Street Lane, on the site of the present flats). He put it in his garden, where it became very dirty and moss-grown. His daughter, Miss Jackson, gave it to the Council during the 1920s after it had been identified for what it was. But the Council promptly lost it again amongst the paving stones in their depot, and it next appeared in the pavement of Carshalton Road. Here the rain soon washed the mud off it: it was recognised, taken up, and with the lettering re-cut, put back beside Margaret's Pool in 1931, where it can still be seen.

Left to right, top to bottom:
*Margaret's Pool, c.1915;
Shepley House, c.1920;
Margaret's Pool. The seated figure is
the artist Tatton Winter taken in the
early 1900s.* (S.L.S.L.);
*Wandle Lodge, Pound Street, with
possibly the Misses Hetherington;
This is thought to be Queen
Victoria's funeral train passing
through Carshalton en route to
London from the Isle of Wight in
January 1901. Strangely the onlookers
have not doffed their hats.* (S.L.S.L.)

ROYAL VISITS TO CARSHALTON

It would be interesting and perhaps instructive to compile a list of the royal and other distinguished persons who have visited Carshalton during its long history. It is sometimes suggested that King William I came this way during the Norman Conquest. There is the celebrated controversy over the question of whether Queen Anne Boleyn carelessly put her horse's hoof down the holy well beside the Parish Church. But it does seem fairly clear that Carshalton has the distinction of being one of the few places in the country where it cannot be said that Queen Elizabeth slept – she only got as close as Mitcham and Beddington.

We have, however, recently discovered that two other Queens of England can be added to the list. Their visits were very brief, and will hardly justify us in styling ourselves as Royal Carshalton, but they should be recorded. In September 1692 Queen Mary, the wife of William of Orange, dined with Sir Robert Howard at his house in Carshalton. The Queen does not seem to have been particularly impressed, since she returned to London immediately afterwards.

But the visit of Queen Victoria to West Street in late January 1901 was rather more dramatic and even briefer: she was only there for a matter of seconds. This is not a deliberate mistake – let us hasten to add that the Queen was, in that uncouth hospital phrase, DOA, dead on arrival. We refer to the exceptionally interesting photograph *(left)* which shows the funeral train of Queen Victoria passing through Carshalton. She had died on the Isle of Wight, and her body was brought up to London – to Victoria of course – from Gosport, and passed through Sutton and Carshalton. It is thought that the picture shows the train on the embankment just about to pass over the railway bridge in West Street. The field below the line is thronged with the citizens of Carshalton, all dressed in mourning, standing to pay their last respects. Strangely, they have not doffed their hats.

ADMIRALS OF CARSHALTON

The Ponds are barely deep enough to take a rowing boat, let alone a battleship, but nevertheless Carshalton has made its own contribution to the naval history of these islands. If Merton has Lord Nelson, and Beddington has Sir Walter Raleigh, we can claim to have provided a home for two distinguished admirals. Lord Anson, celebrated for his famous voyage around the world in the early 1740s, married the daughter of Lord Chancellor Hardwicke, and so came to live in Carshalton House between 1749 and 1752. Admiral Sir Edward Whitaker, a hero of the Siege of Gibraltar in 1704, when the Rock was captured and held against the forces of France and Spain (to remain British from then on), came to live in

Carshalton: he died here in 1755, and is buried in the churchyard. Sir Edward appears to have owned the house in West Street Lane which we know as West Lodge – although there is also a reference to the family at Shepley House, which has not yet been explained.

There is also a third Carshalton Admiral, much less distinguished as a naval commander, but in his way much more important for the history of Carshalton itself – Admiral Bertie Cornelius Cator, who lived from 1787–1864. Bertie was not short for Albert, but was his mother's maiden name. She was the sister of Admiral Sir Albemarle Bertie – so our Bertie already had a naval tradition in the family, on his mother's side, and probably joined the Navy under his uncle's patronage.

On his father's side there was much more of an ecclesiastical tradition, although a rather mixed one. The family descended from John Cator, a well-known Quaker in Herefordshire, who died in 1704. John Cator's younger son, also called John, purchased and rebuilt Stone Court, between 1693 and 1729, and probably married a wife from Beddington as well. This was a short-lived episode in the history of the Cators in Carshalton, and for most of the eighteenth century the London Cators were based in the Bromley and Beckenham area. Bertie Cornelius was the fourth son of the John Cator who obtained the advowson of Carshalton in 1797, Bertie thus becoming brother to one rector and uncle of the next.

Bertie Cornelius was promoted rear Admiral by 1853, and duly became full Admiral. He and his wife Sophia were living in Kent, but they owned William Bates' farm, on the corner of West Street and West Street Lane (where there was a printing shop until 1999). Also, like the other brothers, Admiral Bertie had his share of land in the fields – something over 25 acres of it. When the common fields were enclosed in 1853 these holdings came to form a solid block of land, subsequently called the Cator estate, bounded by Stanley Park Road to the south and the railway line (Carshalton Beeches to Wallington) on the north. Going from west to east, there was a fairly small field to the right of the Glebe Road railway bridge, owned by the rector (W.A.B. Cator), on which Sussex Road would later be built. Then there came a large area, owned by the Norfolk Cators, Bertie's brothers John and Albermarle, which was eventually bought by the Council, partly to build Stanley Park infants school and the rest of it we know as the Stanley Park recreation ground. And next to that was an equally large piece – from opposite Stanley Road to opposite Dalmeny Road – which was owned by the Admiral.

He was coming up towards 70 by the mid-1850s, retired from the sea one, imagines, and apparently decided to use this piece of land in Stanley Park Road to build himself a house. Since he didn't want the common people of Carshalton trespassing in his back garden, the bridge across the railway which led into it was broken down - although you can still see the remains of it along the line from Carshalton Beeches Station. The first reference to the house that we have seen is on a map of 1862, which marks it as 'Admiral Cator's Lodge' – a large square house close to the road, with an even larger courtyard of stables behind it. Unfortunately the Admiral did not enjoy it for long: his wife Sophia died the same year, 1862, and he followed her two years later in July 1864.

Some time after the Admiral's death the south-east quarter of his estate was sold off, and this was used to build another Victorian mansion, which we know much more about, called Anglesey – its name is recalled by street names like Anglesey Gardens and Anglesey Court Road. But The Lodge, after appearing on the OS map of 1867, virtually disappears from the record. A Mr Hoof occupied the house from 1889–93, but it was empty for a long period at the turn of the century, and appears to have been demolished and rebuilt. Certainly the 1914 OS map shows a very different building on the site, with

the new house where the old stables had been (at what is now Woodfield Avenue), and, vice versa, the new stables on the site of the older house. The new house, also called The Lodge, had a succession of fairly short-term occupants from 1906 onwards (one was a Mr C.H. Twidale, who for five years the local directories insisted on calling Mr Twiddle), and it was demolished about 1931 when Stanley Park Road was built up. Anglesey (which had been lived in for 40 years by a Mr and Mrs Gibbs) was demolished at the same time. Nevertheless, the Lodge did not vanish quite without trace. The stables, a building with a sort of two-storey Dutch gable, which, as mentioned, was built on the site of the Admiral's house, can still be seen.

It is one of the nice things about Carshalton that you never know what you can find until you start looking, and there's always something to discover. The stables are now used by a car repair firm behind the petrol station, between Stanley Park Road and Woodfield Avenue: they are worth having a look at, and they serve to remind us of the house where Admiral Cator of Carshalton hauled down his flag.

Right: *The stabling to Admiral Cator's Lodge between Stanley Park Road and Woodfield Avenue used by the Anglesey garage.*

Left: *Anglesey House, built about 1865, off Stanley Park Road.*
(Both S.L.S.L.)

Chapter Four

EDUCATION

BORNHEM HOUSE

Because Catholic schools were not allowed in England, in 1657 the Dominicans had established a school for English boys at Bornhem in Flanders, near Antwerp. After the French Revolution, the French overran the Low Countries; the Dominicans fled to England in 1794/5, regrouping at Carshalton where they tried to re-establish the school. For this purpose they took over a large mansion in Carshalton said to have been designed by Inigo Jones, the famous architect of the first half of the seventeenth century. Armed with this description it was possible to look at a guidebook to Carshalton houses by James Edwards, published in 1799, and he does indeed speak of a high, square brick house 'in the modern (or Palladian) style' – although it took some time to find definite proof that this was the right building. But there was a 'small palace' mid way between North Street and West Street with stables behind it on the West Street side, later to be called Bornhem House. It had all the land up to Wrythe Green, originally known as Shepherd's Close, but in the nineteenth century as French School Orchard

We do have a fairly good idea of what it looked like. There is a brief description of the property when it was insured for £1000 in 1751, a large sum, which suggests a fine house. There are also two rather poor prints of the early-nineteenth century when it was being advertised as a school. It was a handsome seventeenth-century building, about the same size as Carshalton House, although its appearance was not improved by additional wings to the north and south, which were probably added later. It had tall

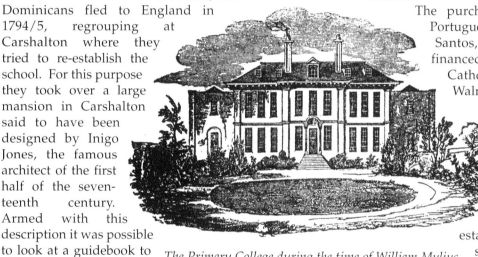

The Primary College during the time of William Mylius, formerly the Byne family house. (H.C.P.M.)

chimneys, an elegant front door approached by steps, and we are told that inside there was a 'grand staircase' and panelled rooms. There was a circular drive in front of the house and behind it a large collection of stables, coach-house, wash-house, brew-house, dovecot, sheds and barns, and also dog kennels.

The purchaser in 1795 was a Portuguese merchant, John Diaz Santos, who was apparently financed by a rich Roman Catholic, a certain Lady Walmsley, who bought the house for the benefit of the Dominican refugees from Bornhem. The project for a Dominican house never really materialised, but they did establish a chapel and a school (under the Revd Br John Ambrose Woods) which acquired about 50 boys. But by 1806 the Revd Woods was the only Dominican left; salaried masters had to be employed; the school fell into debt to the tune of some £6000, and was sadly closed down in 1810.

A year later the school was re-opened as a preparatory school – it eventually acquired the name of the Primary College – by a vigorous 36-year-old Catholic schoolmaster from Chelsea, William Mylius, a well-known author of school textbooks. It lasted for 17 years: but in 1829, saddled with debt and encouraged by Catholic emancipation to return to Chelsea, Mylius moved on again. The owner was now Emanuel Diaz Santos, the Portuguese merchant's son, who had himself become a Dominican and was ordained as a priest, ministering to Catholics in Essex. He died in 1834. The Carshalton house must have been demolished about this time, and the railway company simply bought a couple of open fields, from the local property speculator Jonah Cressingham, 30 years later.

St Philomena's School

In 1893 the Daughters of the Cross purchased Carshalton House and its estate and founded the present school. The Daughters were a Roman Catholic religious order founded in Liège in 1833 by Jeanne Haze, whose religious name was Mother Marie Thérèse. Carshalton House, built in the early 1700s, had been the home of many notable and wealthy people until 1847, when it became known as the Ordnance School and was used as a strictly-run preparatory school for the education of cadets for Woolwich and Sandhurst. In 1868 the Revd Alfred Barrett of North Cheam bought the school. He built extensions and also admitted small girls as pupils. The appearance of the railway in 1888 cut the property in two and the school retained the smaller part – only 26 acres.

When the Daughters of the Cross arrived the property had been unoccupied for several years and required renovation and the addition of more buildings in order to open as a boarding school: St Philomena's College. The boarding school flourished over the next 20 years in spite of the interruption of the First World War, and various requests were made to the Sisters to open schools for local Catholic day pupils. In 1897 a small day school was opened on the west side of the property and in 1914 a secondary school was founded on an adjacent piece of land in West Street. These two schools have now become St Mary's Junior School (rebuilt in the 1960s) and Infant School. By 1931 it was decided to amalgamate the boarding school with the secondary school on the Carshalton House site, thus creating Carshalton House Collegiate School. But by 1945 this grand name reverted to the original name – St Philomena's. The little building in West Street became the Infant School and Kindergarten.

St Philly's, as it is affectionately known, became a Voluntary Aided Secondary School for Girls from 11–18 years. Three form entry was achieved in 1958. Throughout, the school was led by a series of Sisters as headteachers, and Sister Mary Damian's period of office took the school into a close partnership with the local authority and was a period of great expansion. Carshalton House itself was gradually taken into the school and this was handled with skill and foresight. Sister Margaret followed and was the last sister to be headmistress. In 1992 the Governors appointed Mrs Moira Kilkenny as the first lay headmistress, who has continued to extend the good reputation of the school. Now of Technology College status it caters for more than 1000 girls from 11–18 years.

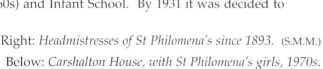

Right: *Headmistresses of St Philomena's since 1893.* (S.M.M.)

Below: *Carshalton House, with St Philomena's girls, 1970s.*

Beynons, Wallaces & The National School

The Beynons were a large, sprawling and confusing family, who set out to baffle historians by calling all their numerous male children either Edward or Edmund, so that it is almost impossible to distinguish one from another. They descended from Edward Beynon, who was certainly in Carshalton by the 1760s (he died in 1800) and who is described as the owner of a 'medicinal warehouse' in East London. It is perhaps significant that they married into two local milling families, the Heaths and the Batleys, both of whom had water mills on the Wandle, grinding drugs and snuff: the Heaths at the Grove Mill, the Batleys at Mill Green. The Beynons were a wealthy family. They lived in the house called Parkfields in Westcroft Road (No. 37) and when the Bramble Haw mansion was built opposite in the 1780s, they owned that too. They also had houses in other places, including Morden and Chelsham; but they seem to have regarded Carshalton as their home village, and quite a number of Beynons are buried in Carshalton churchyard or have church memorials.

In 1821 the Wallaces and the Beynons got together with the rector, the Reverend William Rose, in a scheme to raise, by public subscription, enough money to buy a plot of land in West Street on which to build a school. This was for what was called a National School, jointly supported by the Government and the Church of England, because hitherto Carshalton children had had to go to school in the church, where the rector and the Vestry arranged classes for them. The money was very soon raised; most of it seems to have come from the Beynon family, and the school was apparently built by about 1825, just across the yard from the Old Swan Inn. The building became the Sea Scout headquarters at No. 5 West Street.

During 1825/26 an artist called George Yates went all the way along the Wandle from Carshalton, Wallington and Beddington to Wandsworth, making watercolour sketches of buildings for a new guidebook, which seems never to have been published. He produced a lot of pictures, very quickly, and one of them is of the new National School at Carshalton, 1826, which shows two long, low buildings, connected by a sort of corridor, to form a letter H. Both wings of the building were the same, single storey, with a big skylight on the roof: one wing was to be for boys, the other for girls. But the Tithe Maps of 1839 and 1847 only show the present layout of buildings. We know that one wing was built, because it forms the base of the present building, so there was probably another wing to the north of the present building, where there are now two houses (Nos 7–9 West Street).

But one single-storey building was not enough, and in 1854 the roof was taken off, a second storey built on, and the roof replaced. The boys had the new upstairs; the girls had downstairs, which they shared with a room for Vestry/parish meetings, and a savings bank run by the church. And so matters remained for 20 years.

In 1870 a new system of state education began, and the Education Act of that year provided for each area to have its school board, which would set up state schools. Carshalton got its school board in April 1873, and by November it had taken over the boys' school, and then the girls' school in February 1874 (and in the course of the next two years, the children were moved to new purpose-built schools in Camden Road). Ten years earlier the current Edward Beynon, the Reverend Edward Francis Beynon of Chelsham, had made a will. He left Parkfields and Bramble Haw to a family trust for the benefit of other members of the Beynon family, but a good deal of his money, £4000, was left to a special charitable trust, called the Beynon Trust. This provided charity in the form of clothing and coal for the poor of Carshalton; and about half the money was to be used for the upkeep of the National School in West Street. The sum of £2000 was invested, bringing in the princely amount of about £40 per annum. But in February 1874 the West Street building ceased to be a Church of England National School and became a State Board School. Before anybody could point out to the Reverend Beynon that his will was now a nonsense, the old gentleman himself died on 10 March, a mere two or three weeks after his will stopped being applicable. What was to happen to the Beynon bequest?

In May the rector, the Reverend W.A.B. Cator, attended a meeting of the new School Board, and raised the question: did the National Schools still exist and could the money be paid, or would it have to revert to the Beynon family? Legal advice was sought and it seemed very doubtful that the money could be kept; a second opinion came to the same conclusion; and in February 1875 the executors of the will paid the £2000 to the Court of Chancery until the court could decide what to do with it.

Part of the 1st Carshalton Group, Sir Malcolm Campbell's Own, including Scouts, Cubs and Sea Scouts, who met in West Street, c.1938. (D.Y.)

The rector then petitioned Chancery that the money should be paid to the parish for the benefit of the West Street building. He argued that the building was still used as a Sunday school, and so it could be said that the National School still existed in this attenuated form. It was a very thin argument. But the School Board did not object (which was not perhaps surprising, since the rector was its new chairman); and, with enormous generosity, the Beynon family agreed. So the £2000 Beynon bequest was paid over to the parish for the benefit of the West Street building. Having obtained the money by this somewhat dubious means, nothing more was then heard of it until, five years later, there was a great scandal in the parish about the level of poor relief. A number of complaints were made that money existed in various Carshalton charities, administered in practice by the rector, but it was not being used for the charitable purposes stipulated.

At the Vestry meeting held at Easter 1881, the chair was taken by the churchwarden, Mr John Johnson, and after settling the parish rates for the year, he invited Mr Smith, the local lawyer, to raise the question of the charities. Mr Johnson said that he had been churchwarden for three years, but nobody had ever mentioned the charities to him, and he thought that he ought to find out what they were and what happened to the money in them. He asked Mr Smith to report on the matter. The Reverend Cator immediately objected to this proposal and said that the distribution of charity money could safely be left to him. He was merely following the practice of his predecessors, and in any case he said 'he knew more about the poor of the parish than all the churchwardens and overseers put together.' This remark promptly roused his old antagonist, Mr Greenhill, who commented that whenever the rector saw one poor person, he (Mr Greenhill) could see 300 – but only one got paid!

The meeting was now in full cry, and wanted to know more about the charitable funds and how they were administered. Mr Smith said that he had been obliged to write to the Charity Commissioners to ask them about it. They said that they had twice written to the parish clerk suggesting that the money should be deposited with them, so that they could distribute the interest payable from it. The chairman then complained that the parish clerk had received these letters, but had not told anybody about them. The parish clerk immediately announced his resignation. As regards the Beynon money in particular, Mr Smith said that he had read the will of the Reverend Beynon, which stipulated that the money was to be administered by a trust of nine people, who should be elected annually. It was now 1881, and as far as he could discover, there had been no election since 1876 – and some of the people elected then had by now left the district. He proposed that the money should be transferred to the Charity Commissioners. The rector of course objected to this – and so did his chief supporter, a certain Mr Crow – but they were overruled and the proposal was passed. The Revd Cator then agreed to see that the money was transferred to the commissioners.

What happened after that remains obscure. The West Street building did in fact function as a school for a short time in the 1890s. In 1888 it was used for the Church of England Girls High School, which was the forerunner of the present Wallington High School for Girls. During the 1900s the educational function has been its use for Scouts, in 1914 for the church Cubs and Scouts, also Sea Scouts. (Use by the Sea Scouts was discontinued and the building was restored for domestic use and sold in 1995.) There is still a nine-person Beynon Trust, which includes the churchwardens and a number of councillors. They now administer the Trust's funds for educational purposes in Carshalton.

Left and above: *The National School, West Street, 1870, and the Scout headquarters, West Street, c.1970.*

Chapter Five

LEISURE PURSUITS

Mr Puttock & His Deer

It is not known when there were first deer in Carshalton Park. They were certainly there in the eighteenth century, and they may have been kept there for centuries before that. Little information is available about them until well into the nineteenth century. By this time most of the deer in Carshalton Park no longer belonged to the Taylors, the lords of the manor, who owned the Park, but were simply kept there by the Surrey Staghounds, and were taken off to be hunted about the countryside whenever the Staghounds had a meet.

On the day of the hunt a suitable stag or hind that could give the hunters a good run was loaded into a special wagon, the deer-cart, and trundled off to the appointed place, where it was then released and chased. The deer were not always killed, provided they could run fast enough. It was usual to fix a certain time or a certain distance, at which point the hunt would end. The huntsmen would try to round up their dogs, and the deer-keeper had the much more difficult job of finding and collecting the deer that got away and taking it back to Carshalton, ready for the next occasion.

The person in charge of the deer-cart was therefore very skilled and was the most important and best-known servant of the hunt – an eminent figure in the village. The Surrey Staghounds had a succession of three deermen during the course of the nineteenth century. All of them were famous characters in their time, although very little is known about the first one other than the fact that he was called Gyp, and was renowned for his exploits when he was a huntsman, before he was promoted to driving the deer-cart. He refused to wear boots, and insisted on running after the hounds in his bare feet.

William Puttock, his successor in around 1860, was equally hardy. He was out in all weathers and seems to have had an iron constitution. However, it is likely that he had trouble with his feet, since a cartoon of him, drawn in 1875, depicts him wearing large padded boots and being taken to select the deer for the day's hunt in a chair mounted on a sort of wheelbarrow. He had begun work as a stable lad with Sir Gilbert Heathcote (of The Durdans at Epsom) who was the first master of the Surrey Staghounds. In time, Puttock was put in charge of Sir Gilbert's stables, and when Sir Gilbert's horse, Amato, won the Derby in 1838, Puttock could boast of having done a great deal to help train it. Around 1860 he was given the even more responsible post of being deer-cart man. The deer-cart was kept in the stables at the back of the King's Arms in Carshalton High Street (this stood opposite The Green and was destroyed by a bomb in the Second World War), and Puttock had the cottage by the gate into Carshalton Park at the top of the Square (roughly where the library now stands).

Puttock was deer-cart man for 28 years and was very successful in the post. Regardless of where the hunt went (the Staghounds hunted on the Banstead Downs as well as the South Downs behind Brighton and Eastbourne) Puttock would have to take the deer to the meet. He seemed to have an instinct for which way the deer would run, and (if the deer got clear of the hunt) there would be Puttock waiting for it with his horse and cart at the end of the day, ready to take it back to Carshalton. He was always very pleased at the way he could be home in his cottage keeping warm and dry, whilst the huntsmen were sometimes out until the early hours of the morning, trying to round up the dogs, who had run all over the place as they looked for the deer. But Puttock had a way with everybody, and was immensely popular. He was a great story-teller, and both animals and children loved him. He was such a friendly and genial fellow that if the hunt got out of hand and ran across somebody else's land or damaged their crops and hedges, Puttock was invariably sent along to smooth things down, and he was usually successful.

There was, however, one occasion when even he was unable to settle a dispute. The hunt was out near Fetcham and they were chasing a rather eccentric deer known as Real Jam – all the deer had names, and this one was named after a famous racehorse owned by a member of the hunt. Real Jam had a great propensity for taking refuge in people's houses and on this occasion, hotly pursued by the dogs, it ran into the home of two elderly bedridden ladies, ran upstairs, and much to the ladies' consternation,

Mᵣ Puttick in his Carriage selecting the Deer for the Surrey Stag Hounds.

The Puttocks' cottage in the Square and deer in Carshalton Park.

Mr Puttock driving the deer-cart in the 1870s.

arrived in their bedroom. The deer then stuck its head out of the window to see how the hunt was getting on without it. The dogs, sniffing around in the courtyard, saw the deer up at the bedroom window and promptly also ran upstairs into the ladies' chamber, where they made a real mess. Although Puttock did his best to explain that it was a hind, a female deer, and it was only natural for it to look for a lady's bedroom, the inhabitants were not amused.

Puttock was even more fond of deer than he was of people, so it might be fair to suggest that he was pleased when the deer won. Deer have a great dislike of being handled, but they never minded Puttock. He had the capacity, as he put it himself, to 'charm' them – and just as people are said to sing to bees, or talk to plants to make them grow, Puttock had a sort of incantation with which he could calm the deer down and make them approach him. He would sometimes perform this trick for visitors to the Park if they promised to keep still and quiet, and one of them described it afterwards as a combination of 'a twitter and a chatter'. His best trick, however, was to pull a brilliantly coloured handkerchief out of his pocket, which the deer took as a signal that he wanted to talk to them, so up they would come to him.

He knew each deer by name. There was a deer, another hind, known as Apology, who escaped and was at large for many months, until someone told Puttock that she had been seen near Reigate. Puttock went over there, and along with the local keepers tramped about all day looking for her. Eventually, in the evening, they found her. However, as soon as she saw this group of men approaching, she ran off and was soon two fields away. Puttock made his peculiar call, and she stopped. 'Where are you going, you old fool', he shouted, 'it's only me'. He took out his handkerchief and waved it, and up she came to him. Unfortunately, the other keepers came closer, which frightened her. She struggled and Puttock was unable to hold her, so she managed to escape again. Puttock finally recaptured her months later, when he found her during a hunt near Beachy Head.

There was also a stag, officially known as Ploughboy, who the whole village knew as 'Bacca', because he loved chewing tobacco. He would run after anyone who had some and beg for it. His favourite place was next to the iron gates in Park Lane, and as people went by he would thrust his face through the bars to ask for tobacco. Some people 'fed' him regularly, although he was very fastidious, and would spit the offering out again if it had already been chewed. Although Ploughboy was the son of a famous deer, called Beechmont, who had never been caught by the hounds, Ploughboy himself was hopeless to chase: instead of running he kept stopping to ask people for tobacco. It is said that Puttock often recounted the tale of how Ploughboy had found four unconscious gypsies lying in the mud. Ploughboy had stopped to ask for a wad, but the gypsies

thought he was a gift of a free piece of venison, and tried to grab him. The affronted stag promptly knocked them down, and continued on his way. Eventually this vice brought about his downfall. He became so dissolute that he refused to stay in the Park, and kept jumping out and roaming the streets looking for a chew; he became more trouble than he was worth. Eventually he was sold to a woodcutter in Kent, and ended his days harnessed to a sledge dragging timber about. The last record of Puttock is in about 1888, when he went into the Park one night with his field-glasses to look at a comet. Whilst he was there surveying the sky a stag called The Footman came along and rubbed against him. 'Oh', he said, 'you want to see the comet, do you?' An astonished visitor to the house, who had also gone out to see the night sky, came across the very unusual spectacle of a deer looking through a pair of binoculars, which Puttock was holding in front of his eyes.

Puttock died in November 1890, and was replaced by Tom Ding. Whereas Puttock was eminently sober, and never drank, which was unusual for a huntsman, Ding, it seems, hardly ever stopped. Like Puttock, he had a fund of good stories, but he liked to tell them in the pub, where he could get a few drinks on the strength of them. After one very strenuous story-time in the Greyhound, he came reeling out of the pub and went straight over the railings into the pond. It happened to be local election time, and the next time Ding was passing the parish notice-board, on which the names of the candidates were posted, he was surprised to find that somebody had written his name on the list – and in the column marked 'Occupation' had written 'Professor of Swimming'.

Ding enjoyed driving the deer-cart. It gave him plenty of time to drink whilst waiting for the deer, and better still, after the hunt he had to take the cart back to the stables in the King's Arms, where he could not only get another bottle, but he could also see the barmaid, to whom he was rather partial. His drinking got steadily worse. He was so tight some nights that he was unable to drive the cart into the yard or put the horse away in the stable. One particular night some of the local lads stole the barmaid's dress, stuffed it full of straw, and hung the dummy figure from a beam in the stable. When Ding came roaring home that night and opened the door he thought the girl had hanged herself, which gave him a terrible shock. He was nearly fainting as he fell into the King's Arms, and had to be revived with brandy. After that it is said that he frequently suffered from nerves and had to be revived more and more often.

He was soon quite incapable of looking after the deer-cart, and had to be demoted to being huntsman. However, the Park was gradually sold off for houses from 1892 onwards, and the deer themselves had to go in 1898, so there was no more need for the deer-cart. Ding retired to his cottage in Rochester Road, and seems to have died soon afterwards, in 1902.

BLOOD SPORTS & HACKBRIDGE HOUSE

Carshalton has a long history as a noted centre for blood sports in the 1800s. At the beginning of the nineteenth century, Hassell records that the village was, from this point of view, 'a scene of lively interest', and that the country between Carshalton and Banstead 'was in perpetual activity from the hour that the sporting season commenced in each succeeding year until it was finished.' There were regular meets in spring and autumn, presided over by John Durand, 'the very life spring of the field-sports of the neighbourhood', who owned the Greyhound inn with its stables for the hunters.

In addition to the usual fox hunting, beagling and hare-coursing, the deer from Carshalton Park were owned by the Surrey Staghounds, and were carted up to Banstead Downs to be released

The Earl of Derby's staghounds, from a painting by John Barenger dated 1823. The figures left to right are: 12th Earl of Derby (who lived at The Oaks), Lord Stanley, Hon. G Stanley, Jonathan Griffin. (S.L.S.L.)

and hunted down. There was also a pack of staghounds at The Oaks, which had itself been built during the previous century by an association of sporting gentlemen calling themselves the Hunters' Club. There was fishing, especially for trout, in the Wandle; and the landlord of the Greyhound, which catered specially for anglers, would arrange for parties to visit the great estates along the river whose owners held the fishing rights. And there was also wild fowling in the marshes along the edge of the water.

These were, of course, mainly pastimes for the aristocracy and gentry, although the lower orders no doubt took a share. Certainly there are innumerable reports of poaching. The poorer folk had their own particular blood sports; there are reports of bull-baiting in the early years of the seventeenth century and there was a cock pit at the King's Arms in the High Street. However, the favourite sport, in which all sections of the population joined, was ratting.

There were several rat pits in the area. These were circles of ground with sides about 3ft high, with the sides sloping inwards to stop the rats jumping out. Here dogs and rats fought to the death, and we are told that a terrier with a good reputation for killing rats might have as much as £50 laid on him in bets. The main local supplier of rats in the 1870s, when ratting was still immensely popular, was Mr Gardner, who had a saddler's shop on the north side of the High Street. Later the business was moved across the road to the corner where Barclay's Bank is now

situated. Workmen from the fields would bring rats to him because they heard that he paid a good price.

One day, one of the men who had been harvesting caught over 100 rats whilst doing the threshing. He put the rats in a sack and carried them to the High Street to sell to Gardner. However, Gardner was himself out hunting at the time, so the workman had to hang about and wait for him. It seemed a pity to wait in the road when he was about to make some extra money, so he crossed to the inn – and was soon very drunk. When Gardner came home, he remembered finding the High Street in a state of uproar. 'The street was full of excited people, yelling, screaming, whistling, shouting and running in all directions.' The reason for this, he found, was 'a multitude of rats running about everywhere' – in the road, in the shops and in the houses. It transpired that the labourer, being full of alcohol, had got into a row with a gang of local youths – one of whom had whipped out a knife and slit the sack. No doubt the boy was surprised when over 100 rats jumped out. It is said that the High Street suffered a great plague of rats for several years afterwards, but nothing was done about it: nobody wanted to pay the piper.

The rats bought by Mr Gardner were for the most part supplied to the rat pit in the grounds of Hackbridge House (sometimes called Hackbridge Park). During the second half of the nineteenth century the property was owned by a Mr Edwin Curtis Goad; the Goad family were very enthusiastic supporters of the sport. Unfortunately, little is known about Edwin C. Goad (possibly an American name) although he became the owner of Shopley House in Carshalton in 1887. It is not known when Hackbridge House was built, although it seems likely that it was constructed during the second quarter of the nineteenth century, possibly to replace the Carshalton terminal of the Surrey Iron Railway. It has always been known that a branch line of the Surrey Iron Railway finished up at Hackbridge after leaving the main line at Mitcham Junction; and there is a map, dated 1806, which shows that the terminal was adjacent to the bridge – in fact just about where Hackbridge House stands. The earliest Carshalton station and Hackbridge House either occupied the same site, or must have been very close to one another.

ALEHOUSES & SUNDAY DRINKING

The village had at least four inns by the middle of the seventeenth century. One of them was the White Lion – which was the most important, and may have been the predecessor of the Greyhound. There was also the Feathers, the Owl, and the Unicorn. It is possible that one of these was originally the King's Arms in the High Street (where Somerfield's now stands). By 1700 there was also a public house called The Bunch of Grapes.

In the manorial court records for 1786, Mary Lodge, the wife of Archdeacon Edmund Lodge, a previous rector of Carshalton, claimed that 'the Old Swan Alehouse' with its barns, stables, garden and orchard, had belonged to her father Richard Garrard (of Alton Lodge, 70 West Street) and ought now to belong to her. The court agreed. More to the point, the court record mentions, first, that this was an old pub – and so may well have been built around 1650; and secondly, that the old building had recently been pulled down and the pub rebuilt. As such, it is possible to date the Swan in West Street to about 1780. We know that it remained a public house until 1908, but after that became home to a timber merchant.

We know that the Greyhound Inn dates back to the 1600s, but although there were numerous references to alehouses in the seventeenth century there was no mention of the Greyhound. The earliest reference is in 1706 ('John Watson at the sign of the Greyhound') and it is frequently mentioned after

that. Mr A.E. Jones suggests that the Greyhound was part private house, part public house, so there was a confusion of owners and tenants. But he refers to an 'old customary messuage now used as part of the inn', so the house is probably much older than the pub.

Indeed, alehouses are somewhat easier to identify in the probate inventories, although again this is not specified by the documents and it has to be deduced from the lists of contents. The earliest alehouse in the collection belonged to Robert Sollars, who died in 1691. He left a son, George Sollars – who was his partner 'in the trade of the house wherein the said Robert Sollars lived and dyed' – and various bills to be paid to several vintners and inns in the city of London from whom they were buying wines, brandy and what is called 'strongwater'. Robert Sollars is a bit of a puzzle. He is already well known in the Carshalton records as someone who owned one of the larger houses in Carshalton during the 1660s and '70s. He was assessed for seven hearths under the Hearth Tax, and one source suggests that he had property which later became part of the Greyhound. However, it cannot be assumed that this is an early reference to the Greyhound itself. All the seventeenth-century records of the Greyhound were burnt.

It is not until 1756 that a clear description of the inn is evident. At this point, it is described as a three-storey building with seven rooms on each floor, with the top two being used as bedrooms. Outside there was a yard and an orchard, two ranges of stables, and a granary standing on brick pedestals. There was

The Greyhound in 1970. (S.L.S.L.)

Left to right, top to bottom:
The Swan Inn, West Street, late 1800s;
The Windsor Castle in 1903.
Note the absence of Beynon Road;
The Sun in 1967;
The Fox and Hounds, showing the
demolition of the Chestnut Café in the
forecourt, 1913. (S.L.S.L.);
The Racehorse, West Street, c.1880.
(S.L.S.L.)

also what is called 'a necessary house built on a removable', a well-house up on the Downs, an inn sign on a signpost and a cockpit with cages for 100 birds. It would seem to have been a flourishing establishment, but when the innkeeper, Richard Grandee, died in 1756, his widow, Martha Grandee, declared that the business was much decayed. She launched into a long complaint: she had been left with seven children to support; she was unable to sell the house until the lease ran out; and she had 11 soldiers and two horses billeted on her, which she claimed cost her 2s.0d. a week per head.

It is perhaps not surprising that in 1772 all the most affluent residents had accounts, not at the Greyhound, but at the Fox and Hounds, which was run by a widower called Richard Cronk. This had only four bedrooms, but boasted a busy stables; there were half a dozen coaches for hire, including what is called a glass coach and a post chariot, as well as 22 horses (geldings). Some of their names are listed: Tuft, Toby, Tallboy, Tinker, Whitefoot, Peacock, Robin, Jolly, Blackjack, Poppett and Roundhead. However, all the horses had to be sold in 1772 because Mr Cronk's heirs were two young children, who could not run a business, let alone a pub.

At the end of the eighteenth century the Greyhound was owned by John Durand of Woodcote Hall, Wallington, and later by his son John Hodson Durand of Carshalton House, who sold it to a certain Daniel Tarling (variously described as a victualler of Carshalton and a tailor of Richmond) for £1650 in 1819. A year later Tarling divided up the property. The old hunting stables were kept at the back and were converted into cottages. New cottages were built on the land between the Greyhound and the church/Queen's Well (demolished in 1963). Tarling was essentially a developer. He sold the front of the building for £1550 (only £100 less than he had paid for the whole) to William Tritton, a brewer of Beddington and Wandsworth. The brewing connection passed to Young's Brewery at the Ram, Wandsworth, who have remained owners until the present time. Tarling died in 1829.

Most of the Greyhound documents were destroyed by fire so the map of 1820 is very valuable. Two points of interest should be noted. Firstly, the oldest part of the Greyhound is the western section standing back from the road with the Dutch gables, but the part fronting the pond with bay windows (known as the Swan Bar to locals) was described in 1820 as 'a newly created building' called 'the two rooms'. It is not so new, for it can be seen on the Hughson print of 1806 – the earliest known picture of the front of the building. Secondly, the present car park, once the garden to the old house, caused a problem for Daniel Tarling as it gave no access to his stables at the back. This was solved by giving him a right of way along a path which ran between the old part and the new – two quite separate unconnected

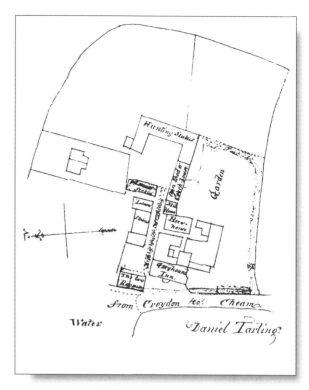

Map of the Greyhound in 1820.

buildings according to the map. Today, when entering the front door, customers can turn either way, but this was not the case in 1820.

The new part was built to enclose what was probably a large open courtyard at the side of the inn. No record exists of when the two parts, old and new, were joined together, but 20 years later in 1849, the Tithe Map shows that this had been done, and the Greyhound as we know it had been formed.

With the variety of inns in the parish, it seems feasible to suggest that drinking was an important part of local life. A note by Dr Peatling sees him complain how difficult it was on Sunday mornings to have to push through the crowds of churchgoers who flocked into the Coach and Horses after morning service. 'Even at one o'clock', he wrote, 'my passage to and from the bar was blocked by a dozen men, with old Miles the verger in the middle.'

But the thirsty churchgoers of 50 years ago had many ancestors, who had to be kept in line by the church officials. Thus in the parish minutes of October 1785, it was declared that from then on all business relating to the parish was to be done in the vestry room and that no money would be paid to settle the accounts of any business transacted in a public house. What caused this resolution to be made is not known. However, it seems likely that one of the parish officers, making merry in the Greyhound or the King's Arms, had unwisely contracted for something which he should not have done, and the church had to foot the bill.

At any rate there was an immediate audit of the churchwardens' and overseers' accounts. Publicans and sinners were a perennial problem. Only two years later, in 1787, a notice was sent by the Parish Council to every innkeeper in Carshalton:

Notice is given to the keepers of all Public Houses in this parish that they are strictly enjoined to shut up their houses during the time of Divine Service on the Lord's Day, and that they suffer no person to remain in their houses to tipple or drink after the hour of ten at night.

To enforce this early version of the licensing hours a beadle was appointed – with a salary of five guineas a year plus a free coat and hat – whose duties were to: 'walk about the several parts of the parish, on Sunday in particular, to remove from hence all idle and disorderly persons.'

Even in Victorian times there was this same conflict between ale and alleluiahs. A particularly neat device is recorded in the 1870s and '80s. The landlord of the Coach and Horses would stand outside on a Sunday and as he heard the sound of the last hymn being sung he would carry two large tin pails full of beer, slung from a yoke over his shoulder,

across the churchyard towards the cottages on Church Hill. Of course he just happened to meet the congregation coming out. They needed little persuasion to purchase one of the pint measures, which just by chance he happened to have with him. The Revd Cator enjoyed his drink and he seems to have turned a blind eye to the practice. However, his successor was cast in a sterner mould, and much to the annoyance of the landlord, prohibited him from carrying beer across the churchyard path. It was, he said, an improper use of holy ground.

Top: *A late-Victorian view of The Hope, West Street, from an original at the house.* (S.L.S.L.)

Above: *The King's Arms, High Street, late 1800s.* (S.L.S.L.)

Left: *The Coach and Horses before 1878.*

'POETRY' FROM THE PAST

Local historians do not usually pay much attention to poetry, although anyone who has read Brightling's *History* will remember that very useful and detailed description of Carshalton in 1855, written in rather uncouth verse. People liked to listen to home-made poems in the way that folk nowadays listen to pop songs. Recitations served as regular entertainment in homes and taverns.

Carshalton local records are full of pieces of peculiar poetry, which were obviously hailed with great delight when some local bard produced them 100 or 200 years ago. Indeed it would not be too difficult to produce a book of Carshalton poetry, containing some of the appallingly bad verse, in which our ancestors recounted some event which caught the popular imagination at the time. It was obviously a favourite occupation to compose parodies of well-known hymns, which were then presumably sung to the appropriate tune. An irresistible subject was the new settlement built in the mid-nineteenth century in the fields beyond Stanley Park Road – the area which was known as Carshalton on the Hill. In local parlance this was known as Jerusalem. A century ago, if you said 'I'm going to Jerusalem', you did not mean that you were going to emulate the rector and make a pilgrimage to the Holy Land. Rather, it meant that you were going up Stanley Road. One explanation for the name is that the new houses were built with Jewish money and many Jewish people lived in them. However, the real reason is probably more biblical – it was Carshalton on the Hill, the city on the hill: Jerusalem. This provided plenty of scope for parodies. One of these poems describes what a cold place the new community was; how one went up Stanley Road and was frozen by the wind whistling across the Downs and the open fields beyond. This was written out and intended to be sung under the title 'Jerusalem the cold 'un'.

One of the oldest and most elaborate of these parodies is called The Carshaltoniad. It was written in 1776 in imitation of the celebrated poem by William Cowper about John Gilpin's Ride, which had just been published. In fact the author gives his name as Ephraim Gilpin, and claims to be John Gilpin's cousin, although he was actually the Revd M. Madan, curate at the Parish Church, who had just been saddled with a new rector, the Revd William Rose, and fairly obviously did not altogether approve of that gentleman's ways. He makes fun of the rector by recording in verse the unhappy episode which followed after a party of gentlemen from Epsom had been on a visit to the rectory during the winter of 1776. This apparently was printed, with illustrations, but it is not known whether any of the original copies survive. A copy of the text was reprinted in the local paper a century later, in 1879.

The poem tells how four gentlemen, who liked to have a good time, hired a coach from the Spread Eagle Inn at Epsom and went to have dinner with the Revd Rose. There was a baronet, Sir Mark Parsons; a local squire, Mr William Noethey; a bluff old seadog, Captain Bevan; and a Mr Thomas Woodman, well known in local society for 'blithe jest and jocund mirth':

> *Four merry blades from Epsom went*
> *At Carshalton for to dine,*
> *To eat the honest Rector's meat*
> *And eke to drink his wine.*

> *The hospitable treat soon showed*
> *The bounty of their host,*
> *For to receive his friendly guests*
> *He spared not pains nor cost.*

> *Good cheer, quoth they; welcome, quoth he.*
> *I'm glad to see you all,*
> *And straightway for to drink their health*
> *He for a glass did call...*

> *They pledged him straight, and thus the wine*
> *And social chat went round,*
> *Till heedless how the hours had passed*
> *The clock at nine was found...*

The gentlemen's coach arrived to take them back to Epsom. So, very merry, they all piled into the coach and set off. It was a pitch-dark night, and in any case they were in no condition to know where they were going. The next thing they knew, the coach had stopped and was flooded with water. They had left the Old Rectory in what is now Festival Walk, had driven straight into the Ponds, and became stuck in the mud. (They had obviously tried to cross the ford by Honeywood and missed it.) It seems they were far too drunk to appreciate what was going on around them:

> *Oho, they quoth, we are set fast*
> *But why they could not think – until they had the*
> *bright idea:*
> *The horses have stopped to drink.*

When nothing happened, they looked out of the coach, saw water all around, and became alarmed:

> *Sadly alarmed, they cried aloud*
> *Some speedy course to take*
> *The river's banks resounded with*
> *The noise which they did make.*

The squire made hunting calls; others shouted for lifebelts and cork jackets, while the old sea captain thought he was back on board ship, and kept bellowing 'Hoist the anchor, and set her head to port'. Mr

Left: *Carshalton St Andrews Football Club, 1904.*

Below: *Carshalton Athletic Football Club, 1920/21. Playing at the time were J. Wadey, J. Newton, W. Hobbs, A. White, B. Massingham, H. Clarke, P. Dicker, H. Buckenham, J. Davies, F. Blundell, J. Cook, Ellis Fitch, T. Fuller, L. Tate, ? Foster, ? Levitt and A. Fuller.* (Both M.F.)

Below: *The First XI outside Bishopsford House, 1987. Left to right, back: Miss D. Lee (scorer), D. Freeman, D. Leonard, M. Cooper, R. Thompson, A. Greenslade, K. Fuller, D. Whitehall (umpire); front: J. Callcut, K. Patel, J. Flint, D. Harrison, J. Flint.* (C.C.)

Woodman commented that they had set their heads to port too long, and if they had only left the rector's port before it got dark, they might be better off now. There was a great hullabaloo, which disturbed the entire village, and people came rushing out of their houses quite unable to imagine why anybody should be sitting, roaring and shouting, in the middle of the Ponds on a winter's night. The banks were ablaze with candles and lanterns as people tried to make out what was happening. Eventually more horses were employed to help pull the coach out of the water. The four gentlemen repaired to the Greyhound to fortify themselves for the rest of the journey home.

Thus ended this auspicious day
With all its mirth and glee.
If such a treat should come again
May I be there to see.

The curate later commented that the gentlemen's visit to the Revd William Rose only went to prove the truth of the old adage: that there was no rose without a thorn.

CARSHALTON FC: 'THE ROBINS'

Carshalton Football Club has its origins in two earlier local clubs. Carshalton St Andrews was founded in 1897 and had a small but enthusiastic group of supporters. They played at the Wrythe Green recreation ground. With the passing of time and the retirement of a number of the players it was decided to merge with Carshalton Athletic in the summer of 1908.

The Mill Lane Mission was founded in 1903 for boys of between 13 and 14 years of age and their pitch was in Carshalton Park. They continued with some success and in 1906/7 were elected to the Croydon and District League, Division 2A and the Surrey Minor Cup. They moved to the Wrythe Green pitch when St Andrews vacated it and changed their name to Carshalton Athletic Football Club. The first match was played on 7 September 1907 against Westbrook (Thornton Heath). The new club had both senior and junior teams and by 1912/13 had won both the Surrey Junior Charity Cup and Division One West of the Southern Suburban League.

The First World War brought a halt to local football for five years but in 1919 play began again, this time in Culvers Park, since the old ground was unavailable, having been sown with new grass. The first match brought a 3-1 victory against Hurlingham Athletic in front of a crowd of around 500 spectators. Plans for building the Culvers Estate led to another move and in 1920 the Carshalton Urban District Council leased the club the present ground in Colston Avenue. The first match was played there on 1 January 1921 and the team was defeated 1-0 by Thornville. The team comprised Messrs J. Wadey,

Ellis, H. Buckenham, Fitch, B. Massingham, T. Fuller, L. Tate, Foster, P. Dicker, Levitt and A. Fuller. The club has remained at the ground ever since and in 1949 the terracing was built. The Robins have continued to flourish and are currently in the First Division of the Ryman Isthmian League.

CARSHALTON CRICKET CLUB

Sir Samuel Barrow, Major Lovelock and Major Mallinson were early patrons of the club when it was formed in 1925. The first games were played on a field belonging to Major Mallinson at Hackbridge. In 1926 the club moved to the Grove field in Carshalton, using the stable as a pavilion. Finally in 1930 the move was made to Poulter Park, a public open space, formerly the grounds of Bishopsford House. The house was closed to the public at that time but the Urban District Council allowed the club to have a pitch there. Teas were served on the lawn at the back of the house and the club prospered.

There was a gap in play during the war years, when the wine cellars of the house were used as an air-raid shelter, and the house itself was hit by incendiary bombs, but survived. The club regrouped after the war, but accommodation was a problem. Not until 1954 did the Council agree to lease some of the rooms in Bishopsford House to the club.

With better facilities things improved again. Tours were made to Holland, and by the late 1960s the club was running three Saturday and four Sunday teams. In 1971 the club entered the Mid Surrey League, which became the Slazenger Surrey League. The club proudly celebrated its 60th anniversary in 1990.

Unfortunately Bishopsford House was destroyed by fire and in 2000 the club merged with Croydon Gas to become the Carshalton and Croydon Gas Cricket Club. Its ground is at Mollison Drive, Wallington.

CARSHALTON CAMERA CLUB

Early in 1950, Band Corporal Peter Stroud of The King's Third Hussars in Germany received a request (which amounted to an order) from his Commanding Officer to design a photographic darkroom and organise a regimental camera club. This was done and, at the first meeting, Peter was elected Chairman. The Third Hussars Camera Club was very successful; its members gained many awards in competitions throughout BAOR.

Whilst on leave in the summer of 1952, Peter attended the first Arts and Crafts Exhibition organised by the newly-formed Carshalton Arts Council held at the Grove in Carshalton. There were a few photographs on display, mainly of postcard size, and not of the standard which had been reached in Germany. He enquired about local camera clubs and was surprised to find that none existed in either Carshalton or Wallington. He discussed the matter with a family friend, James L. Bacon AIBP, Vice-President of the Institute of British Photographers, and enlisted his assistance in setting up what became Carshalton Camera Club.

The first meeting was held at the Fox and Hounds in Carshalton High Street and those who attended included Mr and Mrs Henry Clay, and George Rowbottom (all from Mitcham Camera Club), John Orchard and Reg Wilshier ARPS (from Sutton Camera Club), as well as Barbara Smith and Peter Woolerton. Jimmy Bacon chaired the meeting.

At this inaugural meeting, Henry Clay was elected Chairman, a position which he was to hold for many years. Peter Stroud was Honorary Secretary and Peter Woolerton was Honorary Treasurer. Bruce Nightingale from Putney was introduced in the following week, and he subsequently held all the offices in the club at various times. Later, Jimmy Bacon and Reg Wilshier were elected vice presidents although, sadly, both died within a few years. After several years, John Orchard also occupied the post of Chairman.

Carshalton Camera Club moved three or four times during those early years until finding a permanent home at the hall of the New Presbyterian church, at the junction of Woodcote Road and Stafford Road in Wallington. This was an ideal venue until the club was forced to move once again due to re-development of the site and economic circumstances. It ended up at its present (and also very suitable) meeting place in Butter Hill, on the borders of Carshalton and Wallington.

The club celebrates its Golden Jubilee towards the end of 2002, an achievement of which the members are justly proud. They remain what they always have been – a group of friendly and enthusiastic photographers creating a distinctive atmosphere with the knack of producing interesting and individual photographs which do not necessarily conform to any prevailing fads or fashions.

Carshalton Camera Club is a member of The Surrey Photographic Association, the Central Association of Photographic Societies, and through them, The Photographic Alliance of Great Britain. It is also a member of the Federation of South London Photographic Societies, and a member of the Sutton Arts Council (formerly the Carshalton Arts Council) with which it has been associated since the very earliest days.

CARSHALTON CHORAL SOCIETY

Carshalton Choral Society was formed in 1946 by the late Douglas West, organist at Carshalton Methodist Church. The original intention was to promote musical interest only within the younger fraternity, but the society's membership, currently standing at 70, was subsequently extended to all age groups. The repertoire consists of both religious and secular music, aiming to perform a balance of lesser-known works as well as those more regularly performed. The society holds three main concerts each year, together with a recital of Christmas music. Occasionally it combines with other choirs to perform more ambitious works and regularly performs with the Surrey Festival Choir in Guildford Cathedral.

In its formative years the society was honoured to have Sir Malcolm Sargent as its President and more recently enjoyed the patronage of Sir Harry Secombe.

Since its formation there have been six conductors including Douglas West. This position is currently held by Roy Nicholson. The society is a registered charity in its own right and supports other charities by means of its concert activities.

CARSHALTON LAWN TENNIS CLUB

On 31 December 1911 Sir J. Crichton-Browne signed the deeds for the purchase of land from the Carshalton Park Estate. Sir Crichton-Browne was a doctor and was very keen on outdoor games for young people. It was his wish that part of the land purchased should remain 'open ground', so during 1912 part of the land became Carshalton Lawn Tennis Club.

Most of the members lived in the roads around the club, which lies between Beeches Avenue and Crichton Road. In 1926 Sir Crichton-Browne passed the ownership to six members who became directors and shareholders of Carshalton Courts Limited. After 1938 three trustees were appointed and the club was run by a Tennis General Committee.

Between 1926 and 1938 four hard courts (red en-tout-cas) were laid, leaving four grass courts. Also during this time Mr Edwards, one of the directors, bought a First World War Army hut, which is still used as the club pavilion. During the war membership dropped to 34 in 1941 and sheep and goats grazed on the grass courts, but by the early 1950s membership had risen to 100 and various improvements had been made to the courts. In 1959 the clubhouse was extended by the addition of a veranda, the work being undertaken by club members. With the aid of grants and self-help the club was able to provide new courts and floodlighting in the 1980s and two new courts in 1991.

The junior section of the club was started before the First World War but has been most successful in recent years under the supervision of Anthea Winterton. Coaching is undertaken by the Terry Cooper Organisation. As a sociable 'family' club, friendly matches as well as open and fun tournaments are held along with barbecues and other social events. All of these occasions take place in aid of the Improvement Fund.

Chapter Six

LOCAL FAMILIES

GEORGE BENJAMIN BRIGHTLING

George Benjamin Brightling of Madeley Cottage, Church Hill, Carshalton was a pillar of local society, a churchwarden and a leading member of the local Temperance Society. Additionally, he was one who did not neglect the things of this world: he ran his own building society, and was an agent for such diverse things as insurance and plate-glass windows. Brightling was also the author of *Some Particulars Relating to the History and Antiquities of Carshalton*, first published at Bethnal Green in 1872, with a slightly larger version produced in 1882. This is now quite a rare book. In addition to his historical account, Brightling also wrote a very useful description of what Carshalton was like over a century ago.

Those who have seen a copy of the book will recall the very striking opening, which tells us that 96 per cent of Carshalton consists of fields, of which about one seventh are meadowland. The remainder was used for cultivation of crops, especially peppermint, lavender, thyme, camomile, liquorice, rosemary, hyssop and other herbs. The land has certainly changed since then.

Perhaps even more interesting is a poem, a piece of doggerel really, which he quotes in full, and which was composed by one of the patients at the Royal Hospital for Incurables which occupied the old workhouse at Wrythe Green. The poem was written about 1855, and describes the main buildings, the churches, the schools, the public houses and the shops. He also mentions the residents, although without, as a rule, mentioning names. One can have quite a lot of fun trying to identify and locate them. Here are a few short extracts:

> *It's a neat little village surrounded by hills,*
> *And supports itself chiefly by snuff and corn mills.*
> *There's plenty of places to go and get beer,*
> *As in every village – of that never fear...*

But there was also:

> *A station all covered with roses so gaily,*
> *That the engines come puffing and blowing to daily...*

> *The Rector, the Revd W. Cator,*
> *Who at preaching a sermon is a very first rater;*
> *He divests his discourse of all cant and hypocrisy:*
> *I can't say the same for all church aristocracy.*
> *And the barber, with tricoloured pole at his door;*
> *He's not only a barber, but he's something more:*
> *He keeps the post office, and sorts out the letters,*
> *And every day handles the thoughts of his betters.*

It is interesting to note that there seems to have been a sort of primitive Carshalton Society in the 1850s:

> *There is a society formed for mutual improvement,*
> *And many support this commendable movement.*
> *They're going to have people to lecture and so on,*
> *And I hope the affair will successfully go on.*

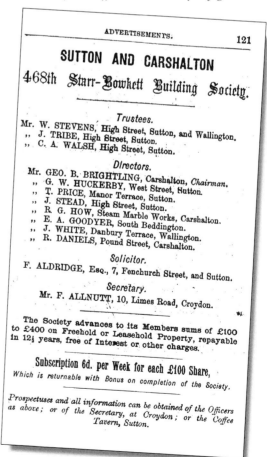

ADVERTISEMENTS. 121

SUTTON AND CARSHALTON
468th Starr-Bowkett Building Society.

Trustees.
Mr. W. STEVENS, High Street, Sutton, and Wallington.
„ J. TRIBE, High Street, Sutton.
„ C. A. WALSH, High Street, Sutton.

Directors.
Mr. GEO. B. BRIGHTLING, Carshalton, *Chairman.*
„ G. W. HUCKERBY, West Street, Sutton.
„ T. PRICE, Manor Terrace, Sutton.
„ J. STEAD, High Street, Sutton.
„ R. G. HOW, Steam Marble Works, Carshalton.
„ E. A. GOODYER, South Beddington.
„ J. WHITE, Danbury Terrace, Wallington.
„ R. DANIELS, Pound Street, Carshalton.

Solicitor.
F. ALDRIDGE, Esq., 7, Fenchurch Street, and Sutton.

Secretary.
Mr. F. ALLNUTT, 10, Limes Road, Croydon.

The Society advances to its Members sums of £100 to £400 on Freehold or Leasehold Property, repayable in 12½ years, free of Interest or other charges.

Subscription 6d. per Week for each £100 Share, Which is returnable with Bonus on completion of the Society.

Prospectuses and all information can be obtained of the Officers as above; or of the Secretary, at Croydon; or the Coffee Tavern, Sutton.

THE BYNE FAMILY

Bornhem House (see Chapter Four), which became the Dominican school, had been known as 'Mr Byne's House' for more than two centuries. The Byne family who owned it, and who presumably built it, had come to Carshalton well before the mid-seventeenth century. There was a Henry Byne who was vicar of Carshalton from 1427 to 1453, but this may just be a coincidence.

It seems the Bynes came from over the Sussex border, from Wakehurst, when a younger son (James Byne) made his fortune by marrying a 23-year-old Carshalton heiress in February 1589. The lady in question was called Sancia Fromond – usually called Sence – and she was the daughter of John and Bennett Fromond, a strongly Catholic family in Cheam and Camberwell. After the Reformation the family had secured the patronage of Carshalton Church, and being Roman Catholic, this made for constant trouble during the reign of Queen Elizabeth. However, as both Sancia and James died during the 1620s, the Bynes inherited an estate in the middle of Carshalton, along with the right to be patrons of Carshalton's church and to appoint the vicar.

The Bynes were in Carshalton for at least five generations – a remarkable span, from the time of the Armada to the Battle of Waterloo. Most of the men were called Henry; and the family made a practice of marrying their cousins. As such they are a genealogist's nightmare, and it is not known what any of them looked like. They were self-effacing, introverted and self-regarding, and yet constantly busy with everybody else's affairs. The reason for this is that they were a legal family. The men were attorneys, and most of the important legal transactions in the neighbourhood were arranged by 'Mr Byne'. It was a very profitable business.

This was especially true for Charles Byne, who had been the guardian of young Nicholas Carew and had had the management of the Carew estates. He owned property in Carshalton, Wallington, Beddington, Woldingham, Ewell, Mitcham, Croydon, Lambeth and Hereford, as well as chambers in London for his legal practice and a pub in Cheapside! Charles Byne died in 1725, followed by his younger brother Edmund two years later.

However, it was Charles who was the seriously rich member of the family. Inside the house, the sum of £2000 in bank notes was found, plus over £8000 in money and £7000 in shares were owed to him (although the latter was in South Sea Company stock so it probably was not worth very much).

The list of house contents in the Carshalton probate inventories gives us a detailed picture of it when it was in its prime. There was the usual long gallery which was home to nearly 40 pictures and what is quaintly called 'an Alarram Clock'; a dozen bedrooms; hangings of crimson mohair or green or blue harrakeen; a flowered satin quilt; a grand staircase with family portraits leading to a great hall; and half a dozen parlours and studies besides a big kitchen. There was also a farm beyond the house, with ancillary buildings including the coachhouse, bakehouse, laundry and so on.

The family were enormously important in the area and were sometimes mistaken for lords of the manor. They lived in this very fine house, steadily accumulated properties in all directions, and became more and more rich. An example of how the family made their wealth is their 1720 loan to Sir William Hammond of Carshalton High Street. They lent him £2500 to buy South Sea Company stock. He had to pay them back with interest, but when the famous 'bubble' burst, Sir William was ruined, whilst the Bynes became wealthier still.

A list of property owned by Henry Byne (IV) in 1725 includes the family's main country estate in Northumberland, two houses in the city of London, the mansion and five other houses in Carshalton, a house in Nottingham, several farms at Mitcham, as well as property in Wallington and Beddington, plus the manor of Woldingham.

It would be foolish to attempt to list all the litigation in which the Bynes were involved, but it is worth commenting on their connection with Carshalton Parish Church. The devout Henry Byne (II) presented the church with a massive silver communion flagon in 1673 and, more importantly, gave the vicar half the rectorial tithes, thereby facilitating the change from vicar to rector. Henry had a son, Henry (III), and wanted the best possible marriage for the young man. In about 1686 young Henry married Elizabeth Herringman, daughter of Henry and Alice Herringman, of Carshalton High Street (Henry Herringman was the most successful publisher of the day and had very good political connections). But the girl, who was only 18, died in childbirth the following January and their only son, James Herringman Byne, died before his father in 1704 when aged only 17. (There is, incidentally, a very striking memorial to Elizabeth (Herringman) Byne on the wall of the Lady Chapel in the Parish Church. It shows a fearsome devil, with scaly limbs and claws, and is quite the most frightening memorial in the church. It is unclear why this should be deemed suitable as a memorial to a young girl.) Consequently Henry (II) was left without a son and heir, and in 1724 his brother Charles inherited, only to die himself a year later.

To understand what happened next, it is important to go back to the 1680s when Henry Byne was appointed administrator of the Carew estates at Beddington during the minority of the infant Nicholas Carew. In 1683/4 Henry's sister Martha married a clergyman called Revd John Nelme, and when two years later there was a vacancy, Henry Byne arranged that his son-in-law (John Nelme) should become rector of Beddington. Four years later, in 1690, a forced vacancy occurred at Carshalton. The Bynes, who were High Church Tory, did not approve of the Glorious Revolution of 1689 (which forced the Catholic James II off the throne), and they refused to take the oath of allegiance required by the new King, William of Orange. As a result, the vicar of Carshalton, Thomas Bradley, did the same. As a punishment, Bradley was expelled from his living. Nobody could expel the Bynes and ironically, because they had the rights of patronage, old Henry Byne was entitled to appoint a replacement. Unsurprisingly perhaps, he appointed his brother-in-law. John Nelme therefore became vicar of both Beddington and Carshalton, and held the positions in plurality until 1703.

John and Martha Nelme also had a daughter, Elizabeth. In best Byne tradition Elizabeth Nelme married her cousin, Charles Byne, who inherited the North Street property in 1724. When Charles died childless in 1725 Elizabeth was no doubt a wealthy woman, but the property was passed to another branch of the Byne family living in Northumberland. The next Byne, Henry (IV), from that county, did not want to be kept out of his grand Carshalton house by a grieving widow. Elizabeth married the rector (William Hillier) and went to live in the Old Rectory at Festival Walk. However, Elizabeth Nelme/Byne/ Hillier was duly widowed again in 1738, and had no desire to lose another home. There was an ongoing lawsuit between the Bynes and the Revd Edmund Lodge of West Street, and in 1738 this was settled by an arrangement under which Elizabeth appointed the Revd Lodge as the next rector and left him the Old Rectory in her will on condition that she could live there with him until she died, in 1781.

The story of the Bynes and Carshalton goes on for another half-century: the last Henry, (VI), died at Reigate in 1815. However, it seems clear that from at least 1750 the North Street mansion was let out to tenants; John Durand, father and son, who are better known at Woodcote Lodge and Carshalton House, had it from 1761 until 1790. (For more information on this, see *The Story of Little Woodcote and Woodcote Hall* by Margaret Cunningham, published by the London Borough of Sutton (Heritage), 1989.) The North Street property was repossessed by Henry Byne for another four years, and then sold for a mere £1100 in 1795.

THE GOOD OLD DAYS
& THE WALLACE FAMILY

Towards the end of the nineteenth century the Sutton firm of printers, William Pile & Co., began to issue the series of little red books which soon became a local institution and were to be found in every respectable home. These books are now of considerable value to local historians. They are of course, the *Carshalton Street Directory* and *Almanac*, which came out every year. Similar publications were produced for other neighbouring places, right up to the outbreak of the Second World War in 1939. In later years the *Almanac* degenerated into a potted history of the locality, but during the nineteenth century it was a much more useful handbook, which included a local Who's Who as well as a report on what had happened in Carshalton during the previous year – a sort of annual report – and a good many pages of miscellaneous information, which was more like a magazine in style.

The *Almanac* for 1884 outlined important facts such as the names of Mr Gladstone's Government, the birthdays of Queen Victoria's children, and the postage rates (1d. for letters 'to all parts of the kingdom'; postcards ½d.). There was also some rather more recondite information, like what to see at Caernarvon Castle, the number of public houses in the United States, and how to cure yourself by willpower if bitten by a cat suffering from rabies – which may not have been so valuable to the average Carshalton resident of the time. Did the people of Carshalton really need to know these things?

There is, however, a more ominous note in the item headed – with heavy inverted commas – 'The Good Old Days': a list of the amounts of wages paid to the workers of Chester in 1597. The reason for putting in this somewhat bizarre item was the evident desire of the editor to reassure the near-starving farmworkers of Carshalton that they were much better off now than they might have been. He obviously hoped they would not appreciate that the value of money had changed since 1597. However, the reality of rural poverty in the 1880s is made clearer by a reference in the 'annual report' to the existence of many societies in Carshalton which were trying to alleviate the sufferings of the farmworkers and artisans, most notably the Carshalton Soup Kitchen. This had been established two years earlier and ensured that the very poor received at least one hot and nourishing meal every day.

The person responsible for starting and running the Soup Kitchen was a maiden lady in her early fifties, noted for her charitable activities and work for good causes: Miss Susan Wallace. She lived with her older sister Mary Ann and their brother James in the big Wallace House, about half way up Pound Street. The reason for such a steep drop from Wallace Crescent to Pound Street, is that the hillside was cut away for the cellars of Wallace House, and to provide a back garden which would be flat and on the same level as Pound Street. Susan's sister, Mary Ann, was not strictly speaking a maiden lady – she was Mrs Wallace, not Miss Wallace. In 1848, when Mary Ann was 20, she had married a Robert Wallace, who may have been some sort of cousin. He died ten years later, childless, so Mary returned to live with her sister. They were always known as the Misses Wallace.

Very little is known about their brother James, who actually owned the house. He was painfully shy, very rarely went out, and lived as a semi-recluse. All he seemed to do was wander round the estate, carrying an axe, because he had a passion for chopping down trees. He also refused to connect the house to the public water supply, even though the pipes ran down the pavement of Pound Street right next to the building. Wallace House relied on its own three wells. The other member of the family worthy of a mention was a younger brother Robert, who was in the Army, and by the end of the century was a retired General living at Brighton. He was very fond of the family home at Carshalton, and when James died in 1903, he came to live in the house with his sisters. After they died in 1908 and 1909 he was actually the last occupant of Wallace House before it was sold off and demolished in 1910.

As a result, Carshalton gained all the houses and shops along Pound Street, approximately numbers 41–75, and all the houses in Wallace Crescent. The loss of Wallace House seems particularly sad because it was arguably one of the most historically interesting buildings in Carshalton. When it was destroyed, most of its history died with it, and as such much less is known about it than many comparable old houses.

There are, however, half a dozen photographs of it and it is very noticeable that the front and back of the house seem to bear no relationship to each other; they look as though they are two different buildings. Indeed, this is virtually what they are. Looking from the side, one can see that Wallace House was built up in slabs, like a series of vertical layers, so that there must have been three or four houses, each slice added on to what was there before. The house was constantly being extended – and one can detect something of this from the description of the house given in the sales catalogue when it was sold in 1910. There was an entrance hall, stairs, then another entrance hall and another set of stairs, because one was now penetrating into the older building which lay behind the front. Similarly, the two big living rooms in the front had two rather large rooms behind them, used as a study and a housekeeper's room. These must have been the living rooms of the older house, because the study is described as boasting some fine oil paintings on the panelling.

The Misses Wallace of Wallace House, Pound Street.

There were a lot of rooms in the house: two living rooms, ten bedrooms and two dressing rooms. This was just as well, since Samuel Wallace in the 1780s and '90s had 11 children, and although two died as babies none of the daughters seems to have married, so they all remained at home. The same thing happened in the next generation, when Edward Wallace and his wife Anna had 15 children between the Battle of Waterloo and the accession of Queen Victoria (1815–37). Again two children died early, but the Wallaces in the nineteenth century required another, smaller house and a cottage in Pound Street, which were used for more members of the family. Even the old house was not big enough.

The curious thing is that all or most of this process of extending Wallace House must have taken place before these big Wallace families existed. We only have definite evidence of one extension: a guidebook of Carshalton dated about 1789 remarks that Mr Wallace had just had his handsome house newly fronted in brick (which could refer to the west front in the photographs). It is unlikely that the Wallaces had had the house for more than a few years at that time. Samuel and Elizabeth Wallace had probably moved in when they got married, which is likely to have been in the late 1770s, since the first baby was born in 1779.

It is not clear who owned the property before the 1770s. It is improbable that the Wallaces were the owners as the building must have been much older. The section behind the west front looks like a typical seventeenth-century or early-eighteenth-century double-pitch roof, and the big roof behind that could very easily be covering a fifteenth-century house. It seems reasonable to suggest that the house originally faced west (and not as one might have expected towards the Ponds) because it was a relic of the days when there was no Pound Street. As such it would have fronted on to West Street, which originally ran right up to the Windsor Castle. All that is left of this is the little piece of road from the Windsor Castle to the gates of Carshalton House (St Philomena's).

Indeed, Pound Street may have originated as a footpath across the Wallace House estate (which is why it ran right up against the house). Most of the land attached to the house was probably across the other side of this path/Pound Street; the land which is now behind the walls of Carshalton House, but was not incorporated into the Carshalton House property until the early-eighteenth century. To compensate for the loss of land on its north side, the owners of Wallace House acquired land on the south side, the area always called The Meadow, which in the 1780s was rated separately, and was marked as having previously been under separate ownership (Ball's land). This took the Wallace property right up to the line of the old High Street (otherwise known as Crooked Lane) which ran along the walls of Carshalton Park. It is still possible to see a piece of the wall in Wallace Crescent and behind Carshalton Park Road. When Crooked Lane was sold off in 1827, Edward Wallace bought up the stretch which ran round the south and east sides of his estate, so that his meadow went right up to the wall of the Park.

So from at least the 1770s through to 1910, during the whole period of the Wallace family occupation, Wallace House was a compact five-acre estate. Four fifths of it was fields, with a nice orchard, and a very attractive old-world flower garden, reaching across from Pound Street almost to Beynon Road and Carshalton Park Road. It had poultry houses, and the family kept four cows in the meadow. Together with the little farms at the end of Pound Street and opposite the Windsor Castle the whole area must have looked very rural indeed. Not that the Wallaces were farmers in the true sense of the word: they just liked to have their own milk and eggs. As a family they were doctors and ran a medical practice. They were Carshalton's doctors for 90 years, from Samuel Wallace who started up in the 1770s to the death of his son Edward in 1867.

The Wallaces seem to have been popular and well liked, at least by those who could afford their fees, although the parish of course paid for them to tend to the poor people in the Wrythe Green Workhouse. The practice must have been a lucrative one so that they could keep up the house and estate, have all those children, get the boys established into the professions, and keep the girls at home. Edward Wallace was certainly a wealthy man, and when he took charge of the practice in the 1820s, he was able to pay a large proportion of the cost of purchasing land for the village school in West Street (later the Sea Scouts building and now No. 5 West Street). Both he and his youngest brother John (who was also a doctor in the village) contributed generously to the construction of the High Street alongside the Ponds, and the new bridge which crossed them (1825–28). Both Edward and his daughter Susan, of Soup Kitchen fame, were noted for their charitable works.

On the other hand there is a suggestion that they were not quite as shrewd as they might have been. Susan had difficulties getting her Soup Kitchen project started. When she proposed the idea in 1881 there was the question of how to raise money for it, so she decided to organise a concert. Unfortunately she held the concert in January, and, as the annual report commented, Carshalton people never go to meetings and functions in January. The concert lost money because the attendance was so low. As such, the Soup Kitchen scheme started off in debt and had to be bailed out.

The best illustration of the Wallaces' näivety is a story which concerns, apparently, Susan's father, Dr Edward Wallace, and which became a classic piece of Carshalton folklore. Being a doctor, Edward had to complete his rounds to visit his patients. To help him get about he had a pony called Tom. It was quite a young pony, but it was extremely fat. It was a great favourite; people were always giving it food and so it became overfed and lazy. Moreover Dr Wallace was very concerned that the pony shouldn't catch a cold, and wouldn't allow him to be clipped. Eventually the pony became so fat and hairy and lazy that it hardly moved at all, and the doctor began to find that he was unable to get his rounds done, let alone cope with emergencies. So he took the horse and sold him to Mr Gardner, the harness-maker and saddler in the High Street, who often bought and sold horses. Gardner knew that Tom was really a good horse, so he got to work on him: he clipped him as short as he possibly could, and he began to give him vigorous exercise. This was easier said than done, because the pony was thoroughly spoiled and not used to harsh treatment, which was therefore much more effective: a touch of the whip and Tom nearly bolted. He began to lose weight rapidly.

A couple of months later Dr Wallace went back to Gardner, and said that he needed another horse as he was struggling to manage his rounds. After trying out one or two, he picked Tom as the horse who looked the fastest, and bought him. Several months later he commented to Gardner that his new mount was the best he'd ever owned – much better than the one he had before. Gardner never told him he'd bought the same horse!

Wallace House. (S.L.S.L.)

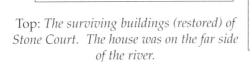

Top: *The surviving buildings (restored) of Stone Court. The house was on the far side of the river.*

Above left: *Window from Stone Court known to be in the Grove in March 1921. A similar window on the theme of the Nativity is in Carshalton Parish Church.* (S.L.S.L.)

Above: *View of the Grove in the 1930s.*

Left: *Pencil drawing of the Grove, signed C.D., 1869.* (S.L.S.L.)

Left: *Old stone with the initials J.R. found at the Grove – possibly the initials of John Ryle.* (S.L.S.L.)

THE GROVE & JONAH CRESSINGHAM

The East Pond was technically private property until the twentieth century. It belonged to the owner of the Grove; more accurately to that part called Stone Court. Everyone in Carshalton knows the Grove, so it is somewhat surprising that very little is known about when the house itself was built, or who built it. It is often assumed that it owes its existence to Sir Samuel Barrow, the last of the long line of landed gentry of Carshalton who made their money from trade and commerce (he was a leather merchant). However, he only bought the property in 1885, yet a drawing of the house dated 1869 exists, in which it looks much the same as today. Furthermore, the house is also shown on the Tithe Map of 1847, which makes the building older than one would suspect at first sight. On top of all this, the name of Mr Jonah Cressingham seems to be inextricably tied to the house.

Jonah Cressingham is the mystery man of nineteenth-century Carshalton and he left a string of question marks behind him. Even his name is a bit of a mystery. He was born as Jonas Crossingham, probably soon after 1790, but died in 1874 as Jonah Cressingham. All the accounts agree that he changed his name, and one of them says that it cost him £500 to do so. This seems a great deal of money to pay for so slight an alteration, and it is not known why he did it. According to one story he was a very poor man who suddenly inherited a fortune and wanted to establish himself as a gentleman, and thought that a change of name was appropriate in the circumstances. Another version of events states that he only did it because his wife, Sarah Ann, refused to marry him until he did so. She was aged 39 when she married him in 1836. She did not long enjoy being a Cressingham: she died unexpectedly two years later. Her rather elaborate tomb is in the churchyard near the south wall of the church, bearing the somewhat sombre inscription from Proverbs (xxvii.1) which, paraphrased, reads, 'You never know what's going to happen next.'

This sentiment is certainly the case with her husband. Jonah was obviously the sort of eccentric person to whom legends naturally attached themselves. This is reflected in the story of his humble origins, for example. It is said that he was so poor that the parish arranged for him to be apprenticed as an act of charity. He became a whitesmith, an iron-worker, although when he received his inheritance he laid down his hammer and announced that he would never do another day's work.

Jonah nevertheless kept his country ways. One of his tenants, John Smith of the Grove Iron Mill along the Westcroft Canal, later said that he was a rough, garrulous man, who would not stop chattering, 'although there was nothing in what he said'. He also kept to ordinary rough country clothes, refusing to wear breeches and a frock coat. Yet even this notion is suspect. A drawing in the Sutton Library shows Jonah as a figure dressed in top hat and black coat, as befitting a prosperous and substantial landowner. Was he in fact poor at all? Although his brother, William Crossingham, remained a tailor – we can trace him from 1803 until 1838 – he was nevertheless able to live in one of the very attractive weather-boarded houses in West Street (No. 12, Yews Cottage). Additionally, their mother, Mrs Mercy Crossingham, a widow, was paying two or three times as much in rates as William in 1810 – so she cannot have been all that poor, even after paying them. Indeed, in the previous year, 1809, young Jonas had been sent to Cambridge University, where he must have been one of the wealthier students, since he paid to dine with the Fellows of his college, Trinity Hall. Incidentally, undergraduates at Cambridge still compete for the Cressingham Prize, which he established in his will. He was almost certainly a lawyer since he was admitted as a member of the Inner Temple. Above all, when he returned to Carshalton from Cambridge he was able to buy a lease of Stone Court in 1817 and apparently took his mother to live with him until she died in 1826.

Whether Stone Court included the gardens on the east side of the river, the area of the Grove proper, is not clear. Certainly there would have been no house there at that time. During the previous century the Grove had been part of the gardens of Stone Court, with many winding paths through it leading to the top of the rise where there was an imitation classical temple in a grove of trees – hence the name. The evidence seems to indicate that Cressingham did lease the Grove as well, and in 1831 a visitor to Carshalton lamented that all the fine trees had been cut down, which is just what one might expect from an uncouth fellow, as Jonah is said to have been.

It is not clear if this was a prelude to building the house, the Grove. The first mention of the house was in 1847, at which point it was leased to a Mr V.B. Currie. It is therefore likely that Jonah had sold his lease for the Grove by then. Being only a leaseholder, he may not actually have built the house.

The actual owners of the estate until 1872 were the Ryle family – and they are even more shadowy figures than the Cressinghams.

Although Jonah only seems to have been a leaseholder of Stone Court, and was to remain so until his death, he was not short of money and soon became one of the main local landowners in his own right. Even in 1827 he could afford to lend somebody £40; and five years later he gave 30s.0d. to the poor of the parish, which was the amount of a fine taken from some poachers convicted by him at Croydon.

Between the 1830s and 1850s he bought up land on a large scale. Much of it was used for building on, as the heavy rise in population led to a severe shortage of housing. He bought a very large area at

Above main: *Carshalton Park House around 1830. Photo of a painting by an unknown artist.*

Inset: *Jeremiah Coleman who lived at Carshalton Park House from 1876–85. He died at Gatton Park aged 80 in 1939.*
(Both S.L.S.L.)

Above: *A Victorian photograph of Carshalton Park House showing the Victorian bay windows.* (S.L.S.L.)

Left: *The Coleman family in Carshalton Park, c.1880.*

Rosehill, and most of the Wrythe, including the old workhouse, which he leased out as the Leicester House school. He had nearly 20 small fields over towards the Wallington boundary, and he leased a further 90 acres around Woodmansterne Road. He owned several places in North Street, including what is now the Roman Catholic church, but which at that time was leased to the Methodists. He bought the snuff mill on the Westcroft Canal and gave it to another relative, George Crossingham, to run – George himself had taken over the West Street house. When the snuff mill became the Grove Iron Mill in about 1868, Jonah bought the steam engine to work it. He also had a lot of the land where the new houses were being built along the roads to Sutton, as well as property at Banstead, Cuddington, and a house in Sussex.

On top of all this, he inherited a fortune, but not until 1851. This included most of Tulse Hill, where he became lord of the manor, and a large part of Brixton. Again this was turned to profitable account through development. It seems that the inheritance had originally been given to his sister, Mercy, back in 1807, but perhaps they had both benefited at that time, as this would have coincided with the date Jonah went to Cambridge. It seems likely that Jonah also received his sister's share of the wealth when she died without having children.

There are no records that show Jonah Cressingham had any children and the story ends with his death in 1874. Already Stone Court and the Grove had been reunited, since it seems that the Ryle family also died out. Both houses were bought by the rector, the Revd William Cator. It is said that he was one of the richest men in Carshalton, and had taken a lease of the Grove in 1856. Ten years later, in 1885, Sir Samuel Barrow seems to have bought the Grove, which is where this saga began.

THE SLAVE TRADE & THE TAYLOR FAMILY OF CARSHALTON PARK HOUSE

'Rule Britannia', wrote Thomas Arne in 1740, as whilst Britannia rules the waves 'Britons never never shall be slaves'. Yet even as he wrote, large numbers of British subjects were slaves. They weren't all on remote West Indian islands: many of them were in this country, as it was very fashionable for wealthy families to have black servants. Carshalton was no exception – the Hoskins, the Scawens and the Fellowes all had black servants who were baptised and in due course buried in Carshalton churchyard. The last of these was Samuel Mudian in 1841, who was a slave at Carshalton Park House, even though the slave trade had been abolished well before his death. Mr Jones has suggested that he probably began life as Samuel the Bermudian, from Bermuda.

As far as records show, only two Carshalton residents were actually engaged in the slave trade itself, running ships to West Africa in order to acquire negroes to sell in the Caribbean. One was Sir John Fellowes of Carshalton House (who at least made partial amends by losing most of his money and by leaving the parish the Water Tower); the other was George Taylor, who had extensive sugar plantations on the West Indian island of St Christopher/St Kitts, and made a very large fortune. He then retired to Carshalton, bringing some of his slaves with him: his will, dated 1810, refers to 'all my negroes' along with his animal stock, 'live and dead'.

The villagers of Carshalton, whilst they appreciated the willingness with which George Taylor allowed visitors to walk round his park and look at the deer (you could usually do so, if you asked at the lodge in the High Street), were not very much in favour of his wealth; they thought it was tainted by the slave trade. The tradition grew up in the village that the Taylors would only have the Park and be lords of the manor for three generations. In fact the villagers got it slightly wrong: five members of the Taylor family over four generations owned the Park.

George Taylor bought the Park from James Scawen of Stone Court in 1781, and three years later he did what the Scawens had always intended to do, but had never done: he built Carshalton Park House. As such he is the first person to be recorded as being taxed on 'the new house' in 1785. There is a lively controversy amongst local historians surrounding the question of whether there had been a house in the Park before 1785. It seems most likely that when George Taylor took over his new house on the corner of Brookside and Carshalton Place in 1785, no house then existed in the Park. His great-nephew, Edward Estridge of Queen's Well, recorded his memories in 1889 and was very firm that he had been told there was no house in the Park before his uncle owned it.

The building that George Taylor constructed was a relatively small two-storey house, which had a Gothic-revival front facing the canal, and a much more classical south front facing towards the Park. There are two known pictures of it. One is a print by John Hassell produced in 1817, in which the building looks very romantic, with horses and cows alongside the rushing waters of the canal. The other is a much calmer picture by an unknown artist working in about 1830. It is a well-known work showing the deer in the Park, with the orangery and the Parish Church in the background. It was owned by the aforementioned Mr Estridge.

There is also a very early photograph of Carshalton Park House, perhaps dated around 1860, which surprisingly shows a three-storey building. It appears that the roof of the house had been raised and a new top floor inserted – only to be taken away again a generation later. All the later photographs show the house restored to something like its original size, but with Victorian bay windows inserted into the south front. It is very difficult to date these changes, partly because the Taylor family must have approved and presumably paid for them. There is no evidence that they actually lived in Carshalton between the early 1830s and the late 1880s, or again from 1900 until the house was demolished in 1927. There is instead a long list of tenants. As such, the only time one can be sure the Taylors were here after about 1838 was when they were brought here for burial.

George Taylor died in 1814, at the age of 80, and his younger brother John succeeded him until 1832. Carshalton Park then passed to their nephew, another John, a young man (aged 32) who may not have been married at that stage because his eldest son was not born until 1837. This child, William Taylor, was born and baptised at Carshalton.

A list of Carshalton inhabitants liable for jury service in 1838 states that the Taylors had moved to Hackbridge, and the first of the many tenants (William Riversdale Grenfell) was living at Carshalton Park. Since it seems unlikely that anybody would go to the trouble of building an extra storey on the house just before moving out, it seems reasonable to surmise that it was the first John Taylor (George's brother) who did the work on the third storey. However, he died in 1832, and the print showing the original house is supposed to show the property as it was in 1830. Perhaps he enlarged the house for his nephew at the very end of his life (although nephew John stayed there a mere five years).

The photograph of the three-storey house shows two small children playing in the garden, which it names as the Aitken children. James Aitken, the second tenant, appears to have been at the Park by 1844 – although perhaps as a sub-tenant at first, because his actual lease is dated 1851. He obviously liked living there because the Aitkens stayed until 1869. Since a photograph is unlikely to have been taken before about 1855, perhaps these were in fact Aitken grandchildren. However, Peatling recorded that the attic storey was removed during Mr Coleman's time at the property. Jeremiah Coleman was a senior partner in the big Norfolk mustard and starch business and was the fourth tenant of Carshalton Park from 1876 until he died there in 1885. If Peatling's information was correct, and the reduction in the size of the house and the other alterations dated to around 1880, the impetus must have come from the Coleman tenant rather than from the Taylors, who were now living some distance from Carshalton on the South Coast (Southampton, Torquay). Added to this, in 1880 the Taylor heir, John William Frederick Blake Taylor, was only a boy of 13.

When this young man came of age and inherited in 1888, he decided to bring the Taylors back to Carshalton, and his eldest child, Sybil, was born at the Park in 1890. Despite this, the writing was on the wall: by 1892 a substantial part of the Park was put

up for sale, and the restored Taylor residence did not survive into the twentieth century. The local council managed to save what is now called Carshalton Park in 1912, but the house was reduced to its immediate gardens between Talbot Road and the High Street, and that too duly went during the 1920s.

According to village gossip, the last of the Taylor squires was ruined by 'fast women and slow horses'. This is probably a slander – the Taylors were simply examples of a national trend. Between 1880 and 1930 it is estimated that about a quarter of the land in England was sold off. There had been a very severe agricultural depression which began in the late 1870s and lasted until the end of that century. Tenant farmers who actually worked most of the estate could not continue, so the older ones retired, and the younger ones sought pastures new in the colonies. At the same time the completion of the direct railway line from London to Carshalton and Sutton by 1870 made the whole area ripe for dormitory suburban development. There was a ready market for the sale of land for housing – the proceeds from which could now be invested far more profitably in such things as stocks and shares rather than land for its own sake. To top it all there was a new threat to the landowner: death duties (whereby tax was levied on property after the death of the owner) were introduced in 1894 and proved so profitable that no government, of whatever party, was prepared to reduce them. Indeed in 1919 the duties were virtually doubled, and occasioned the great wave of estate sales in the 1920s. At least the Taylors neatly arranged their dying to avoid that: J.W.F.B. Taylor had inherited as far back as 1867 (when just one year old), and did not die until 1932, well after Carshalton Park House had vanished.

WOODCOTE LODGE: THE SCAWEN SCANDAL & JOHN DURAND

The largest and most grand house in Wallington, known as Woodcote Lodge or Little Woodcote, belonged to Carshalton and paid its rates to the Carshalton Vestry. Local historical records abound with references to Woodcote, but there are so many places with this name in the neighbourhood that it is extremely difficult to sort them out. Much of the evidence remains confused and seemingly contradictory.

However, the house existed in the middle of the eighteenth century since it is shown on the John Rocque map of 1762. Ten years earlier one of the great ladies of Carshalton, the Countess of Pomfret, who was living in the village, notes in her diary that she had just been over to Woodcote to have dinner with Mr Thomas and Mr William Scawen. This indicates that, like so many local properties, Woodcote Lodge was part of the enormous empire that first Sir William Scawen and then his nephew Thomas, of Carshalton Park, built up in this part of Surrey.

Thomas Scawen, as monarch of nearly all he surveyed, had a very large collection of relatives, many of whom were accommodated in the various houses which he owned. It is not known which particular relative first had Woodcote Lodge. It may have been his brother Lewis, since in 1732 Lewis swore homage to Thomas Scawen as lord of the manor. But Lewis died in 1740, and the first definite information we have is that their younger brother William was living in Woodcote Lodge in 1752.

William Scawen appears to have lived there until 1775. It transpires that he was rather a nasty old man. He never married, but in 1763 he took a 14-year-old girl into the house to live with him, and told the local people that she was his wife. The girl, Jane Butterfield, stayed with him for 12 years. Perhaps William was genuinely fond of her, at least for a time, since he arranged to leave her £20,000 in his will. However, something appears to have gone wrong. In 1775, when Jane was 25 or 26, William suddenly cut her out of his will. Soon afterwards he was found dead; he had been poisoned. Jane was arrested and charged with murder. There was a celebrated trial at which all the juicy details of their scandalous liaison were dragged out into the open and caused a great sensation. However, the supposed Mrs Scawen had apparently been very popular with her neighbours. These revelations seem to have increased her popularity and there was general rejoicing when she was acquitted of the charge of murder. She was able to show that one of William's peculiarities was to experiment on himself with various drugs and poisons, and she suggested that on this occasion he had simply miscalculated the dose. The jury, no doubt swayed by the spectacle of a beautiful woman in distress, gave her the benefit of the doubt.

The house was presumably sold off with the other Scawen estates in the years around 1781 and although the evidence is by no means conclusive, the owner during the next decade seems to have been a certain John Durand.

Durand, who may have been of French Huguenot descent, first appeared in Carshalton in 1761 having just retired from life at sea. He was then in his early forties, and having made a handsome fortune as captain of a merchant ship belonging to the East India Company, he pursued the ambition of buying himself the life of a gentleman. He purchased a great deal of land in Carshalton, particularly around Barrow Hedges, and was one of the largest farmers in the district. He also retained his commercial interests with an East Indian shipping firm at Rotherhithe, and an office in London. It was to assist these enterprises that he determined to buy himself a seat in Parliament – an act of folly and impertinence, according to one of his opponents. He paid around £4000 for a seat, and secured a succession of Government pocket boroughs (Aylesbury 1768, Plympton Earle 1775, Seaford 1780). This gave him the contacts he needed and during the 1770s he secured a series of lucrative contracts to supply the Army and Navy during the American War of Independence.

Durand was obviously a very successful businessman, but it is doubtful that he gave his political masters good service. The Government's election manager remarked that he was 'extremely slack', and there is no record that he ever spoke in the House of Commons. In 1780 it was said of him that:

... no man understands the Multiplication Table with more comprehensiveness and precision of intelligence: but in the laws of his country, or in duties of a legislator, there is perhaps no individual more completely ignorant.

Durand was too busy enjoying life in his great house at Woodcote: under the Window Tax of 1784 he was assessed for no less than 82 windows. When he arrived home he would order a flag to be hoisted on top of the building, and this was a signal that he was ready to receive company. This was, says one account, a universal invitation to all desirous of partaking of his festivities, to join his hospitable board. The memory of these feasts lived on long after his death: it was known as the 'golden age' of Carshalton. Many of these entertainments took place after hunting, in which Mr Durand took the lead. He was described as 'the very lifespring of the field sports of the neighbourhood'. Fox hunts, stag hunts and hare-coursing upon the Downs followed one another in rapid succession. 'The country in the vicinity of Banstead', it was said, 'was in perpetual activity from the hour that the sporting season commenced in each succeeding year until it was finished.' It was probably this interest which led Durand to purchase the Greyhound Inn, with its numerous stables, as a meeting-place for huntsmen.

Apparently the local Vestry, the Carshalton Council of the time, thought that he was living too well, and that they should benefit from some of this wealth. In May 1786, the parish clerk noted that a report had been received which suggested that when Mr Durand purchased Little Woodcote the rates had been fixed too low. Durand was summoned to attend the parish meeting to have his rates increased. He declined to attend. He was then asked to send

Woodcote Hall (formerly Lodge) in 1987. (S.L.S.L.)

87

details of how much land he had bought and what it cost. This made Durand come to the meeting, but only to declare that he had no idea of the exact figures. He was told to come back again; he did not appear. Letters were sent to him every week but he did not answer them. It was not until a year later that he was eventually persuaded to put in an appearance – at which point his rates were raised by 50 per cent, an extra £50 a year. It may be supposed that Durand was deeply mortified at this treatment, but he only had to pay the increased rates once, since he died the following summer (July 1788) and his son inherited his property. There are no records of a Mrs Durand, but she may have come from a local family named Hodson (who built Wandle Cottage in Pound Street as a hunting box). Their son, John Hodson Durand, married a Miss Hassell of Beddington the month after his father died. It may be that the couple had been courting for some time but had not wed because the old man had not approved of the match.

For a time the younger Durand kept up his father's reputation as the leader of the local sporting fraternity. He was particularly keen on chasing hares, and regular meets were held on the Downs. In 1796 he presented the Carshalton Cricket Bowl (now in the care of the Heritage Centre) which carries one of the earliest pictures of the game of cricket. He directed his father's East India shipping company; he continued to make money and buy property. One of his houses was used for the Dominican school in North Street. He even owned Carshalton House for a few years, although he sold it again in 1800.

Soon after this something unknown happened that made him give up the fast and furious life of a sporting country squire. He withdrew from local life and shut himself away in his house at Woodcote, refusing to come into the village. We last hear of him, about the time of Waterloo, living the secluded life of a recluse at Woodcote Lodge. From this time onwards the house, which had been so central to Carshalton affairs, disappeared into the obscurity which it still enjoys.

The house itself is still worth a visit: Woodcote Hall, in Park Hill Road, at the corner of Woodcote Avenue, has an interesting octagonal lodge (which has been restored). It is not often that one has to go to Wallington to see an important piece of old Carshalton – but there it is.

SOURCES FOR CARSHALTON RESIDENTS

As far as the records show, Strawberry Lodge appears to be the only Carshalton house built in the seventeenth century and this is a particularly difficult century to deal with. All the records of the manor court for the Tudor and Stuart periods are either missing or unpublished, so there are only a few scrappy extracts before l682. There is only one map, but it does not show the dozens of place names

in Carshalton, which were no doubt perfectly familiar to everyone in the 1600s, but which are almost meaningless today. Similarly, there is no list of residents. Perhaps one day a family history society will transcribe the registers of births, marriages and deaths at Kingston. As things stand, however, there are two main points of interest.

Firstly, in 1660 the monarchy was restored in England after 15 years of Cromwell and the Commonwealth. Parliament believed it ought to be nice to Charles II (in case the Cavaliers took too savage a revenge on the Roundheads) and so it decided to give the King a present. Even in those days Parliament was very good at giving away other people's money; it ordered a voluntary tax on all property owners, in order to pay off the King's debts. Although the tax was voluntary, it was seen as an opportunity to declare one's loyalty to the restored monarchy. In fact, although Carshalton was a relatively Royalist area, it has been calculated that only 40 per cent of those who might have paid actually did so. Nevertheless this does provide a partial list of names and occupations of Carshalton residents on 7 September 1661. This list was edited in 1982 by Cliff Webb for the West Surrey Family History Society as a *Calendar of the Surrey Portion of the Free and Voluntary Present to Charles II, 1661*. Out of the 20 people in Carshalton who paid, six were classified as gentlemen/gentry (whereas places like Sutton, Cheam and Beddington only rated one gentleman each). Top of the list, paying £50, was the distinguished lawyer Sir Edmund Hoskins, who was lord of the manor of East Carshalton (remember that the manor was divided in two in the 1600s). His manor house was probably in North Street, between the Sun public house and the railway line. Opposite him there was another lawyer, Henry Byne, paying £1, whose house was on the site of Carshalton Station. Nearer the Ponds was the house which had replaced the medieval manor, Stone Court, occupied throughout the seventeenth century by the Burrish family: here George Burrish paid £5. Another gentleman, John Morgan, paid £2. There are no records of which house he owned.

A notable omission from the list is that of the lord of the manor of West Carshalton (the so-called Burton half of the manor), who was another well-known lawyer, Dixey Long. He lived at the Old Farm, the predecessor of Carshalton House, and as he had taken this from the staunchly Royalist Burtons, he was understandably not thrilled by the restoration of Charles II.

Instead, the list included two gentleman who had dealings with Dixey Long. There was Robert Sollers, who paid £1. His family claimed a two-fifths share of the manor of West Carshalton or Kinnersley (its medieval name was Kenwardesley), apparently on the grounds of property in the area of Pound Street – although Dixey Long refused to recognise this claim. The real mystery, however, is Thomas Carleton, who paid the second highest amount (£6), and who may (Mr Jones suggested) have been related to Dixey Long. Certainly Edward Carleton, presumably his son, gradually acquired the Old Farm Estate and is the first person known to have lived in the present Carshalton House by about 1700. It had always been clear that the Carleton family lived in Carshalton before that time, but it has never been known where the original Carleton House was, but if Thomas Carleton paid £6, it must have been an extensive estate.

The second point regarding the list of residents, that the editor of the *Calendar* very sensibly points out, is that the only real comparison with his list are the lists of returns for the Hearth Tax. As unpopular a rate as the Poll Tax, it did not last long. In 1662 Parliament authorised a tax of 2s.0d. per hearth from all ratepayers (which thereby excluded the very poor). Village constables were ordered to send in an annual return of how many hearths each ratepayer had, and were given powers of search, in order make sure people were not operating illegal fireplaces. There was such a fuss about all this that the tax was abolished in 1689, one of the achievements of the 'Glorious Revolution'. In 1940, the Surrey Record Society published the lists of who had how many hearths in 1664. However, there is no record of the Carshalton returns for the first five years, or of 1673/4. The returns are infuriating as historical evidence: they simply give a total figure for the number of hearths each person had, but without specifying how many houses the figures related to. As such, a person with two or three houses would appear to be the same as a person with one very big house. The total also included not only hearths in places like stables, but also things like blacksmith's forges or industrial stoves. The result showed the two people in Carshalton who paid the most; one was the lord of the manor, Sir Edmund Hoskins, with 18 hearths (presumably because he had more houses than just the manor house), and Josias Dewye with 14 hearths (presumably because his gunpowder mills would have had all sorts of ovens for making charcoal).

The number of hearths for a big house with outbuildings was ten: both Dixey Long at the Old Farm and Mrs Dorothy Burrish at Stone Court had ten; and there were half a dozen medium-sized properties that had between seven and nine. The great surprise once again is Thomas Carleton, who regularly paid for 13 hearths, the third highest total in Carshalton. Thomas Carleton seems to have had a house which was bigger than Stone Court or Carshalton House, putting him in the same league as the lord of the manor. Is there another big house in Carshalton? Looking at the only seventeenth-century map of Carshalton (the so-called Arundel Castle map) there is just one candidate marked – a house we really know nothing about and labelled as The Bury/Berrie, which was eventually demolished in 1792 and replaced by another, this time called Elm Grove. The estate covered the whole of the area from Butter Hill across to Wallington Bridge, fronting on to London Road, and running back as far as the modern railway line, including the whole of today's Butter Hill estate. These few facts may be enough to suggest that the Berrie was the Carleton family house during the 1660s.

There are two other distinguished residents worthy of note, whose names do not figure in local history books, but who appear on the Hearth Tax lists. In 1665 there was a medium-sized house (six hearths) occupied by the 40-year-old Earl of Oxford: he was Aubrey de Vere, twentieth and in fact last Earl of Oxford, who had been a Royalist leader during the Commonwealth. His estates had been confiscated by Parliament for disloyalty; Cromwell had him arrested and tried for treason three times (he was designated commander in chief of the Royalist armies waiting for Charles II's return). When Charles was formally invited to return from exile, de Vere was one of the people sent to ask him; and he carried the sword of state at Charles' coronation. From then on he was one of the country's leading soldiers, a privy councillor, and a very great man.

The other distinguished name in 1665 was Francis Coventry, a man who can easily be bracketed with de Vere, but whose career had gone the other way. His father was the first Baron of Coventry, Keeper of the Great Seal under Charles I. Francis, with his two brothers, Henry and William, had shared Charles II's exile in Holland. He had done much undercover work for the Royalists, and when Charles regained his throne, he might have anticipated a glittering future (both of his brothers became secretaries of state). For some reason, however, Francis Coventry had had enough, and in the early 1660s he announced his retirement from public life and withdrew to the countryside. In 1665 he took a tenancy of the manor house at Carshalton from the Hoskins family, and the Hearth Tax lists tell us that he was still there ten years later – and indeed had increased his number of hearths from 18 to 23.

What is historically interesting about this is that it represents a sort of reclamation of Carshalton by the Government. For centuries, like Beddington, Carshalton was one of the circle of manors around London which the Government of the day had liked to control. During the 1640s, during the Civil War, Carshalton was pre-eminently Royalist. There had been a marked shift to Parliamentary control during the Commonwealth of the 1650s, which was reflected in the very low take-up rate for the voluntary 'present' to Charles II in 1661. By the early and mid 1660s Carshalton seems to have been 're-colonised' by Government ministers and safe Royalist families, which allowed the parish to resume its traditional function in the administration of the realm. Even in the seventeenth century we find that Carshalton enjoyed being what it had always been before.

Top: *The Black Dog, North Street.* (S.L.S.L.)

Above: *The Police Station (left), before 1920, looking east down Pound Street towards the Ponds.*

Right: *Village policeman by the church wall outside Woodman's butchers shop, c.1920. The number of Metropolitan Police based in Carshalton grew to over 50 by the beginning of the twentieth century and included two mounted policemen. The Pound St station opened in 1848, was demolished in 1920 and replaced by an enlarged Margaret's Pool and flower beds. The force transferred to the Police Station in Stafford Road, Wallington.*

Chapter Seven

COMMUNICATION & SERVICES

THE PONDS BRIDGE, STAGECOACHES, INNS & OLD PHOTOGRAPHS

The road alongside the Ponds, the railings, and the new bridge across the middle of the Ponds, were built by public subscription between 1825 and 1828. The builder was a man called John Weller, and he had to tackle the problem of what to do with the traffic whilst the work was being done. This was particularly important while he converted the old bridge into the new bridge. He issued an instruction that horses and carts must go round, and not try to cross the bridge whilst he was working on it. However, this was strongly resented by Mr Sendall, the innkeeper of the Black Dog public house in North Street, who argued that he had always driven over the Ponds road bridge and wasn't going to stop now. So when he drove up to the bridge John Weller stopped him and they had a stand-up fight, during which Weller knocked Sendall off the bridge and into the water. From then on, so the story goes, the new bridge was known by the locals as, 'Weller's Arch – or Sendall's Dip', because as one went up, the other came down.

The Swan Inn, West Street, c.1870.

The first authorised vehicle to cross the new bridge in 1828 was a coach drawn by six horses driven by Daniel Brown, the owner of the Carshalton stagecoach firm which operated from the King's Arms in the High Street. For 2s.0d., he would drive people to Gracechurch Street in London in an hour-and-a-half flat if they sat on top of the coach (3s.6d. inside). It was an old, established firm which had been operated by a man called Hickerson as far back as the 1780s (he only charged 2s.3d., but the journey took three hours). The coach left Carshalton at 8am, so that you could be in the City in time for lunch at 11am, and then return in the afternoon (2.30pm in winter; 3.45pm in summer) to be home by the time it got dark. On Sundays, however, instead of leaving at 8am, the coach left at 7am. Respectable Carshalton citizens did not linger in bed on Sunday mornings.

A popular ditty of the time went:

Daniel's horses cannot go
because they have no corn
But here comes Blucher well
run in with his bugle horn.
(Chorus):
Blucher for ever; and Daniel
in the river –
A knife in his heart, and a
fork in his liver.

Daniel Brown's coaches survived for a time, but the coming of the railways in the 1840s largely put an end to the London stagecoach business. In the 1850s there was still a stagecoach running from the Swan Inn in West Street (opposite No. 2 West Street) to Holborn, and the fare had dropped to a shilling, presumably to compete in some way with the trains.

Although the stagecoaches stopped at the King's Arms in the middle of Carshalton High Street, the actual coaching office where a ride could be booked and where the horses and coaches were stabled, was on the other side of the High Street. Here there was also a blacksmith with his forge to shoe the horses and mend the wheels. All this was opposite the King's Arms, by the old fairground and market-place, at the back of Haydon's butchers shop and slaughterhouse. It was an old building called Summer House, which had its own yard (Summerhouse Yard) and numerous outbuildings. It was destroyed in the early 1940s by the same bombs that destroyed the King's Arms and Haydon's. In 2002 Somerfields occupies the King's Arms site; Haydon's is the pay-and-display car park; and

The first tram at the junction of Ruskin Road and Park Lane, 27 October 1906.
The man with his hand resting on the starting lever was a director of the tram company.

A tram accident at the corner of Park Lane and Ruskin Road, 1 April 1907.

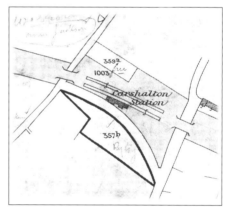

Top: *Steam train arriving at Beeches Halt, later Carshalton Beeches Station, c.1909.*

Above left: *Carshalton Station, c.1870.*

Above right: *The site of Carshalton Station from the Tithe Re-apportionment Map of 1886.*

Left: *Horsebus* Lady Madcap *passing Queen's Well, c.1900.*

Summer House has been replaced by the Park Lane Pharmacy. The land behind the pharmacy is the remains of a field which Daniel Brown rented (from Sam Killick) as grazing pasture for his stagecoach horses.

The probable reason for the name 'Summer House' was that in the eighteenth century the term 'summer house' not only meant a garden greenhouse but rather referred to the house in the country, to which people retired in summer from their winter town-house residences where they were surrounded by society. Villages such as Carshalton were full of summer houses belonging to various lords or ladies, so the coaching office was probably originally one of these.

More is known about the building's later history. By 1870 it had been bought by the Haydon family, who are said to have substantially altered the appearance of the house (and there was certainly a Victorian square bay put on the front of it). It kept its connection with horses, since in 1900 it became the home and office of the Gardner family, who were saddle- and harness-makers and riding instructors with shops in both Sutton and Carshalton for over a century. Gardners had Summer House until the early 1930s. Even at the end of the 1930s there was, appropriately, a car-hire firm operating out of Summerhouse Yard.

There is a photograph of Summer House which can be dated to about 1936. This is interesting because the water along the road has been paved over, but the railings still remain. In its last half a dozen years Summer House became the Carshalton Estate Office run by the firm of estate agents Benians & Wallis, with a firm of solicitors conveniently upstairs (Carter & Barber). It was also possible to order coal there.

In the later 1930s it was also used as a special constables' police station, as the Carshalton branch of Toc H, as well as the meeting place of a somewhat esoteric organisation calling itself F Squadron of the Legion of Frontiersmen.

The photograph shows that on one side of the front door there are the brass plates of the lawyers; on the other side there is a photograph of a pin-up girl in a glass case. This is because part of the house was used as a photographer's studio run by Max Rosher. The Roshers were a Nottingham family, presumably of German extraction, who moved to Carshalton in 1927. The family comprised William Rosher (Charles William Christopher Jacob Rosher), who died in 1933, his sons Karl Frederick and Max, and his wife Sarah, who went on living in Talbot Road until 1950. The house later became the Wilks family home.

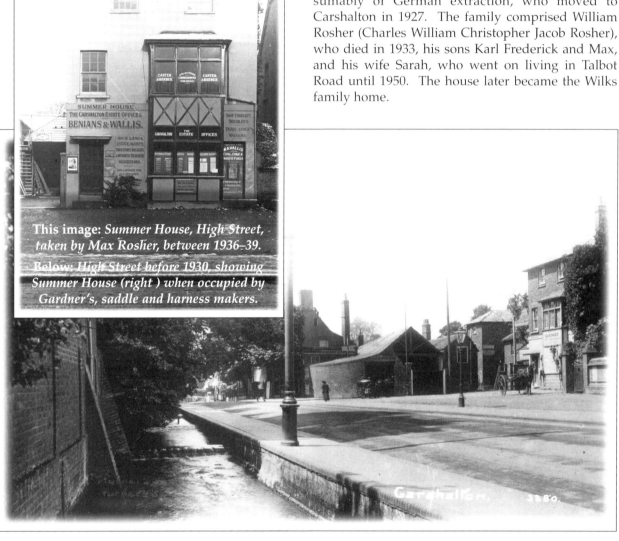

This image: *Summer House, High Street, taken by Max Rosher, between 1936–39.*

Below: *High Street before 1930, showing Summer House (right) when occupied by Gardner's, saddle and harness makers.*

Chapter Eight

MEDICAL MATTERS

THE OPENING OF THE COTTAGE HOSPITAL

There were celebrations in Carshalton to commemorate Queen Victoria's 80th birthday on 24 May 1899. All the streets were decorated, and the Ponds were floodlit. There was a great carnival and parade accompanied by massed bands. This was followed by a group of men on horseback wearing historical costumes, and a procession of decorated bicycles. There was also a march past of representatives of local societies and social clubs, like the Masons, the Free Foresters and the Oddfellows. The highlight, however, was a column of nine fire brigades from places as far away as New Malden, Thornton Heath and Guildford, as well as the local ones.

All this took place in the evening, and for many people the great event of the day was the ceremonial opening of the new Cottage Hospital, which had just been built in Rochester Road. Prominent politicians from both parties had been invited to the opening. There was the Lord Chief Justice for the Conservatives; but the guest of honour was Lord Rosebery, who had been the Liberal leader after the retirement of Mr Gladstone, and who had driven across to the ceremony from his house at Epsom.

Lord Rosebery had probably lunched well, and when called upon to make a speech was in jocular humour. The proceedings had opened uneasily when all the 'common' people, who were supposed to sit at the back, had come forward and occupied the seats at the front reserved for the local VIPs. To smooth things over Lord Rosebery began by commenting on the way in which class divisions were being eroded: members of the aristocracy now rubbed shoulders with quite ordinary people, meeting them in railway trains and at football matches and race meetings – indeed, working men were even now allowed to play golf. These somewhat patronising remarks apparently went down better than they perhaps deserved to, and the noble lord warmed to his theme. 'I want to ask myself a question', he said. 'Is there any real advantage in being better off, in being rich as opposed to being poor?' (At this point a rude fellow in the audience began to make hooting

noises and had to be thrown out). 'After all', said Lord Rosebery, 'both rich and poor eat dinner – and you can't eat more than one dinner at a time, however well off you are'. He admitted that the Romans had a method of doing it: but he thought that was disgusting and not suited to delicate constitutions. 'You can't', he went on, 'wear more than one suit at a time – however rich you are – and you can't ride more than one horse (unless you've been trained by a circus)'. In short, he was saying that nobody can do much better than anybody else, regardless of their circumstances. There appears to have been a considerable amount of noise by this time, but Lord Rosebery apparently thought the audience was just indulging itself in loyal cheers, and was led to the conclusion that it was really better to be poor than rich. If you were poor, he claimed, you weren't tempted to indulge in luxurious living, but had plain honest fare, which was much better for your health. In fact the only benefit he could think of was that if you were ill and rich you could afford much better medical attention. However, now, he said, Carshalton had removed even that distinction by building a local hospital for everybody to use.

Clearly, the proceedings were a riot. The local newspaper did rather spoil the effect by commenting the following day that if Lord Rosebery really felt that way about being rich, then the only logical thing he could do would be to sell all that he had, and give it to the poor. The newspaper claimed, rather sourly, that Lord Rosebery was far too concerned about the welfare of the poor to seek to burden them with all the disadvantages of his wealth. It went on to suggest that the lord wished to keep them poor and healthy and out of hospital.

THE WAR MEMORIAL HOSPITAL

This hospital was opened in the Park on 30 July 1924. It was built as a memorial to those who had died in the First World War, and also to replace the Cottage Hospital in Rochester Road. There were initially 26 beds at a cost of £23,000. In 1930 the hospital was extended, more than doubling the number of beds to 58, and a 20-bedroom nurses' home was built, a gift

Top: *The Cottage Hospital with some of the staff, c.1900.*

Above left: *The War Memorial Hospital, The Park, 1920s.*

Above right: *Postcard of the Cottage Hospital soon after opening.*

Left: *Aerial photograph of St Helier Hspital.*

(S.L.S.L.)

of Major W.J. Mallinson, the President. By 1947 there were 62 beds housed in four wards, as well as a massage clinic which was provided in 1932, an operating theatre which had opened in 1935, and a large house, Lyndhurst, which was aquired to provide extra accommodation for the nurses. With the National Health Act this hospital became part of the St Helier Group.

DEVELOPMENT OF ST HELIER HOSPITAL

When the much-needed St Helier Hospital was being built in the late 1930s the existing hospitals were Sutton General, Carshalton War Memorial Hospital, The Nelson (Mitcham), Wimbledon Hospital and several chest hospitals. Tuberculosis (TB) had been rife but with modern treatment chest hospitals gradually became redundant and were ultimately closed in the 1960s. Queen Mary's Hospital for Children had opened in 1909 and had 900 beds and cots for children, mainly for pulmonary TB, joint conditions and poliomyelitis (infantile paralysis as it was known world wide). Gradually less provision of this sort was needed. St Helier Hospital was planned in the 1930s and built on the site of a pig farm. The foundation stone was laid by Queen Mary in 1937. The well-known actor Eric Porter remembered his mother taking him to see the ceremony. Dr Ferguson was Medical Officer of Health for Surrey at that time. The nurses' home was named after him. The lower part of that building is now occupied by the outpatient and physiotherapy departments.

The first matron was Miss Bertha Wood who had previously worked at Kingston Hospital. She had been trained at Guy's and saw herself essentially as an administrator. She must have been the first matron not to wear a dress and a frilly cap. She wore a suit! Miss Wood bemoaned the fact that Morden Hall, the proposed alternative location for the hospital, had not been chosen. With a London postal number and the proximity of the underground she thought that there would have been less staffing difficulties at Morden. She retired in 1956 and was followed until 1969 by Miss K. Bomford, the last matron as such.

During the Second World War, in spite of its camouflage, the hospital was bombed. Sister Kingdon lost an eye from flying glass and the house of Dr Barrington Brooks, the Medical Superintendent, was demolished. The hospital re-opened in 1941 using the lower floor only. The maternity unit was used as a surgical unit for servicemen. (There was a dispensary basket which still had painted on it 'Male Maternity'!) Many babies were born on the estate during the war, giving much work to Miss Whip and Miss Cook, the District Midwives. The School of Nursing was founded by Miss Maisie Mackenzie in 1941 and a large School of Midwifery followed.

The League of Friends was started in 1951 by Miss Hoole, followed by Mrs Petch, Mrs Truphet and Mrs Mary Moore. The League has raised many £1000s to facilitate the purchase of various equipment, such as scanners, curtains and chairs, which have all added so much to patients' comfort. The National Health Service was introduced in 1948 promising 'care from the cradle to the grave' but Miss Hoole realised that there would be items which the NHS alone would never be able to provide.

Elizabeth the Queen Mother visited St Peter's Church and the estate in 1962. She was very impressed by the massive white building of the hospital and asked to return the next year, so in 1963 she presented the prizes to the nurses and student midwives. Part of the outpatient department is the Springall Unit, named after Richard Springall, who was the Hospital Secretary during some very difficult years when major remedial work had to be done to the structure of the building. It was said that a cheap, non-quick-drying cement had been used in the original building and this, together with the effect of salts in the water, had caused cracks to appear. Parts of the hospital were in danger of collapse. Cementation Ltd carried out the work from 1963–65. Steel piles were driven deep into the ground below the foundations for support and the whole operation caused much noise, inconvenience and cost. The original cost of the building had been £2 million. It was opened when it was in some respects still incomplete because of the outbreak of war.

Latterly the increase in the cost of treatment, new services and the need for expansion have led to financial difficulties. The hospital has attracted severe criticism, but excellent work is still carried out there and many local people have only praise for the treatment they have received at the hospital.

SMALLPOX & THE DOCTORS WALLACE

One of the recurring features of Carshalton history is that local doctors were often regarded as great nuisances and a danger to the public. This is particularly true of the vaccinators, those who preached the value of new methods of inoculation against smallpox, and who believed in what they were doing so much so that they went around giving their services free of charge to the poor people of the parish.

Smallpox was one of the great curses of the past, feared only a little less than the plague itself, even though it was sometimes more deadly. For example, in 1641 nine people in Carshalton died during the year: six of them from smallpox. One of the great advances of medical science was the development of inoculation. During the eighteenth century people were inoculated against smallpox by the method known as 'variolation': a mild attack of smallpox was deliberately induced in children – to immunise them against a worse one – by inserting pus from smallpox blisters under the skin and into the bloodstream. On the whole it was a fairly effective method, reducing the number of deaths from smallpox from some 15–20 per cent (one in six) in those who were not treated to about 2 per cent in those who had been inoculated. However, it had some drawbacks. In the first place, one could not be sure that the attack of smallpox induced by the inoculation would be a mild one. Secondly, even if it were a mild attack, the patient could still act as a carrier of the disease, and could infect anybody else who was not protected. And although many doctors thought that inoculation would give life-long protection; as we all know now, jabs only give temporary security and have to be renewed.

There was the sad case of Harriet Truncheon of Woodmansterne. She was born in, or around, 1799, and was probably inoculated in 1800 or 1801 (her younger sister Eliza was inoculated at the age of two in 1804). Harriet then had a mild attack of smallpox, recovered, and was pronounced to be immune. When she was 12 or 13, like most poor country girls, she was put into service, and became a servant in Croydon. As happened to so many young servant girls away from home, she was pregnant by the time she was 14, and was delivered (as the records put it) of 'a child of her mishap'. Wanting to give the child the same protection as herself, she had the baby inoculated too. The child duly had its mild attack of smallpox but to her great surprise, poor Harriet herself caught smallpox from the baby; and mother and child were packed off home to Woodmansterne in 1815. There they promptly proceeded to infect all the other members of a large family, even though all the younger brothers and sisters had been 'done'. To make matters worse they also infected the family living next door, who were not inoculated: four of them were very ill indeed, and two of them died.

The surgeon who had inoculated poor Harriet at the beginning of the century was Carshalton's doctor, Samuel Wallace, who had come to live in Wallace House in Pound Street in about 1780, and was to die there about 1826. He was a great believer in inoculation: more importantly, he was one of the pioneers of the new method of vaccination discovered by Edward Jenner. Jenner tried using cowpox material against smallpox, and for his cowpox material or 'vaccinia' he suggested taking the liquid or lymph from blisters on the udders of infected cows. His first experiments with this were carried out in 1775, but he didn't actually test it on people until 1796. Its importance was very quickly recognised – the Royal Jennerian Society was formed in 1803 – and go-ahead young doctors began using the new method and holding surgeries to which poor people could come and be vaccinated free of charge. It is clear that a doctor from London held surgeries at an inn at Kenley in 1804, and another from Croydon at the vicar's house in Woodmansterne in 1805. The only drawback of the new method was that the lymph had

to be transferred from the arm of an inoculated person to the arm of the person being inoculated. This arm-to-arm method meant that the doctor had to have a patient at the right stage to take round with him to one of these surgeries, which had therefore to be hurriedly arranged at the last moment.

It was obviously far more convenient if you could have the vaccine available by itself in a form in which it could be carried around, and within a couple of years this had been produced and was known as 'dry matter' or 'dried material'. The first recorded use of this dry material locally was in November 1807 when, again at Woodmansterne, Dr Wallace's eldest son, Edward, himself a doctor too, vaccinated seven children with it and recorded complete success. The records then show that he, and his younger brother Dr John Rowland Wallace, went on using the new method at Woodmansterne until the records themselves cease in 1831. Like most improvers, the doctors were attacked and condemned by the ignorant and the stupid, and those with vested interests to protect. Ridiculous stories were rife; it was said that children who were inoculated with the cowpox would start to moo – and some might even grow horns!

Woodmansterne's rector, the Revd Gilbert Buchanan, was a cleric who was strongly in favour of inoculation. He, like others, kept a record of vaccinations in the register of baptisms, so as to be able to prove that the children of his parish had both spiritual and physical immunity. It is not clear whether a similar record was kept at Carshalton, but it seems inconceivable that when three distinguished Carshalton doctors pioneered the vaccination, they would have given it to Woodmansterne children and not to Carshalton ones. All three Wallace doctors were noted for their work amongst the poor of the parish, especially at the workhouse (Leicester House) on Wrythe Green, so it would be very surprising to find that they were not performing inoculations there too, as acts of charity.

Both of the younger doctors, Edward and John, survived into the 1860s, and were greatly respected and loved for their good deeds amongst the poor. When Brightling came to write his *History of Carshalton* in 1872, he dedicated it to:

... the honoured memory of the two warmest and truest friends that this village ever possessed. The names of Edward and John Rowland Wallace were for a long series of years associated with every effort to promote the temporal and spiritual advancement of this place. Not for the praise of men, but for the love of God did they freely give their time, their talents, and their means, to serve their poorer neighbours; and He will surely not forget their works and labour that proceeded of love.

Their pioneering work in vaccinating the poor against smallpox was one of the things that Brightling had in mind.

Chapter Nine

THE RIVER WANDLE, MILLS & MILLING

THE WANDLE & ITS WATER FLOW

The Wandle has for centuries been one of the busiest rivers of its size in the country, and therefore attempts to interfere with the flow of water have always been strongly resisted. Even the Domesday Book recorded that there were 13 corn-mills – and perhaps more – between Waddon and Wandsworth, using the water of the river to turn the mill-wheels, and by 1600 the number of corn-mills had risen to 24. However, from the fourteenth century it becomes apparent that this water power was also being used to help the local cloth trade. There were mills for grinding dyestuffs, fulling-mills, and by the eighteenth century the banks of the Wandle were among the chief centres in England for bleaching linen and printing calico. By 1805 no less than 40 undertakings were making use of the water flow in the river, and this use was kept up until the local cloth industry collapsed at the end of the nineteenth century. Due to this tremendous activity, any drop in the supply of water in the Wandle has always been a cause of great anxiety.

A water shortage always coincided with Carshalton Ponds drying up. As early as 1610 there are records showing that in times of drought there was so little water coming out of the springs at Carshalton that the inhabitants dug ditches to keep what water there was for their own cattle and refused to let any of it go down the river – to the intense annoyance of the mill owners. However, the mill owners got their own back. When the amount of water coming down the river wasn't strong enough to turn the mill-wheels, they used to build dams across the river to pen back the water and so build up enough water-power to turn the wheels when the dams were opened. In 1610 the mill owners would dam up the river for six hours a day in winter, and anything up to 12 hours a day in summer. This, of course, was exasperating for the people in Carshalton. Not only did they have to hump their bags of corn from one mill to another, trying to find one that was working in order to get their corn ground; but the practice of damming up the river had the effect of making the river above the dam burst its banks and flood the surrounding meadows. Even as far back as the fourteenth century, there is a case of a gentleman from Southwark who was fined for flooding the common land at Carshalton by damming up the river.

So it is understandable that for hundreds of years every attempt to take water out of the Wandle has been fiercely resisted. The first known case was in 1610 when one of the King's chaplains had the bright idea to make some money by selling water in London from the springs which fed the Wandle. He asked the King for permission to take a tenth part of the water from the river and run it through an underground pipe from Waddon to the city. This resulted in a huge outcry: the people of no less than 13 counties said that they used the mills on the Wandle – and this scheme would make the mills work shorter hours than ever – so the project was abandoned.

But since then there have been a number of other attempts to interfere with the water of the Wandle. In the 1790s it was even suggested that the river should be done away with altogether and converted into the first part of a canal to run from London to Portsmouth. In 1849 there was a plan to divert the river into huge reservoirs on Wandsworth and Wimbledon Commons to supply water to the expanding suburbs. And in 1906, one of the railway companies tried to get permission to sink a deep well at Carshalton and draw out two million gallons per day. All these attempts were defeated by the opposition of local people. But in 1966 Sutton District Water Company proposed a scheme to sink a bore hole at the Oaks, waterproof Carshalton Ponds and maintain their water level by pumping back water from downstream in times of drought. This proved popular, for not only was the resulting water for local consumption but the future of the Ponds was guaranteed.

SOME EARLY MILLERS

In 1661 the eminent gunpowder manufacturer Josias Dewye came to Carshalton and leased, then bought, the estate called Bacons on which three gunpowder mills had been established at the end of the Civil War. It was Josias Dewye who then built Strawberry Lodge as a second house on the estate. Strawberry Lodge still survives but Bacons was demolished in the middle of the eighteenth century (it stood at the bend in Denmark Road), and was replaced by Shepley House. Dewye had a partner or manager called Boreman, who seems to have been in charge of the gunpowder mills. These mills were on both sides of the river at the point upstream from the Hack Bridge where the Carshalton Wandle joins the river coming from Croydon at Watersmeet, just opposite Wilderness Island. So the estate had land both in Carshalton and in Wallington, and the land next to the mills on the Wallington side became known as Boreman's Mead, after Mr Boreman.

Boreman's name is sometimes spelt Boerman – he was a Dutchman and probable Huguenot refugee. The Huguenots came to England from France and the Low Countries during the sixteenth and seventeenth centuries to escape religious persecution. They settled in large numbers in East London and at Wandsworth. The French are traditionally held to be responsible for introducing silk printing, and then calico bleaching and printing, while the Dutch, who specialised in the making of copper utensils, used water mills to hammer out sheets of copper.

Although Josias Dewye took most of the Bacons' estate – the Strawberry Lodge and Shepley parts – out of Carshalton House ownership, Burton's Mill remained attached to Carshalton House. It therefore passed to the Carleton brothers early in the eighteenth century. According to Mr Jones' history, the Carletons, who were tobacco merchants, converted a mill to grind snuff: but there is no real proof of this, nor indeed any evidence that there was a snuff-mill at Butter Hill until much later in the eighteenth century. After the Carletons were bankrupted the mill passed to Sir John Fellowes. In 1732 Thomas Scawen bought the mill and the Moor from the Fellowes family. So although it is possible to trace something of the history of the mill it is not clear when it was converted from a corn-mill to a copper-mill. There is a reference to Mr Carleton's copper-mill in 1707, which seems to be the earliest mention. There was later a lease by Sir John Fellowes in 1720 to Charles Parry, a copper miller from Mitcham, who is known to have supplied sheets of copper to the Royal Mint for coinage.

Burton's Mill then went to a Huguenot, a Dutch coppersmith from Whitechapel called William Thoyts. His name is possibly a corruption of Te Hoyts, and comes from Frisia in North Holland. As one might expect, the Carshalton officials of the day could not cope with this, and he turns up in local records with a variety of anglicised names like Thorpe and Thwaites! Despite this, Thoyts was a significant figure in Carshalton history for about 40 years. He was in the area between 1732 and about 1769, after which he or his family transferred to Merton Abbey, having already developed another copper-mill at Willow Lane on the Mitcham boundary. He was a very distinguished name amongst Wandle industrialists. He specialised in making copper plates for printing calico and prospered. The rateable value of his property doubled during the 1740s. He had a mill house at Butter Hill, but he appears to have lived in Westcroft (at the corner of the High Street and Westcroft Road) until 1761. He then moved to a smaller house 'at the Field Gate', although it is not clear exactly where this is. He also owned a timber-frame house and cottage – which may be at Butter Hill, but the description simply reads 'near the George alehouse'. This is the only known reference to a George alehouse in Carshalton, so it does not shed much light on the location of the dwelling. It seems likely that he had a very fine house built at Butter Hill, which was later known as Thursley, because it is always described as a former copper house, and Thoyts was the last copper miller at Butter Hill. On one side it had the old mill house known as Burnside (aka Burntside), next to Butter Hill Bridge, and on the other side there was a cottage with the river running under it, so that the mill was actually standing on an island. In Thoyts' time the island was nine acres in extent, and was known as the Moor, or later Scawen's Moor after he bought it in 1732. It is a little difficult to visualise it now because the railway line and embankment cuts it in half. The Vinyl Products factory and offices in the twentieth century stood on the same island, which stretches from Mill Lane right up under the railway embankment to Wilderness Island. (By 1999 this had become a housing estate on the south side of the Wandle.)

When the copper-mill stopped being used as such around the late 1760s, perhaps 1770, it was not converted to a snuff-mill but became a calico-printing factory, and the fields over towards Wallington, like Boreman's Mead, were used for calico bleaching. The introduction of calico bleaching and printing at Butter Hill and at what became the Shepley estate, was the work of the man who replaced Thoyts as the most important miller in Carshalton – George Ansell.

It is important to stress the point again: there is no clear evidence of snuff milling at this time. George Ansell took a lease on the Butter Hill bridge site from Thomas Scawen in 1770, which gave him the copper-mill site, and this was confirmed by James Scawen in 1775. By now Ansell was branching out into paper milling; but it seems the development of snuff- and madder-mills at Butter Hill occurred in the 1780s. The old snuff-mill is the only surviving building at Butter Hill – and Carshalton's oldest mill building.

THE REYNOLDS FAMILY & CULVERS

The event which seemed to Brightling the most important in recent Carshalton history was the collapse of the Carshalton calico industry in 1872, and the subsequent sale of the great bleaching grounds along the Wandle at the Culvers six years earlier in 1866. The Culvers estate, 280 acres of grassland, was reduced to only a quarter of its original size. Previously it had stretched right across northeast Carshalton, from North Street by the station all the way over to Hackbridge and down the river to Mill Green at Beddington Corner. However, 200 acres were sold off, and so began the process of covering all this land with houses, a tide of bricks and mortar which eventually engulfed the Culvers itself nearly a century later.

Cloth had been made in Carshalton since the Middle Ages, but what brought immense prosperity to the industry was the development and great popularity of the cotton and linen cloths, known as calicoes, during the eighteenth century, which used cotton from the new empire in India. Before it was dyed and printed with patterns, this cloth had to be whitened, which was done by spreading it out in the fields along the river, pouring the high-quality river water onto it, and letting it bleach in the sun. In a good summer the cloth would bleach in a month. There were about a dozen calico mills and manufactories, bleaching and printing cottons and silks along the Wandle from West Croydon to the Mitcham boundary, but three-quarters of these were in Carshalton.

The great expansion in the industry came after about 1760 and it really became big business with the appearance in Carshalton during the 1770s of Foster Reynolds, then aged about 40. His family came originally from Chichester in the early-seventeenth century, but by the 1750s they were established at Southwark, where his father, Thomas Reynolds, was a cloth-maker in the City of London. In 1734 Thomas had married Mary Foster, the daughter of a Southwark leather-maker. It was very much a milling family. When his father died in 1771 Foster Reynolds took over an extremely prosperous business, and moved up the Wandle, first to Mitcham, and then to Carshalton, where he bought the Culvers estate, and proceeded to make a very large fortune indeed. By the time he died in 1797 his Carshalton calico firm, specialising in bleaching and the production of Irish and Russian linen, was said to be the largest of its kind in the world.

An indicator of this prosperity is the fact that by this time the estate included three large houses. The first was the Culvers itself, a large old house, which certainly dated back to the beginning of the seventeenth century, at the end of what is now Culvers Avenue on the island formed by the division of the river into two streams. The first definite information comes from an insurance policy of 1744, which states that it was a timber-frame house in the middle of a 'whitening ground', surrounded by a cluster of outbuildings, including a flour mill and mill house (which is now known as Carshalton Mill). The name of the estate means 'the pigeons' or 'the doves' – a 'culverhouse' was a dovecote, of which there was one at the Culvers. Dr Peatling, who knew and photographed the house, says that it was much older than it looked and suggests that it might have been the original mill house. The bell on the roof, used as a fire alarm, carried the date 1623 and it was still there in 1920. The house itself was rebuilt and enlarged to about double its size in 1850.

The second residence on the estate was Wallington Cottage (later called Culverside) on the Hackbridge bank. It was also enlarged and modernised in the middle of the nineteenth century. The third house was built in 1786 on the Carshalton bank and called The Limes – not because it had a splendid avenue of limes, but for the much more prosaic reason that there was an old pit in the grounds used for quarrying chalk to make building lime. It also had a walled garden which was used for growing grapes.

When, incidentally, the estate was broken up after 1866, these three houses came to form their own separate estates, and it is some indication of their value that they housed two of Carshalton's three richest men. The Culvers was bought for £25,000 by Peter Gassiot, a great friend of John Ruskin, and Chairman of Kew Observatory. The Limes soon went to a very odd character, a wealthy Jewish clothing merchant from Holborn, Maurice Moses. When he came to live in the house as a landed gentleman he thought it was appropriate to change his name, and, instead of being Mr Moses, became Mr Beddington – although the locals still insisted on calling him 'Beddington Moses'. The third richest man was the rector.

Probably the reason why the estate had three great houses was that Foster Reynolds had eight children. There were three sons to be provided for: Thomas, William and Jacob. William and Jacob carried on the running of the calico business (which also included corn-, leather- and dye-mills), and William, the senior partner, was so rich by 1816 that he was able to buy the grandest mansion in the area, Carshalton House itself. He lived there for 20 years.

The eldest brother, Thomas Foster Reynolds, who looked after the London end of the business, was a very splendid person, driving his coach and four up to his City office in great state on weekdays, and to Croydon on Sundays. Also a very eminent figure in the scientific world, he was one of the founders of both the Royal Horticultural and Zoological Societies. It was therefore extremely mortifying when his young son, Thomas Forbes Reynolds, barely 21, created a great scandal by eloping with the daughter of his neighbour, Mr Daniell of Morden Hall, a director of the East India Company. Frances

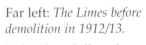

Far left: *The Limes before demolition in 1912/13.*

Left: *Alarm bell on the roof of the Culvers, about 1900.*

Below and top: *The Culvers, south view, in the early 1900s, and somewhat later.* (All S.L.S.L.)

Daniell was already engaged to Lord Marjoribanks (he gave her a watch at Croydon Fair in October 1822 as an engagement present). Only a month later the impetuous young Thomas Reynolds slipped into Morden Hall, bribed one of the maids with the gift of a workbox, and carried off Miss Frances – still wearing her watch – to Gretna Green. There was a dreadful row, but the runaways were at length forgiven, and suitably remarried at St George's in Hanover Square.

However, this had further repercussions. The Reynolds were a prominent Quaker family, and leading figures at the Croydon Meeting House. They were often in trouble with the Carshalton Vestry for refusing to pay tithes, but when the young man married a non-Quaker, he was cut off from the Society of Friends, which greatly upset the rest of the family. Nothing seemed to go right after that. Thomas tried entering into the family business, but found that he had no interest in selling calicoes. His wife died in childbirth in 1831, and he was broken-hearted. He decided to make a fresh start, went up to Cambridge and qualified as a doctor, but never really practised. He then spent the rest of his life living a rather miserable sort of exile in a house in Beddington on, as the account puts it, 'the wreck of a good fortune'. Worst of all, he had to attend Church-of-England services. He heartily disliked Beddington's rector, who, he said, preached his sermons copied from a book, and spent most of the service deciding which of his more important parishioners he should invite back to the rectory to share his 'excellent ham' for supper.

The Quaker attachment to the Reynolds, however unfortunate it may have been in this particular case, was a vital connection in the case of Thomas' brother. William Foster Reynolds and two of his children, his son Foster and his daughter Ellen, married into the enormous intermixed clan of the Gurney and Fry families – virtually aristocracy amongst the English Quaker families, with immense wealth, generated particularly though banking. This was, of course, a very valuable connection for an industrialist. The Frys and Gurneys were themselves intermarried with other rich Quakers such as the Barclays (also bankers) and the great brewing family of the Hoares. Perhaps the most famous member was Elizabeth Gurney, better known as Elizabeth Fry the prison reformer. She was linked to the Reynolds by three marriages: William married her cousin; Foster married her daughter; and Ellen married her nephew.

It was this last marriage, of Ellen Reynolds to Samuel Gurney in 1837, which was most significant for Carshalton, because they came to live at the Culvers, and had it rebuilt. The last of the Carshalton Reynolds, Ellen's brother Charles, was supposed to be in charge of the calico business, but he was something of a layabout, and did little more than live in Wallington Cottage and act as a sort of bailiff for the estate. In any case the calico business was by this time only a small part of a great Quaker commercial and industrial complex, and was of diminishing importance. Technological progress was making the old traditional bleaching methods obsolete, and there was a certain lack of interest in running the firm. The Reynolds and Gurneys were now more interested in leading the lives of country gentlemen, and Samuel Gurney devoted himself to stocking the waterways of the Culvers with a vast collection of rare and beautiful waterfowl. The local calico industry was on its way out; the end came with the collapse of the Gurney bank, a financial crash of epic proportions, which rocked the commercial world – and for Carshalton meant the selling and break-up of the Culvers estate between 1866 and 1870. It was the end of an era.

The much smaller estate was bought by one of Carshalton's most distinguished residents, John Peter Gassiot, in 1886, then nearly 70. He may have bought the Culvers as something of a retirement home; indeed he died ten years later on the Isle of Wight, but while he was in residence a string of eminent folk came to Carshalton to visit him, including Ruskin.

Gassiot had started off in the Navy when he left school, but when he was 21 he married, had 12 children, and joined the family firm of Martinez & Gassiot, wine shippers between London and Portugal. He made a fortune out of port wine. Gassiot himself became famous for holding Spanish dinners, but his real love was science, especially the study of electricity, and his house on Clapham Common had the best-equipped laboratory in London. A Fellow of the Royal Society, and a founder of the Chemical Society in 1847, he was also Chairman of the Observatory at Kew Gardens and had a great interest in fauna and flora. The exotic collection of trees and waterfowl at the Culvers attracted many people to the locality.

Mr Gassiot was also a local magistrate and benefactor. He gave the Wrythe Green Recreation Ground its drinking fountain and paid for the building of the mission church of St Andrew's at the Wrythe – but of course this too, like the Culvers, is no more.

THOMAS GELLIBRAND

When Thomas Gellibrand died on New Year's Day in 1826 he owned some 20 buildings beside the river at Butter Hill, including a water-wheel and pumps. He was a calico printer by trade, who in 1817 had taken over the Ansell cloth-mill and used the old copper-mill opposite (later known as Thursley) to grind dyestuffs – indigo and logwood are listed in the contents. He seems to have had only one servant living in his house. He did not possess a sword, but he had a gun, and was obviously a keen fisherman. He also enjoyed his cellar, which contained two-dozen bottles of French wine, two-dozen bottles of madeira from the West Indies, no less than 18-dozen (more than 200) bottles of port, and 24 bottles of gooseberry wine, which he perhaps made himself.

Samuel Gurney and his wife Ellen (née Reynolds). Charles Reynolds of Wallington Cottage stands alongside. The Culvers may be seen in the background (right). Photograph of a painting by Friedrich Wilhelm Keyl, RA, exhibited at the Royal Academy in 1851. Keyl was a pupil of Landseer (MS).

Above: *The Limes, late-nineteenth century.*

Right: *Culverside, formerly Wallington Cottage, c.1900.* (S.L.S.L.)

Above right: *Gassiot Lodge, c.1870.*

SOME MEDIEVAL MILLS

Adam le Gale lived in Carshalton c.1300 or earlier. In return for their faithful service to him, he gave his servants Roger de Leybourne and his wife Agnes possession of a house (albeit for a fee of 20s.0d. of silver). In addition he told them that he only rented it from the Abbot of Chertsey, and they would still have to pay an annual rent to the Abbot, which hitherto he had been paying himself. The grant has been copied into the cartulary of the great Benedictine monastery of Chertsey. Although there appears to be no further reference to this house, the cartulary does show what else was owned by the abbey in Carshalton.

As mentioned, c.1300 Roger and his wife Agnes rented a house from the Abbot of Chertsey. Leybourne derives from the medieval name for the River Wandle, the Leydebourne. This information, copied into the cartulary, also says that the house in question is next door to the house of Richard the goldsmith on one side, and the mill belonging to the Abbey of Chertsey on the other. In case people didn't know where that was, the charter adds that the house is between the river and Mill Street (Mullestrete). This is surely the earliest known reference to Mill Lane, which then ran nearer the river than the present road. The mill referred to is the mill in the Grove, the Stone Court mill, known as Town Mill during the 1300s and 1400s, more usually the Upper Mill after that.

In around 1359 the manor court at Carshalton heard a complaint against the Abbot of Chertsey that he had in some way damaged or blocked the highway at the Town Mill, and the monks were told to clear it up. We can trace their possession of this mill back through the cartulary. It first appears in 1200 when the abbot paid John Comyn four marks sterling for it (possibly for a lease) and in 1278/9 the abbot paid Sir William and Joan Ambesas another ten marks of silver for the same mill. It wasn't until 1321 that Sir William stopped charging the abbot a fee for grinding his corn and malt there. Whether this is the mill recorded in the Domesday Book for Carshalton it is impossible to say for certain, but it is quite likely. The Town Mill was the main manorial mill for Carshalton, and from the fifteenth century went together with the manor of Stone Court. The Gainsfords had it by 1480 – so it wasn't affected by the Dissolution of the Monasteries in the 1530s – and it simply went on grinding wheat and malt for 800 years, mostly for the benefit of whichever family owned Stone Court. (The owners, of course, employed millers to do the actual work for them; the Popes in the eighteenth century, for example, and the Charringtons in the nineteenth.) When the Scawen trustees sold up in the 1780s, the mill passed for the first time into separate ownership and for its last century was no longer attached to Stone Court itself, although it has since been reclaimed. It was rebuilt in the 1830s, and finally stopped work in the mid-1880s by which time it was in disrepair. Surprisingly, there is no visual record of it. It was restored by the London Borough of Sutton in 1989 but subsequently vandalised and in 2002 awaits further restoration.

Other mills in Carshalton during the Middle Ages were held by a different monastic house. The great priory of Augustinian Canons at Merton, in control of Carshalton Church from the 1100s to the Reformation, had a mill at Carshalton by the later 1300s. It is uncertain whether this was another mill in the middle of Carshalton – perhaps Honeywood – or was a mill on the canons' land at Hackbridge.

There were at least three medieval mills by the 1400s: the Town Mill, mentioned above; the Chamberlain's Mill; and the Fulling Mill. All three appear in the manor court records and are mentioned in 1482. In 1620 the three mills are shown on Carshalton's earliest map. They appear to be the same mills, even if by that time they had changed their names. By 1620, the Town Mill at Stone Court was known as the Upper Mill; the map also shows Middle Mill at Butter Hill; and the Lower Mill where the two branches of the river join above Hackbridge.

One of the witnesses to Adam le Gale's charter was Richard de la Chambre or (in Latin) de Camera – Richard of the (King's) Chamber. The Chamberlains appear on many local documents during the Middle Ages. Little is known about their mill in Carshalton, except that it was the forerunner of the Middle Mill at Butter Hill. In 1482 there was a complaint at the manor court that Nicholas Gainsford had allowed trees to overgrow the highway between his mill (the Town Mill/Upper Mill) and the Chamberlain's Mill. Presumably the latter was a corn-mill, but there is no record of it producing flour during the eighteenth century. It seems to have become everything but: a copper-mill, calico works, snuff-mills, paper-mills, all these clustered round Butter Hill Bridge as part of the vast Ansell industrial empire (and there is still one of the snuff-/paper-mills remaining beside the bridge). However, there is no sign of corn-mills until the 1830s, when a new one appears to have been built alongside the south-east bank of the river, and called (rather confusingly) either the Lower Mill or the Farm Mill. This was operated for half a century by the Ashbys – surprising since they specialised in running windmills (Brixton, Croydon Common, Banstead and Wallington). It continued under other millers (Henry Denyer is the best known, from a local postcard which is often reproduced) and went on grinding corn until about 1912. During the 1900s the mill was greatly enlarged and rebuilt, especially after Vinyl Products Ltd took it over in 1954/5. Part of the original mill building, which ran alongside the river, and could be easily viewed from the BP car park in Mill Lane, was incorporated into one end of Shed 15 which was painted blue. In 1998 the BP site in Mill Lane was replaced by housing, but part of the old snuff-mill by Butter Hill Bridge is still visible.

THE PONDS IN 1283 & 1884

It is a curious coincidence that the first known reference to the Ponds is also connected with rowdyism. In 1283 one of the archdeacon's officers, Peter of Ewell, with two of his clerks, was passing through Carshalton, but does not seem to have been made very welcome – medieval archdeacons were never popular. When they got to the Ponds, 'violent hands' were laid on them by 'certain sons of iniquity', a fight ensued, and blood was shed. Finally the mob seized Peter and threw him in the water, where he almost drowned – no doubt the water was deeper in those days. It is not clear what the upshot was, except that the perpetrators were excommunicated by the archdeacon. Local tax collectors should be warned!

In 1884 a heatwave went on well into the autumn – and it had begun early. Even in May the records tell us that the days were growing longer and the sun hotter, so much so that a water cart was being used to deal with the dust swirling off the roads. This caused a rumpus when it went out to water the roads on Sundays as well as weekdays, which some people thought was shocking as it was defiling the Sabbath.

By June the Ponds were smelling strongly and 'stank so offensively as to be not only a nuisance but a positive danger to health.' Complaints were made that the local council (i.e. Board) had neglected to clear them out for many years, but the Board said that it would be dangerous to dig up such 'a mass of filth' in the hot weather, and the matter was deferred. In any case the cesspits were contributing their own quota of smells, and the Board was busy discussing whether it could afford sewers. These discussions were held in private – no press allowed – so that, says the writer:

... the public is quite in the dark as to what, if anything, is being done. But whether the Board has done all that it might have done is a question which we need not discuss here.

However, there was fear that there might be an epidemic of Asian cholera, which it was thought might be brought across from France, and an emergency service was instituted. The Board agreed to a regular weekly refuse collection – which was when it all began.

Above: *West Pond, c.1900, showing the ford.* (S.L.S.L.)

Left: *East Pond, March 1922, showing a Council notice warning people not to drink the water.* (S.L.S.L.)

Snuff & Paper at Butter Hill

Following the development of printing, paper-making was introduced into England just before 1500, and by the middle of the seventeenth century there were about 50 paper mills in the country. Most of the paper they produced was brown, which was used, as it still is, for wrapping paper or as cardboard. Although attempts were made it proved uneconomic to manufacture white paper until the early 1700s. Then came the great expansion in the English paper industry, and between 1740 – when the first records of paper being made in Carshalton appear – and the end of the century, the number of paper-mills in the country doubled, and the amount of paper produced multiplied fourfold.

Most of the eighteenth-century records of Carshalton, like the Rate Books and Vestry Minutes, are written on paper actually made in Carshalton, and excellent paper it is. Paper not only needs water to drive the mill-wheels, but also very high-quality water to make the pulp for white paper – and the Wandle was ideal for this. The water was also needed to clean the material from which the pulp is made. It was not known in those days how to use woodpulp – that came in about 1850 – so all sorts of things were used to make the pulp, such as straw, thistles, nettles, even rhubarb. But the basic ingredient was rags (although they also used old ship sails and rope for brown paper). Because of the volume of rags that had to be sourced, it was convenient to be near London, which was the centre of the very profitable old rag collection trade. There was also a 'raghouse', a warehouse for storing rags, in Mill Lane during the 1740s.

Carshalton, then, was very well situated as a place for making paper. There was a close connection between Carshalton and Maidstone, the great paper-making centre in Kent; and in the early-nineteenth century when the whole industry was divided up into five main areas, Carshalton ranked as one of the five, alongside Maidstone, Wells, Manchester and Leeds. Carshalton paper was very big business, and very profitable; even a small mill and a few workmen are capable of making a great deal of paper.

The earliest paper-mill in Carshalton appears to be the Scawen paper-mill, which can be traced back to 1744. It was halfway along Mill Lane – Paper Mill Lane as it then was – which became the site of the Distillers/BP factory before becoming housing in 1998/9. There has been a mill, and probably a bridge, at Butter Hill since the Middle Ages, and we know that one of the three village corn-mills – the Middle Mill – was in the vicinity up to the seventeenth century. By the eighteenth century there were several mills in the area around the bridge, and the earliest specific reference to this particular building dates from about 1770, when it was used as a paper-mill. It was much smaller than the big paper-mill further along Mill Lane, but it was also much more distinguished in that the paper-maker was Christopher Patch, who had a national reputation for the manufacture of fine-quality paper. He was very proud of this reputation and was always looking for improvements. When in the 1790s there was a quarrel between the English and Scots paper-makers over who had been the first to use chlorine in the water to bleach the rags for the paper, and who therefore had the patent rights to use this process, the English won the debate by citing the case of Christopher Patch of Carshalton. He had tried doing this in 1789, although he found it too expensive for normal use. Like other paper-makers, Patch complained bitterly about the excise duty levied on paper manufacture – and the better the paper, the more duty had to be paid.

It was therefore a considerable shock to Patch when he was hauled before the Court of Exchequer in the 1780s and accused of defrauding the Customs and Excise. The trouble was that he made a well-known type of paper called 'large thick post'. This included rather a lot of letters, and the brass stamp which he used to print this on the paper wouldn't take all the letters. So instead, he used to stamp the paper with 'thick post', and then write in the word 'large' afterwards. The excise officer thought he was trying to cheat the excise, and pay the lesser rate of duty levied on smaller paper, so charged him with fraud. He had to wait a long time for the trial, and became more and more upset and depressed about the whole affair and this slur on his good name. Although he was in fact acquitted at the trial, he literally worried himself to death, and died, aged 64, in 1792. His wife Ann and their son Christopher carried on with the business but the next blow fell in 1806, when the mill burnt down.

The Patch family were only tenants, and had never actually owned the mill. By the end of the 1770s it had been owned by the Wallington calico manufacturer George Ansell, and came to form part of the complex of half a dozen mills which made up the Ansell industrial empire.

The Ansell Milling Empire

Both the Reynolds family of Culvers, north of the Hackbridge, and the Shepleys, south of the bridge, used the river for milling corn, leather and oil – and for bleaching and whitening linen or calico. Both owned lands bordering on the possessions of a third family – the Ansells. This family not only combined milling with calico manufacture, it also used the river water for another purpose, the making of paper.

It is probable that the Ansells can be traced back to the cloth-making family of that name who were in Southwark in the sixteenth century. George Ansell is first mentioned in 1765, when he was 33/34 years old, and was a partner with a certain Robert Barker

Left to right, top to bottom: *Butter Hill c.1900, showing (left to right) Thursley, Burntside, Denyer's flour-mill (to the rear) and the snuff-mill;*
Burntside, Butter Hill. (S.L.S.L.);
Snuff-mill, Butter Hill, early-twentieth century;
The front door of Thursley, Butter Hill. (S.L.S.L.);
The windmill described variously as Short's Windmill and Windmill, Banstead Lane. A possible candidate for the Carshalton Windmill.
(S.L.S.L.)

Above: *View looking
downstream with the
snuff-mill (left) and
Burntside (right), at
Butter Hill,
c.1870.*

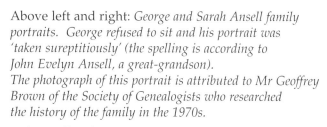

Above left and right: *George and Sarah Ansell family
portraits. George refused to sit and his portrait was
'taken sureptitiously' (the spelling is according to
John Evelyn Ansell, a great-grandson).
The photograph of this portrait is attributed to Mr Geoffrey
Brown of the Society of Genealogists who researched
the history of the family in the 1970s.*

Left: *Snuff mill, Butter Hill, c.1900.* (S.L.S.L.).

of Wallington in a calico-bleaching and printing firm. They owned a good deal of the land alongside the river, right across from Wallington Bridge to Butter Hill, and down towards Hackbridge. In particular they used the area called Boreman's or Bowman's meadow to spread out the calico in order to bleach it. Much of this land is actually in Wallington, but by the 1770s Ansell had his headquarters in what had been the Scawen copper-mill, just to the east of Butter Hill Bridge. He married his wife Sarah in 1772 and they had eight children in the space of 12 years (George was 52 when the youngest was born).

During the late-eighteenth century the Ansell interests expanded rapidly. George not only took over the Butter Hill paper-mill, but in 1782 he bought the much bigger paper-mill along Mill Lane when the Scawen estates were sold – this meant both paper-mills were in his ownership and he controlled the Carshalton paper industry.

He didn't actually run this second paper-mill himself: it was left in the hands of the existing millers, William Curteis and his sons John and Thomas Curteis. William Curteis lived in the mill house called Vandalis, later 84 Mill Lane. He is also shown in the rate books to have been milling at Carshalton Windmill from 1803–8. This windmill was on the Sutton border at the corner of the Ridgeway and Chalgrove Road.

The Ansells don't seem to have manufactured paper themselves until the first decade of the nineteenth century. By the 1780s they had this very valuable complex of mills in the same area: the old Butter Hill copper-mill used as the calico factory; the Mill Lane paper-mill; and the Butter Hill Bridge paper-mill.

Nevertheless, George Ansell himself remained essentially a calico manufacturer, and in June 1785 he formed a new firm, with a London office, and a new partner, Francis Morier, presumably a Frenchman. Ansell seems to have 'gone into Europe' and in particular seems to have traded with France. Unfortunately this arrangement only lasted two years, because in the autumn of 1787 Morier set in motion a scheme to defraud Ansell of £5485. Morier pretended that he had sold 1300 pieces of calico to various firms in London and Manchester. In fact he had secretly shipped this hoard of cloth over to France, and, before Ansell could ask for payment, had fled to Scotland. Of course, when Ansell sent bills to these London and Manchester firms asking them to pay for the cloth they were supposed to have bought, he got some very rude answers. He promptly thought that these firms were trying to diddle him, and started legal proceedings against them. In fact the judges seem to have held that the fraud was against these firms rather than against Ansell, and so the firms were liable. Some or them paid up, two of them went bankrupt, and Ansell still lost a lot of money. Morier indeed caused a vast amount of

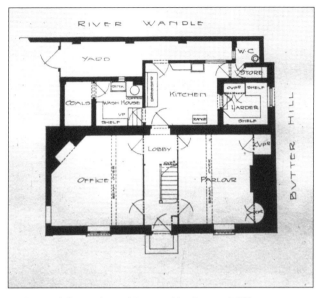

Ground-floor plan of Burntside, Butter Hill. (S.L.S.L.)

damage and confusion before the affair was finally cleared up in 1793. By this time England was at war with France again, and Ansell himself had not long to live. He died in June 1797 and is buried at Woodmansterne.

His wife Sarah then took on the job of keeping all the Ansell concerns going until their boys were old enough to take over. The eldest son William does not appear to have lived locally: perhaps he took over the London end of the business. However, the four younger sons – George, Charles, James and Robert – took one of the Carshalton mills each, and then proceeded to swap round with bewildering rapidity. They had at least three substantial mill houses to live in: Burntside, a sort of seventeenth-century farmhouse; and next door to it in Butter Hill the very handsome eighteenth-century Thursley (although both were knocked down between the wars). Along Mill Lane was the third house called Vandalis, built about 1785, and only demolished in 1970. So the Ansell brothers had three good houses in Carshalton to use – and they needed them. Three of the four were married, and between them they produced 20 children.

There was also the eldest daughter, Fanny, who had a further six children after she married another local calico manufacturer, Benjamin Bailey, who was soon taking a full part in running the Ansell complex. Ben Bailey was an interesting character, who later in life regarded the supreme moment of his career as being the occasion when he saw King Louis XVI, before he was guillotined during the French Revolution. Bailey is important in local history because in about 1800 he bought the site of Stone Court and the Grove, which would be just after the Stone Court mansion was demolished. Therefore he is probably the person responsible for converting the outbuildings of the mansion into the house that is now known as Stone Court. He doesn't seem to have actually lived in it himself – he had his own house next to his calico factory up at Beddington Corner.

So in the early years of the nineteenth century there was a very large and sprawling colony of young Ansells in Carshalton. However, as their numbers grew, so their business declined as they encountered a series of misfortunes. The Butter Hill mill burned down in 1806, and was then rebuilt in much the same form that it is in today – most mills burned down sooner or later: this was a normal occupational hazard. It is hard to tell how much of the old building was destroyed in this fire, and how much had to be reconstructed to form the present buildings. It appears that even before the fire the mill had been divided in half and had two water-wheels. It became a double mill, with the part nearer the bridge being a paper- and flock-mill and the part at the other end being a mill for grinding snuff and madder. It was still shown divided this way in 1850.

The real trouble came with the ending of the Napoleonic Wars. The first to go was James Ansell, who was running the paper-mill in Mill Lane. He had to mortgage the mill in 1813, which suggests that he was in financial difficulties, and two years later, in 1815, he was declared bankrupt. In the course of the next two years James, together with his brother Robert, who had a share, was obliged to sell the paper-mill to a London stationer, Nathaniel Muggeridge – who paid £5000 – and for the rest of the century the mill was run by the Muggeridge family, although they kept the Ansell name for the business because of the high quality and reputation attached to paper made at the Ansell mill. The next to go were the elder brothers George and Charles – George was running the calico factory and Charles the paper-mill at Butter Hill – and both were declared bankrupt in 1815. At the hearing it was said that George had been living on credit for several years, buying large quantities of 'calicoes, quiltings, muslins, cottons and stuffs' and drugs and dyes to print them with, which he couldn't pay for – and that Charles had done the same with paper. Charles even owed his coal merchant £289, which was particularly unfortunate, as the coal merchant in question (Joshua Bennett of Wandsworth) also happened to be one of his brothers-in-law. The brothers did try to start up again: they rented a calico-mill at Merton in 1823 – but three years later they were declared bankrupt again. They don't seem to have been very good businessmen.

Meanwhile Benjamin Bailey was sharing in the general financial catastrophe. In 1817 the local authority complained that Bailey had not paid his rates (they came to £8.2s.0d.) but he was declared to be bankrupt, and the debt was written off. He seems to have kept his Beddington Corner calico business going until about 1830, but he had to get rid of his Carshalton property – which explains why the Grove became a separate property from Stone Court for most of the nineteenth century. Bailey had to sell

it off – and eventually a separate house was built on it (which is why today, there are two houses in the Grove).

By this time the Ansells no longer owned the building – nor any other mill. Indeed all the Ansell property seems to have been sold off at about this time. The various brothers repeatedly went bankrupt one after the other, and the only one who recovered anything out of the wreck was the youngest son Robert – the only one who did not go bankrupt. He was able to go on occupying, although no longer owning, the Butter Hill mill and the mill house, Thursley. He carried on until he died in 1865, and was then succeeded by his younger son, also called Robert, who eventually died, unmarried, in 1905 and brought the Ansell mill story to an end. The building seems to have been disused for much of the early part of the twentieth century, and in 1912 most of the mill machinery was cleared out and the remaining wheel dismantled. One of the old millstones was left outside the door of the building, and it stood there until the Borough Council buried it under a new pavement in 1968 (although it has since been suggested that they should dig it up again). From the 1920s until about 1950 the building was used by J. Boughton, who, by a curious coincidence, made parchment and vellum (mostly for use on dance-band drums). Since then it has been used by a succession of light engineering firms such as Gray Gauges Ltd in 1973, and STR Printers in 1999.

The mill has long been a favourite subject for painters and photographers, and there are more pictures of it than most other places in Carshalton. It has no great architectural merit, but it has a very considerable historic interest for Carshalton, and so it seems vital that it is preserved. The building was threatened with demolition in 1979 but fortunately has so far survived.

Postscript

Both Robert Ansells, father and son, not only made snuff in the ordinary way of business, but they also had a contract with the Customs and Excise. When a load of smuggled tobacco was seized it was sent down to Carshalton, where Robert ground it up into coarse powder, which made it easier to dispose of. This seemed such an awful waste to Robert Ansell that he decided to give it instead to the workhouse, so that the poor people of the parish could use it instead of snuff. However, the other snuff manufacturers objected to this practice and it had to be stopped. Instead the ground-up tobacco was put in a boat and taken out to sea, where it was tipped overboard. This is perhaps a silent commentary on the decline of the Ansells. From operating one of the best paper-mills in the kingdom, it was reduced to grinding up tobacco to be thrown into the sea. There is surely no need to comment further: 'snuff said.

THE WANDLE CALICO INDUSTRY

Steadily increasing demand for water combined with years of drought have pushed the water table down below the level of the pumps and have dried up ponds and rivers, particularly in South-East England. So far the Wandle has escaped the fate of rivers like the Ver and the Darenth, but even a reduction in the amount of flow threatens water purity. It was water quality which made the Wandle Valley a great area for bleaching calicoes. This industry had reached Mitcham by the middle of the seventeenth century, and we know that there was calico bleaching at Mill Green by 1700, at the Culvers by 1740, Hackbridge in the 1760s, and in the course of the next century all the way to Croydon. Less well known is the story of colouring and putting designs on the cloth: calico printing. Both Carshalton and Wallington were of special importance in this respect.

In 1754 Carshalton House acquired a new owner in the form of a young businessman of Huguenot stock who was becoming very wealthy through his connections with various North-German trading interests. He had in fact married the daughter of a very prominent Hamburg merchant – although he soon became a leading figure in the East India Company. His name was George Amyand. His father was employed at the court of George II; his elder brother Claudius Amyand was already a member of Parliament, and in the same year that he came to Carshalton George himself was given a Parliamentary seat: he sat for Barnstaple from 1754 onwards. It was his widespread business interests which made him enormously wealthy. He was able to loan the Government very large sums to finance the Seven Years War; which in turn gave him even more lucrative contracts, particularly to provision the Army in Hanover; and he was duly knighted in 1764. Like so many business tycoons, he was obviously a workaholic, and he simply wore himself out and died two years later in 1766 (when Carshalton House was sold to Thomas Walpole, a

relative of one of Amyand's business partners). When Amyand was buried in Carshalton Church, at the age of only 46, it was said that his 'keen and arduous pursuit' of wealth had 'so worked the capillaries of his brain' that it 'wore them down to a filament, which distorted the whole constitution and dissolved the entire frame.'

One of George Amyand's earliest businesses was a partnership he formed in the late 1740s with one of his German contacts, Johann Anton Rucker, later to be naturalised in 1745 as John Anthony Rucker. Rucker himself came to live in Carshalton at a later date. In 1764 he was a tenant at Wandle Hall (Strawberry Lodge), although he is better known for his mill at Phipps Bridge (Mitcham), where he may have built the house known as Wandle Villa, now owned by the National Trust (this matter appears to be disputed). Amyand and Rucker, who had offices in London, had a firm of calico printers, and it was they who were responsible for introducing a revolutionary new method of printing calicoes into England which involved the use of copper plates – very suitable for the Wandle with its many copper-mills, and had been invented in the mid-1750s by a man at Drumcondra near Dublin. Soon after he came to Carshalton, Amyand arranged for the inventor, Francis Nixon, to come to England and become a partner with himself and Rucker for printing calicoes by this new method. Although Nixon himself died in 1765, the year before Amyand, the business continued as Nixon & Co. until 1789 when Rucker retired to the large new house he built for himself at Wandsworth.

Another Irishman, William Kilburn, born in Dublin in 1745, came over to work in the Wandle mills and began to make a reputation for himself as a designer and printer of both calicoes and wallpaper. In about 1777 he was engaged by James Newton to be manager of Newton's calico bleaching and printing business in Wallington. Newton was closely connected with the Ansell family of Butter Hill. Both Newton and the Ansells had mills at

Designs for chintz by William Kilburn, 1788/94. (V&A)

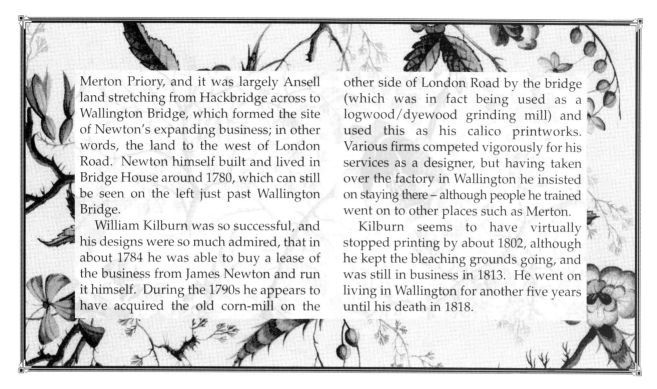

Merton Priory, and it was largely Ansell land stretching from Hackbridge across to Wallington Bridge, which formed the site of Newton's expanding business; in other words, the land to the west of London Road. Newton himself built and lived in Bridge House around 1780, which can still be seen on the left just past Wallington Bridge.

William Kilburn was so successful, and his designs were so much admired, that in about 1784 he was able to buy a lease of the business from James Newton and run it himself. During the 1790s he appears to have acquired the old corn-mill on the other side of London Road by the bridge (which was in fact being used as a logwood/dyewood grinding mill) and used this as his calico printworks. Various firms competed vigorously for his services as a designer, but having taken over the factory in Wallington he insisted on staying there – although people he trained went on to other places such as Merton.

Kilburn seems to have virtually stopped printing by about 1802, although he kept the bleaching grounds going, and was still in business in 1813. He went on living in Wallington for another five years until his death in 1818.

WATER-WHEELS & THE GROVE MILL

The following story was related by the *Sussex Weekly Advertiser* of 19 October 1818:

Mr J. Harrow worked in one of the Carshalton paper-mills in Mill Lane, which had a very big water-wheel, and he walked out on to one of the plank bridges over the river, and leaned over to oil the wheel. Unfortunately the plank bridge gave way, and to save himself from falling into the river, he grabbed hold of the water-wheel, and tried to push himself back. Even more unfortunately his sleeve caught on a piece of metal on the wheel, and he was carried round with it, 'turning him over and over in its progress'. When the wheel went up it bumped him against the brickwork of the culvert above the wheel; when the wheel went down it nearly drowned him in the water underneath – and of course he couldn't get free, but was just carried round and round.

Hearing his shouts for help, his workmates rushed out of the mill, and decided that the only thing to do was to stop the wheel. To do this they had to shut off the water. So they heaved on the levers and closed the sluice gates. Unfortunately, just as the gates were closing, the wheel brought Mr Harrow round again – and he got shut in the floodgates. This at least got him off the hook. Sadly, his left leg was squashed quite flat and had to be cut off – and he did not survive long afterwards.

Water-wheels, then and now, are pretty lethal things, which have to be treated with respect. One of the very few water-wheels of the Wandle still surviving is the wheel in the Grove, although it has been constantly vandalised. This mill has one of the longest histories of all the Wandle mills. It is the Carshalton manor mill recorded in Domesday Book, which means that it was probably an Anglo-Saxon mill. It appears to be the corn mill attached to Stone Court during the thirteenth century; but then there is a rather confused patch in its history; and it is not mentioned again until 1445, when it is called the Town Mill. There seem to have been two millers: Reginald atte Church/Chirche (who was accused of blocking up the flow of water in the mill pool so that the road was flooded) and William the Miller (who was accused of making excess profits).

By 1482 it was Nicholas Gainsford's mill, the Upper Town Mill, and was described as three mills under one roof; two for flour and one for malt. It was operated by the Pope family until 1779, when it was bought by John Hilbert, the great Wandsworth miller, who also had Croydon Palace as a calico factory. He or his family rebuilt the mill early in the nineteenth century, but from 1801 it was Charrington's mill and the younger Charrington, Robert Linton Charrington, kept it going until 1879. It was continued for a few years into the 1880s by James Bristow, but was rapidly becoming ruinous and falling down of its own accord. The lady who had Stone Court, the rector's wife Mrs Cator, removed it altogether in 1887, except for the wheel, which was converted to turn a dynamo for electricity. It is an interesting wheel. In 1808 it was one of a pair of 15ft breastshot wheels (it is still possible to see the mounting for the other wheel) but it does seem in a curious sort of way to be made up of two parts: half the construction is much lighter than the other half. It may be that it is a combination of two still older wheels. There is no date on it, so its age is unclear. Still more curious, there seems to be no picture of the mill at all; all the alleged old photographs of this mill are actually photographs of the other Grove Mill, the mill on the Westcroft Canal.

The Cottage in the churchyard, 4 High Street, late 1800s. The Woodman's thatched barn is on the left.

The Servers at All Saints, c.1912. The Revd G.B. Vaux is fifth from the right at the back. (J.H.)

Chapter Ten
THE PARISH CHURCH

SOME SIXTEENTH-CENTURY INCUMBENTS

The Carshalton rectory and its location have changed with the centuries, and there are half a dozen Carshalton houses which have been the homes of rectors. In the sixteenth century the position was even more difficult because there was not only a rector, but a vicar as well – and apparently there was both a rectory and a vicarage (although the latter was probably more like a curate's cottage). The reason for this duplication is that after the Reformation the rectorship and the property going with it were bought and sold like any other property. Thus one could easily have a layman as rector, and he would therefore appoint a cleric as his vicar to take the actual services.

One of the first of these lay rectors was a man called John Fromond or Fromans, who bought Carshalton's rectory in 1556 and lived there until he died in 1580 (when he passed it on to his son). He must have been a fairly rich person, and he had married a lady called Benedicta Draper, the daughter of one of Henry VIII's jewellers, who came from Camberwell. When he bought the rectory he obtained a house and a cottage – probably the Parsonage House and the vicarage, a tithe barn, dovecot, orchard, garden and 270 acres of farmland, presumably out in the common fields. The old Carshalton tithe barn seems to have stood by Margaret's Pool between the end of West Street and Pound Street: probably where the corner of the convent wall stands. So he was a wealthy man; the tithes were paid to him, not the vicar; and he could well afford to appoint a vicar to do the job of being the parish priest. Unfortunately he just seemed incapable of getting on with his vicars – and he went through a whole string of them. In 1568 the vicar complained that Fromond had not been to communion for five years – naturally, he didn't last long. The next vicar complained that Fromond was unable to mend the broken church windows and the following year the vicar complained to the bishop that the rector had failed to repair the chancel. So after several warnings, the bishop excommunicated the rector in 1569. Nevertheless, he survived, but there were

further complaints in 1570 about lack of repairs to the church. In 1573 yet another vicar complained that the rector was not looking after the vicar properly, and was keeping him short of food. All these matters went to the episcopal court – the court of the bishop of Winchester – and the bishop must have been heartily sick of Fromond.

If Fromond did not like vicars, so that there was constant friction, the other sort of people that he could not abide were millers, and there were several lawsuits in which local mill owners complained about Fromond's behaviour. His neighbour, who was named Ralph Hurlstone, had a mill near Fromond's rectory and complained that when Fromond wanted fish he went out and caught them in the mill-tail. To make it worse he had several streams of his own running by the house, but he refused to clean them out – with the result that they got blocked up, and this annoyed all the millers because it cut down the flow of water to their mills. Additionally, when a cart-horse went to drink in one of these dirty streams, it just fell over and died – and Fromond refused to pull the dead horse out, so the whole river became polluted. However, the worst thing of all, something which apparently shocked the whole village, was that John Fromond the rector played bowls on his lawn on Sundays. There doesn't seem to have been much of the Drake spirit about Carshalton: the village really didn't take to Fromond. However, what could one expect? He was a Roman Catholic, and he came from Cheam! Perhaps he didn't like Carshalton either.

Fromond's parsonage may well have been near the tithe barn in West Street/Pound Street. This has led previous writers to suggest that Fromond's rectory was on the site of the Old Rectory in Festival Walk, and was the house which preceded the present building (late-seventeenth century). This idea would not have been impossible, and the biggest objection to this site – that there weren't any mills nearby – would not have applied in the sixteenth century, because there seem to have been two at that time. One was on the lake in the grounds of Carshalton House (the sluice and foundations were still visible in 1921 when the lake was nearly filled in to make a playing field) and the mill-tail would be the stream along Festival Walk. The other mill may have been at the other end of this stream, where it joins the Ponds, attached to the north side of Honeywood. It has been known for about ten years that there was a much older building embedded in the end of Honeywood, but to our great surprise we find that photographs of the 1870s and 1890s seem to show it.

AN EARLY VICAR OF CARSHALTON

The vicar of Carshalton from 1612 was named Peter Dawson or Danson. He was not in the vicinity very long because in 1618 his uncle, the vicar of Camberwell, died, and he took over the living of Camberwell from him, although it is possible that he may not have actually given up Carshalton until 1624. He was half Irish. He may have been appointed to Carshalton in the first place for his very strong Roman-Catholic sympathies. Later on he in fact hid and gave shelter to a Roman-Catholic priest who was trying to escape the authorities. He seems to have been a very active and energetic man, until the Civil War broke out in the 1640s, and with the Puritan control of London, he was thrown out of his living by Parliament in 1644, and branded as a 'malignant', a Royalist and a Papist. Although he was subsequently reinstated, he seems to have become very depressed by the great national crisis and simply gave up and let things run down. It is not clear

where Peter Dawson/Danson lived when he was vicar of Carshalton but there is a persistent tradition that he lived in the fifteenth-century house next to the east end of the church, used as Kingston's butcher's shop (latterly the Old Ducks Wine Bar). He rarely held services, and when he died in 1652/3 it was said that he had not preached a sermon for the last 12 years. As there wasn't much to do, he literally 'went to pot' – he took to drink. Obviously this was not approved behaviour, so he had to do it secretly – he used to lock himself in the church and drink there – and was sometimes discovered by his clerk lying on the altar dead drunk. He could not really afford this lifestyle so he exhorted his parishioners to give alms to the poor – and then he went and emptied the poor box. It is possible that this is Puritan propaganda as it doesn't seem in character from what we know of his earlier life. Peter Dawson/Danson was in fact one of the founders of Wilson's Grammar School at Camberwell in 1615, and the uncle whom he succeeded as vicar of Camberwell was Edward Wilson himself.

So there was a close link between Carshalton and Wilson's School right from the beginning, and for the next 200 years the vicar or rector of Carshalton was always automatically made one of the governors of Wilson's School. The establishment was moved to Wallington from Camberwell in December 1974 and the historic link between Carshalton and Wilson's continues.

Main: *The Old Rectory, Festival Walk.* (S.L.S.L.)

Inset: *Victorian photograph of Honeywood showing the mill on the right-hand end.*

THE MISSING RECTORY

Carshalton had an incredible number of rectories; the place is littered with them. In the early days, when the rector was a mere vicar, he probably lived close to the church. Three buildings by the church are said to have housed the parish priest: Dame Duffin's Cottage (now demolished, *see page 6*) by Anne Boleyn's Well, the end of Kingston's butcher's shop (later to become The Old Ducks Wine Bar) and the cottage in the churchyard (4 High Street). Then came the rectory in Festival Walk; the new rectory in the High Street (now replaced by the shopping precinct); at one stage the Grove was used as a rectory; and most recently No. 2 Talbot Road. Records show that there was yet another one, but it has long been unclear as to where it was. When Mr Jones produced his *Directory* in 1973 he suggested two other specific buildings. However, it is possible that two further properties may have housed the parish priest.

The reason why local historians disagree on this subject is that it appears that it stood in that square of land between West Street Lane and Carshalton Station, with West Street on one side and North Street on the other. This is a very central part of old Carshalton (there ought to be plenty of information about it) and yet in practice it is a nightmare for the local historian. It has a large number of listed buildings within its boundaries, but there is a limited amount of accurate information about them. This block of land was well defined by the 1600s. West Street Lane was the old road from Stone Court to Sutton, which gave it a definite southern boundary. North Street is a medieval road and West Street certainly existed and is known by that name in the seventeenth century (although it was sometimes called Wrythe Lane). The northern boundary of this area also seems to have been clearly defined by this time, particularly by the 1650s when the Bynes built Bornhem House, roughly on the site of the station.

On the earliest map of Carshalton, the Arundel Castle map of about 1620 (*see page 33*), one can see this block of land clearly marked out. Unfortunately this map reveals virtually nothing about the area in question: it is a complete blank within its boundaries, except that there are two houses shown in North Street at the corner with West Street Lane – by Beechwood Court, opposite the Sun. A lot of time elapses before the appearance of Rocque's map of 1765, which shows this area packed with buildings, looking very much like it does today. It is not until the first Tithe Map of 1839 that a detailed picture emerges, but that of course is too late for our purposes.

Revd Hillier, who died in 1738, was followed by Revd Edmund Lodge from Bristol. Hillier's widow, Elizabeth Hillier (Nelme) [for further information see the Byne family under Local Families], did not want to leave the Old Rectory, which she thought was Byne property and her home. She wanted the new rector, Edmund Lodge, to live there with her – either as a lodger, or perhaps she thought she could then marry him, and keep it all in the family. But Lodge wasn't interested (there having already been an enormous and ongoing quarrel between his family and the Bynes about property ownership). Apparently a wealthy man, he bought himself a new rectory and got himself a wife as well (in the form of Mary Garrard, whose father, Richard, owned Alton Lodge in West Street, No. 70). Elizabeth Hillier apparently went on living in the Old Rectory until she died in 1781.

Revd Lodge left Carshalton in 1759, when he was promoted to archdeacon, and in the 1780s his Carshalton house passed to his son, also called Edmund. The young Edmund – he would have been 30 years old in 1786 – was even wealthier than his father. He not only had his father's old rectory house, but he also acquired Alton Lodge as well through his mother. Both these Carshalton houses were let out to tenants – although he seems to have used the rectory as a sort of country residence – but he spent most of his time at his very fine house in London in Bloomsbury Square, which was more convenient for his work. He was to become a very famous antiquarian and genealogist, one of the Heralds at the College of Arms, and the founder of Lodge's Peerage. When he died in 1839 he was the oldest member of the Society of Antiquaries, and immensely respected. He never married, but his sister Mary lived with him and kept house for him.

The Lodges had two houses: one of them, as outlined above, was Alton Lodge, 70 West Street; the other was the former rectory. Where was this rectory, the original Lodge house? Where did the Lodges lodge? When James Edwards visited Carshalton in about 1789, and made a list of important houses and owners, he wrote:

In the street which lies a furlong north of (the entrance to Carshalton House) is a small genteel house in the possession of Mr Wood; and a little further on a neat white boarded house occupied by Mr Richards: both belonging to Edmund Lodge.

The neat white boarded house, a little further on, occupied by John Richards, is Alton Lodge. Where was the small genteel house, with Mr Wood in it, not quite so far north? The traditional (and most likely) answer to this (originally put forward by Peatling) is the house which went by the name of Colstonfields, No. 44 West Street. It was demolished around the end of the Second World War and is now the car park for the Hope Inn. According to a Mr Ward Evans, who lived there before the war, and indeed before 1918 as well, this was the Revd Edmund Lodge's house, which he purchased as a rectory in 1738, buying it from a lady called Parkhurst, who lived at Epsom. So that house dated back to at least the 1730s.

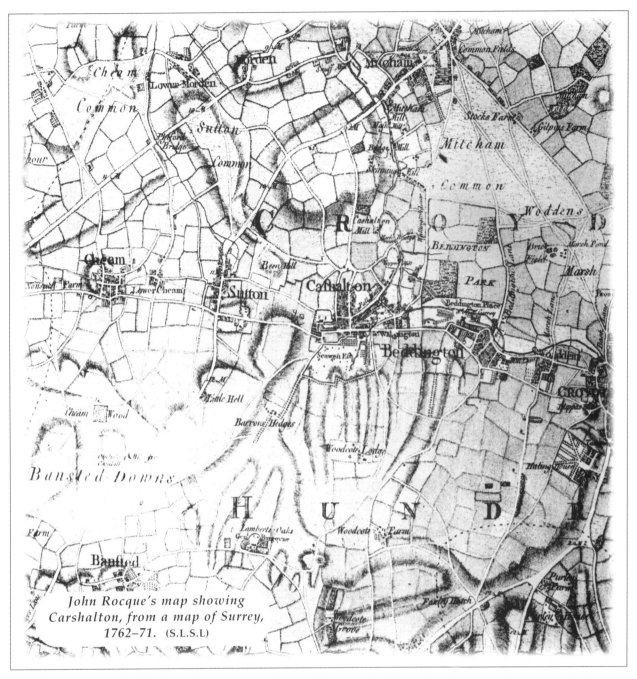

John Rocque's map showing
Carshalton, from a map of Surrey,
1762–71. (S.L.S.L)

Left to right: *Woodman's butcher's shop, later Kingston's, by the church path, in 1916.* (S.L.S.L.);
Front door of Alton Lodge, 70 West Street, c.1900. (S.L.S.L.);
London House, 42 West Street, September 1967, long after the demolition of Colstonfields.

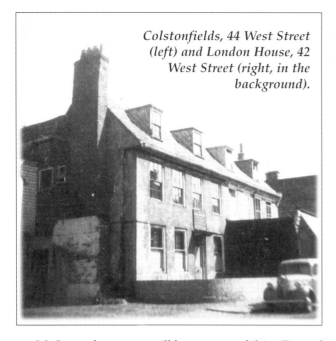

Colstonfields, 44 West Street (left) and London House, 42 West Street (right, in the background).

West Lodge, West Street Lane, 1981.

Mr Jones, however, will have none of this. First of all he points out that there was a third Lodge house in 1789, owned and occupied by the younger Edmund Lodge himself. This was the house on the corner of West Street Lane and North Street, called Beechwood – which has since given its name to the flats called Beechwood Court. Was this house of 1789 in existence in 1738? There appears to have been a house on that site, according to the maps of 1620 and 1765, but whether it was the same one is not clear – and there is no very obvious way of finding out. The three-story brick house with a slate roof was demolished in the late 1930s, probably 1937. However, there is no pictorial record of it, apart from a corner of it visible in the distance on a photograph of the Ponds, where it looks like an eighteenth-century house.

Mr Jones, nevertheless, seems to prefer another and more ingenious alternative for the location of the original Lodge house of 1738. He doesn't think that Colstonfields was grand enough for a wealthy rector's house, and he has been intrigued by the house which lies behind Colstonfields: the house called West Lodge (25 West Street Lane). This is much more 'genteel', and has the peculiarity of a front door at the side, in West Street Lane, which appears to face west towards West Street. In brief, Mr Jones suggests that West Lodge was the original Lodge rectory of 1738, and that it originally fronted onto West Street, which is why it faces the way it does. According to this, the house called Colstonfields was built into the front garden of West Lodge early in the nineteenth century – and the construction of other buildings soon followed to make up the present West Street frontage. Thus West Lodge, next to Beechwood Court, appears to be the missing Carshalton rectory.

This is an interesting speculation, but there still appear to be two fatal objections to it: one is that there is not a shred of evidence to connect West

Lodge with the Lodge family, either father or son. A fair amount of its history has been traced (although there are gaps) and it seems to have been built about 1730 – a Byne family property, but one which was leased to Sir Edward Whitaker, a retired admiral, who had been second-in-command and a hero of the Siege of Gibraltar in 1704. Sir Edward died in 1735, and is buried in Carshalton churchyard. The house passed to his nephew, Samuel Whitaker, who duly followed his uncle to Carshalton churchyard in 1740 – and there was possibly his son, another Edward Whitaker, a London coffee merchant, who also ended up in Carshalton churchyard in 1762. By 1786 West Lodge had passed into the hands of a family called Clarke, and it stayed with them until at least 1850. So there does not seem to be much room for a Lodge in West Lodge. The other, and even more damning, objection to Mr Jones' idea, is provided by a photograph of Colstonfields (*top left*). This is clearly an early-eighteenth century house, not one built into a front garden after 1800 – and what is more interesting, the picture makes it obvious that Colstonfields originally included the house next door, No. 42 West Street. These two houses were initially all one house, a large and distinguished early-eighteenth-century dwelling, quite grand enough for the wealthy Edmund Lodge to have bought as his new rectory in 1738.

It seemed strange that there was no information about No. 42 West Street, now called London House. The reason for this of course is that the history was already there – in the form of Edmund Lodge's first house. Half the house has gone: it went when No. 44 was demolished in about 1948. However, the other half, No. 42, still exists – and the Carshalton Society was very pleased to be able to help and encourage the restoration and renovation of this property. The Society did not realise at the time that it was another of Carshalton's rectories.

THE BECKENHAM LINK: ROSE & CATOR

During the eighteenth century the rector of Beckenham, the Revd William Rose, was also the rector of Carshalton and divided his time between the two parishes. He was popular and very hospitable, remaining as rector in Carshalton for 52 years. The advowson (the right to appoint the rectors of Carshalton) was held by the Rose family. In 1797 they sold this right to John Cator of Beckenham so that when the Revd William Rose died in 1829, it was up to the Cators to decide who should be the next rector of Carshalton.

Mr Cator, thought to be William Albemarle Bertie, mid 1800s.

Well, they had plenty of choice. There were six Cator boys in the next generation, all nephews of the John Cator last mentioned, the children of his brother Joseph Cator and Diana Bertie, the admiral's sister. The two youngest Cator boys do not feature: the Revd Thomas Cator married the daughter of the Earl of Scarborough, and went off to spend his life in a Yorkshire rectory. The youngest, Peter Cator, became a successful barrister in Kent. All the other four Cator boys came to have a bearing on the history of Carshalton.

The head of the family, the eldest son, yet another John Cator (John Cator V), also lived at Beckenham, but it was he who established the main family home in Norfolk, where the Cators still had a presence in the twentieth century. He, and his son Albemarle Cator, who succeeded him in 1858, would not be worth mentioning here, had it not been the case that they had acquired ten acres of land in the common fields of Carshalton to the south of Carshalton Park. Nor would the second son be worth mentioning – he was later to become Lieutenant-General Sir William Cator of the Royal Artillery – except that in 1820 he and his wife Penelope produced a son, blessed with the traditional Cator names of William Albemarle Bertie. The third son was future rector Charles and the fourth, Bertie Cornelius, later became Admiral.

The Reverend Charles Cator was the next appointment in 1829. He had already distinguished himself in 1809 by marrying a Yorkshire lady with the singular name of Philadelphia Osbaldiston. He was hardly one of the parish's more illustrious parsons. In the course of the next six years he managed to get into debt, then into prison (for not paying his bills), and finally he was declared bankrupt. He was forced to resign in 1835, and banished to a remote Yorkshire village for the next 40 years. Since he is still listed as rector of Carshalton in 1849, 14 years later, one suspects that he may have retained the title,

and the relatives who replaced him, a cousin called Vernon and then his nephew William Albemarle Bertie Cator, came as technically vicars or curates. At any rate, in 1849 Charles is still credited with holding the glebe, the land which went with Carshalton Church (and which was free of tithes), including the rectory in the middle of the High Street, and the Grove field behind it. There were also some six acres in Long Furlong, again land in the common fields beyond the Park. However, other records show that William Albemarle Bertie, who was also a nephew of Admiral Bertie Cornelius Cator (see 'Admirals of Carshalton'), became rector in 1845 and died in Carshalton in 1884 having purchased Stone Court and the Grove, and so restored them to the ownership of the Cator family.

NEWS ABOUT THE PARISH CHURCH IN THE LATE-NINETEENTH CENTURY

From long before the Reformation Carshalton Parish Church – All Saints – was at the centre of controversy. It was the source of arguments which often divided the local community. Even as late as 1920 there was a fierce argument about whether spitting should be prohibited in church, and, if not, whether spittoons should be provided – as, parishioners were told, was the custom in European churches. This 'spew in the pew' debate, which probably wasn't taken too seriously, pales into insignificance against the rousing events of 30 years earlier.

By the 1880s there was a general feeling that church life was at a low ebb in Carshalton (by this the established Anglican church is meant: all the evidence is that the Dissenting and Roman Catholic churches were flourishing). The rector, the Reverend W.A.B. Cator, was coming to the end of his long reign of nearly 40 years, and had patently ceased to take much interest in the church and its services. Later on, one of his parishioners recalled:

During the Reverend Cator's time we had the same hymn every Sunday morning without fail. It was the hymn 'A few more years shall roll'.

This set the tone for the rest of the service, which was very lugubrious, and the rector's sermon, which was a lengthy reminder

The Revd Lord Victor Seymour and his wife in the late 1800s.
(J.H.)

that Judgement Day was coming. For the afternoon service there was a litany, with some prayers for the evening service added on: but Mr Cator refused to have an evening service; and when a few members of the congregation arranged one amongst themselves, he generally refused to attend. The congregation had to make a special collection in order to be able to pay a curate, Mr Graham, to come and take it. (Records reveal very little about Mr Graham, except that he lived at Wrythe Green and had a very big nose.)

Concern was also expressed, not only about the services, but about the condition of the church itself. There was a fear that the foundations were being shaken by the constant passage of horses and carts past the building; the churchyard was unkempt and neglected; and ivy was climbing the walls and eating into the stonework. More serious was the feeling that an old medieval church was simply not adequate for a rapidly expanding, lively suburb: the church, wrote a contemporary, was 'picturesque but inconvenient'. There was a strong feeling that improvements had to be made. The Revd Cator had carried out extensive alterations back in the early 1860s, which greatly increased the number of seats: but these changes were now pronounced to be out of date, and therefore ugly. It was felt that here at Carshalton – as all over the country – there should be wonderful new Anglican churches built so that they could accommodate all the rapidly rising populations as soon as they were converted to the Church of England. Big, new churches represented the missionary endeavour of the Victorian church. Carshalton, which seated 600, was deemed not big enough.

Obviously nothing was going to be done whilst the Reverend Cator remained in charge, but he suddenly died towards the end of 1884. The family cast round for a suitable replacement, and found him in the person of a young man, the Reverend Lord Victor Seymour, born on 6 March 1859. Lord Victor had only a few months' experience of parish work, but he possessed two very valuable qualifications for the job. He was a man of rank, the fourth son of the Marquess of Hertford; and he was engaged to marry Elizabeth Cator, daughter (one of 14 children) of a rather distant cousin of the previous rector. It would keep the position in the family.

In his reminiscences, written 40 years later, long after he had left Carshalton, the Revd Lord Victor suggested that he found Carshalton a very odd place. Having listed some of the notable residents in the big houses, he commented:

I will not mention any more of the residents: but truth compels me to add that some of them were quite unlike any people I had seen before, and no doubt they regarded me as an oddity too.

He certainly came with a reputation for being young and vigorous, and George Brightling, the local historian and churchwarden – who also liked to think of himself as energetic – felt that something ought to be done to impress and please the new rector. Lord Victor was installed three days before Christmas 1884, and George Brightling thought that he would enjoy some carols on Christmas morning. He organised a large party of carol-singers, and at six o'clock

Main: *South side of the Parish Church during alterations. Note the absence of crenellation on the tower and the chimney on the outer south aisle.* (S.L.S.L.)

Inset: *St Andrew's Church, Carshalton.* (J.T.)

in the morning they went along West Street to cluster outside the window of the house where the new rector was staying (now No. 30 West Street). The rector was woken by vigorous singing outside, but he refused to go out in his nightshirt. Brightling complained that although the carol-singers sang and sang, there was no sign of life within, and they eventually left, sadly shaking their heads at the idea that their new rector was a very sleepy fellow.

They could not have been more wrong. Lord Victor was very much a new broom, and a stormy 15 years ensued. He records that his first action on entering the church was to throw out all the mops and brushes, buckets and pails, which the cleaning ladies usually dropped out of sight behind the altar rails or left propped up against the altar itself ready for use. This action was to be symbolic. In the first place Lord Victor was a protagonist of the ecumenical movement: the parish, he records, could not decide whether to suspect him of being a Papist in disguise or, even worse, a secret member of the Salvation Army. This last remark was the result of an event which astonished the parish. Having commented that it was a pity that the Salvation Army, if its members really were the Christians that they claimed to be, did not hold their parades in church, the usual congregation at the Parish Church was thrown into a state of consternation on the following Sunday. The doors suddenly opened and in marched the Salvation Army, with drums beating, bringing with them all the poor in the parish that they could find, and filling every corner of the church.

Lord Victor recorded afterwards that they were very well behaved and kept fairly quiet – although there were some unusually lusty 'Amens', and every now and then enthusiasm got the better of some member of the Army who would shout out 'God bless you my Lord'. Lord Victor emerged with an entirely unexpected reputation as protector of the Salvation Army. He recorded his belief that his parishioners no longer threw members of the Salvation Army into the Ponds or hauled them through the mud – which had been the normal way that Carshalton treated the Salvation Army. Only a few years previously a Salvation Army march at the Wrythe had broken up under a hail of mud, stones and flour bags. The residents were a violent lot at Carshalton in those days.

However, Lord Victor did not keep his new 'converts' – a little later, in 1892, the Salvation Army built its own meeting house or citadel at the corner of North Street and Wrythe Green. New mission churches were built, such as St Andrews at the bottom of Wrythe Lane in 1886 and the first Good Shepherd church – known as the 'tin church' or the 'iron church' – in Stanley Park Road in 1890. Meanwhile Lord Victor had insisted that the Carshalton rectory in the High Street (now the shopping precinct) should be extensively re-built to make

a suitable home for himself and his new bride – he married Elizabeth Cator in September 1885. What he really wanted to do above all was to knock down the Parish Church, and build a new one.

Not surprisingly, this proposal caused a furore, and Carshalton was split between those who wanted to renovate and restore the old church, and those who wanted a new building. Ironically, the bulk of the population (those who were not Anglicans, nor churchgoers) and what Lord Victor disdainfully termed 'the public house element hostile to religion' were in favour of conservation, of keeping the old church. Their motive, however, was not preservationist pure and simple: they recognised that restoration was cheaper than new buildings, and they were afraid that to build a new church would lead to an increase in the tithes, which they bitterly resented having to pay. By today's standards, the proposals sound quite modest. At a meeting in 1889 the architects (the celebrated firm of Blomfields) explained the scheme and the cost was estimated at £10,000. It was announced that work would begin when half this amount had been raised.

The rector made strenuous efforts to get funds, and after only a year it was stated at the Vestry meeting in December 1890 that £5000 had been subscribed, and permission was sought for the work to begin. To the rector's dismay, the meeting voted against a new church. This was hailed as a victory for democracy: the battle cry was raised that the church meant 'people, not buildings'. The local paper commented that Carshalton was suffering from having two lords: the lord of the manor, who promised everything and did nothing, and the lord of the rectory, who did everything and promised nothing. Both were trying to turn Carshalton into a new heaven and a new earth. There was a violent paper war.

The rector promptly retaliated against the rejection of his plans by demanding that a referendum should be held, at which only members of the congregation could vote. He declared that he would be present at the poll to ensure that everyone voted properly. Ladies from the congregation toured the district to canvass the voters and compel them to come in. As one scurrilous contemporary poem, called 'Meditation amongst the Tombs', was phrased:

Twas a wintery day near the end of the year,
With a dull leaden sky growing cheerless and drear,
When some elderly spinsters of gentle degree,
Who disseminate tracts with small packets of tea,
Braved the sleet and the snow, ransacked alley and slum
(Though it can't be denied that they looked very glum),
Their mission and earnest endeavour to find,
And ensnare every voter, though halt, lame or blind.
For their dear little parson a fresh craze has found,
And declared he will pull the old church to the ground.
There, in place of the ivy-clad, time-honoured pile,
Would build a cathedral, ritualistic in style.

It is a dreadful poem, and it deserved to fail: the rector's tactics were highly successful – as the poet lamented:

The parson sat snug by the voting-room fire,
Where the slightest dissent soon stirred up his ire.
And at last, with the help of each feeble old crone,
This dear little man got the way of his own.
Yes, the doom of our temple is finally sealed,
And pickaxe and crowbar destruction now wield.
And the tombs of our dearest, by navvies o'ertrod,
Till it's hard to distinguish the acre of God.

Fortunately a survey of the tombstones was made before work began.

In point of fact financial considerations made it desirable to keep more of the old church than had originally been intended. For example, the tower and bells were reprieved at a fairly late stage. Nevertheless, the side of the old church facing the Ponds was removed, and what was virtually a new church was built onto it, double the size, so that there are almost two churches now in the one building. A memorial stone was laid in the new chancel on 3 October 1891.

The rector scored a great triumph over his critics by getting a member of the royal family to come and lay it. She was a daughter-in-law of Queen Victoria, the Duchess of Albany, the widow of Prince Leopold. She had been to Sutton earlier in the year; and the rector felt that if she could go to Sutton, she certainly ought to come to Carshalton – and come she did. There was a great procession down North Street, with the road so thickly decorated by bunting and flags donated by Carshalton traders that it is said the railway bridge was quite hidden from view. The procession then journeyed down to the High Street to have lunch at the new rectory, before visiting the church, and then on to a reception in Carshalton Park. The whole of Carshalton was on holiday. Never, said the local paper, had so many people gathered in the village – and there was not a single inharmonious note to mar the proceedings (although in the next paragraph it reported that pickpockets had made a great harvest in the crowd). In fact this royal visit provoked a furious outburst from the opposition:

Who tricked a Royal Duchess, who?
To win her smiles to pay the screw…
For 'twas a low, disloyal thing:
A Royal Lady here to bring
Our parish quarrels to partake,
For show and ceremonial's sake…
The crumbled bones in death outcried
Against the wrecker's hateful pride,
Whilst royalty was duped to play
The partisan, then hie away…

Remember, Carshalton, beware!
You guides of royalty take care,
Let not your charges intermix
With local fights or politics.
Oh, what a wasteful deed was done
On Wandle's bank at Carshalton.

The controversy now became really vicious, and the pamphlet warfare reached a degree of bitterness which one might expect to find in medieval and Reformation tracts. The rector was accused of trying to sell Carshalton to the Pope, of grinding the faces of the poor to get money for his new church, and of threatening damnation to those who would not pay.

For example, there is a spoof sermon in verse, which was attributed to the rector. The implication is that he was preaching it to the poor at the Wrythe on 17 November 1891. The text claims that he 'fell among thieves':

I'll Romanise the people; I'll have them follow me;
I'll let them know I have the power
To bind and to set free.
I am the only telephone
By which their prayers can reach
The seat of mercy up above
Within the golden street.
So the parish priest I mean to be,
Their sole and earthly king…

Although most of it is too dreadful to include here, the text continued:

Treat thy neighbour as thyself,
The scriptures plainly say.
But what's the Book to me?
I live in modern day.
Do I follow Christ?
Or do I follow Rome?
When a man can't pay his tithes,
I'll sell him out of home.

Of course these tactics simply did not pay off. They merely alienated sympathy by being so vicious and scurrilous. The preservationist mob enjoyed a brief moment of triumph in 1892 when the money ran out, and the rebuilding came to a halt:

There stands our new Temple, a shapeless great hulk,
With hoarding enclosing the unfinished bulk.
And there it will stand while moons wax and wane:
The dismal result of a project insane.

Not surprisingly the conservationists' jubilation was short-lived – the residents weren't going to put up with this sort of thing, and soon money for the new church was flowing in again, and the rebuilding continued.

The last service was held in the old church on 21 November 1892, and the first in the new part of the building took place a week later. The services had to be repeated in duplicate and triplicate because so many people were now coming to church to see the new building and find out what all the fuss was about. The new building was consecrated the following year, and although work continued for another 20 years, the issue had been settled. Carshalton was to have its new cathedral, despite all the arguments for preservation. The vicar was not called Victor for nothing.

A NOTE ON MODERN RECTORS

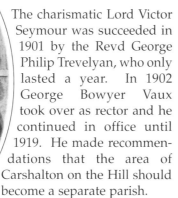

Father Corbould. (K.W.)

The charismatic Lord Victor Seymour was succeeded in 1901 by the Revd George Philip Trevelyan, who only lasted a year. In 1902 George Bowyer Vaux took over as rector and he continued in office until 1919. He made recommendations that the area of Carshalton on the Hill should become a separate parish.

Father Corbould took over in December 1919. He was an extreme Anglo-Catholic whose services differed little from those of the Catholic Church before the Second Vatican Council of 1962/5. A figure of some controversy, he would often dress in cassock, douillette (long double-breasted overcoat) and 'soup plate' hat, with the addition of frock-coat and top hat when visiting London. Small boys were apt to shout 'There goes the Pope', when he passed, thus attired. He worked for the unity of the Catholic and Orthodox Churches with the Church of England and is said to have been awarded a medal by the Greek Orthodox Church. Much of the fine decorative work by Sir Ninian Comper was added to the church during his time. Father Corbould lived in the rectory in the High Street and was unmarried. He died in 1957.

His successor in 1958 was the Revd Leigh Cameron Edwards, a Welshman by birth, who was less extreme than his predecessor. He officiated for the next 43 years and must have christened, married or buried someone from most families in Carshalton. He became a well-known and loved figure. He lived at first in the Victorian rectory, but moved to a new building in Talbot Road. Twice married, his eight children all took their turn at serving or singing in the choir.

During his term of office St Andrew's at the Wrythe was closed by the bishop in 1959 and the Good Shepherd Church, formerly a daughter church, became a parish church in its own right in 1965.

Revd Leigh Edwards about to cut the cake when celebrating his 50th anniversary as priest, 1991.

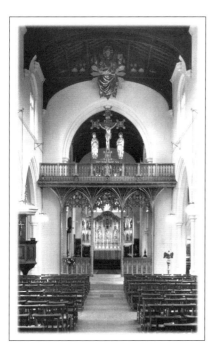

Interior of All Saints facing west, showing Comper work, 1968.

All Saints interior facing east, 1968, showing more Comper work.

Gilders working on the organ case designed by Sir Ninian Comper in the 1930s. (K.W.)

Chapter Eleven

OTHER PLACES OF WORSHIP

HOLY CROSS ROMAN CATHOLIC CHURCH

The Catholic Church in Carshalton grew out of the parish of Sutton, which was established at the turn of the twentieth century. It took over the Methodist Church in North Street some time after the Methodists moved to Ruskin Road in 1911. Originally this building was a Mass centre served by a visiting priest from Sutton. By 1931, with the burgeoning population, the diocese of Southwark decided that Carshalton could become a separate parish. Money was scarce and by the outbreak of the Second World War only the front half of the church and presbytery (priest's house) had been built. The original church remained tacked on at the back and became the hall for the parish. It could also be opened up to the half-built 1930s church by drawing back the partitions to serve the large congregations at Sunday Masses. Visibility and audibility were poor from the hall (old church) into the new church but it had one of the first public-address systems relaying the sermon from the pulpit to the hall using a carbon microphone, a valve amplifier and small box loudspeakers. The rest of the service was in Latin and could be followed in the people's own illustrated Latin missals with English alongside.

Entry was gained through a porch, which lead into the back of the half-built church with the choir and organ opposite this side entrance. A bicycle shed was outside. The presbytery was joined alongside the eastern end of the church. It is said that the first parish priest, Fr Albert Jenner, insisted on the presbytery being built before the church was completed. He opined that parishioners would always find the money to build a church but would forget about providing a presbytery for the priest if that had to be built later. So the presbytery was large enough to serve visiting priests and the bishop's entourage coming to stay. In more recent times, its size has proved invaluable, as it has facilitated all sorts of

things going on in the parish. Fr Jenner was there until he died in 1939.

Fr Anthony Kavanagh was the next parish priest. He was very outgoing, formed a large catholic social club, and had many social links with other parishes and groups throughout Carshalton which was quite unusual at the time. He died suddenly in 1960 while still parish priest. The funeral cortège was very long – when everyone walked to All Saints cemetery behind the hearse, traffic came to a complete standstill. The plot was provided by one of his many acquaintances.

This unsatisfactory arrangement of old and new in the church was of course thought to be only temporary until the rest of the money to complete it had been raised. However, the arrangement continued throughout the war and into the 1960s. Under the leadership of the parish priest, Fr Patrick Daly, in 1963 the push was made to sweep away the hall and complete the church almost to the 1930s design. The front section continued in use in spite of dust and dirt. A new parish priest, Fr Albert Ryan, came at the start of the building work.

This is the church you see today – amazingly the features of the 1930s could be closely matched and only a keen eye can spot the slight mismatches. In the mid-1970s the Sanctuary was re-ordered, under the Vatican II auspices, to have an altar facing the people and the communion rails were largely removed. Fr Luke Verhees (*above, with his dog*) came in 1989 when Fr (then Canon) Ryan retired as parish priest. He continued to live close by in Beechwood Court and acted as an assistant priest for weekday and Sunday Masses. Although the two had very different ideas, the arrangement seemed to work quite well. He retired in 1996 to live at Heathfield Priory, Cross-in-Hand (a rather apt place name) in Sussex with one of his sisters, and another sister worked as a nurse there; so all the remaining family was together. He died in June 1998.

There was no parish hall with the completion of the planned church, so additional land was rented from Victor Seymour and British Rail. A parish centre of a steel frame and wood cladding construction without foundations but with a design life of 10–15

Church of the Good Shepherd, Stanley Park Road in 1929. (V.M.)

Main: *The new Church of the Good Shepherd, Queen Mary's Avenue, 1930.*
Inset: *War Memorial outside the Church of the Good Shepherd before 1930.* (Both V.M.)

years was erected in 1970. This building became increasingly problematic and had to be closed in 2001, having lasted double its expected life! What comes next has not been decided. Following a small fire in the church, improved sound and lighting were installed in 1999 and the resultant refurbishment has made a new colourful church out of the old.

A splendid view of the church can be gained from the railway station platforms and trains. Its good open position close to Carshalton village and surrounding estates means that the number of parishioners remains high and will seem to continue for the years ahead.

ST MARGARET'S ROMAN CATHOLIC CHURCH

St Margaret's is in Fir Tree Grove, off Stanley Park Road. It was founded in 1934, as an offshoot of the Sutton diocese, the first priest being Fr Frederick Rhead. Bishop Brown, a Scot, named the church after St Margaret of Scotland, whose figure decorated the top of his crozier. He also donated a statue of the saint. The parish priest during the 1950s was Fr Albert Tomei, who remained there until 1975, when he sadly met his death in a road accident. The first tin church was replaced in 1980 by a new dual-purpose building which could be used as a church or meeting room. Fr Cyril Elkington designed the building and acted as priest until 1985, when Fr Kevin Pelham took over.

THE SALVATION ARMY IN 1884

Ever since early summer some local members of the Salvation Army had begun to march through the streets of the village on Sundays, usually ending up with a prayer and hymn meeting on Wrythe Green. At first this had attracted little attention, but during October the meetings began to get larger and very rowdy. As soon as the Salvation Army formed up in a circle for the prayer meeting they were surrounded by several hundred locals, who would shout rude remarks and when hymns were announced, would start singing a different hymn in opposition. Then they would jostle the Salvationists, and fighting would break out, and the police were called in.

By November, 'the riot became so great' that the Salvation Army had to take to its heels, and was chased across the Wrythe by the mob, who caught the leader of the Army, named Bashford, and rolled him in the mud. Then the lord of the manor, Mr Taylor of Carshalton Park House, got involved. He sent his solicitor to tell the Army that it could not use Wrythe Green any more for its meetings, and he would sue them if they tried. However the Salvationists refused to be daunted. Next Sunday they were out again, but as they paraded down the High Street they were bombarded with bags of soot and flour and other 'signs of disapproval'. They then tried to hold a meeting on a piece of waste ground, but Mr Taylor sent the village beadle after them, and the meeting was forbidden.

They tried again the same afternoon, and formed a procession along Mill Lane. They were, says the account, 'followed by a crowd of close on a thousand people, who cheered, groaned, sang and shouted as no mob but a British mob can do'. The police were out in strength, however, and it was thanks to them that the Army eventually got away relatively unharmed. They never tried to hold an open meeting again.

The Army now meet at their citadel in Green Wrythe Lane.

THE CHURCH OF THE GOOD SHEPHERD

The first church, a small iron building, was erected in Stanley Road in 1890, and in 1900 a larger iron building became the second church in Stanley Park Road, the material from the first church being used to erect a church hall. The site for the latter was next to the garage, now occupied by shops. As the church flourished and the population grew it became necessary to plan for a third church, and an area of land was purchased from the Carshalton Urban District Council. Building work began in 1929 to a design by Martin Travers.

In appearance it resembled a Spanish mission church. The building was consecrated by the Bishop of Southwark on 8 May 1930. The Revd Corbould would not give his consent for the Good Shepherd to become a parish church in its own right and it was only after his death that the Revd Leigh Edwards gave his assent. The Revd Basil Tuffield was instituted and inducted as first vicar in December 1965. The Revd Gordon Jeff followed from 1979–86 and since 1987 the incumbent has been the Revd Christopher Wheaton.

THE BAPTIST CHURCHES

In 1895 the Mill Lane Mission was founded in Palmerston Road. The building was enlarged to take a larger congregation, but over time the numbers fluctuated so that by the end of the Second World War they were a mere handful. With the encouragement of the Carshalton Beeches Baptist Church and the appointment of Sister Blodwen Rees as full-time pastor there was a big improvement. In 1954 the congregation moved to Strawberry Lodge, a Grade II listed building built to replace Bacons in the late-eighteenth century. The present building was built by Josiah Dewey and inhabited subsequently by a series of mill owners including the Foster Reynolds family. The foundation stone for a new church alongside the Lodge was laid in December 1969 but the church outgrew this and a newly refurbished

Strawberry Lodge and rebuilt Baptist Church were opened in 1996.

At the southern end of Carshalton, interested Baptists began meeting in a shop in Banstead Road on 12 October 1929. By 1931 they had purchased a plot in Banstead Road and the foundation stone for a church hall was laid on 18 April; the hall duly opened on 27 June. The Carshalton Beeches Baptist Free Church was officially formed the following month. The church expanded so much that another hall had to be opened in 1933. The Second World War caused some dislocation as well as damage to the church – first by a land-mine and later by a doodle-bug. Repairs and extensions were made and the church has gone from strength to strength.

THE METHODIST CHURCH

The first chapel for Methodists in Carshalton was opened on 16 July 1861 in North Street. Local Methodists, who had no meeting place, approached Sir Samuel Gurney, MP, who lived at The Culvers. He leased them some land, made donations to the building fund and laid the foundation stone at the opening of the building. Church members grew rapidly over the next 50 years and outgrew the chapel, so a new site was procured in Carshalton Park, next to the tramway in Ruskin Road, and a second church was built. The foundation stone was laid on 30 September 1911 and under the leadership of the Revd Frank Cooper there was a further period of expansion.

The population grew after the First World War and the second church was beginning to be too small for its swelling congregation. The church treasurer was Major William Mallinson who lived at The Grange in Wallington. He contributed the money for a third church, to be built in memory of his father, on land adjacent to the existing church. This building, now the current Methodist Church, was opened on 25 September 1926. The previous 'second church' became The Ruskin Hall, and left the Methodists with a fine complex of halls and associated rooms which have been well used over the years for both church meetings and community events. The Ruskin Hall was used as what was known as a 'British Restaurant' during the Second World War, which provided cheap (and rather unappetising) lunches in times of shortages. Subsequently the kitchens were used to prepare meals for local schools.

There has been a flourishing day nursery in the hall for nearly 40 years, up to the time of writing. The Ruskin complex is also the meeting place of a dancing school, the flourishing Carshalton Choral Society, the Ruskin Players and for over 50 years the home of the Carshalton Women's Fellowship, founded in the 1930s. Weekly meetings of Scouts, Cubs, Guides, Brownies, Beavers and Rainbows also take place here as well as numerous Church activities.

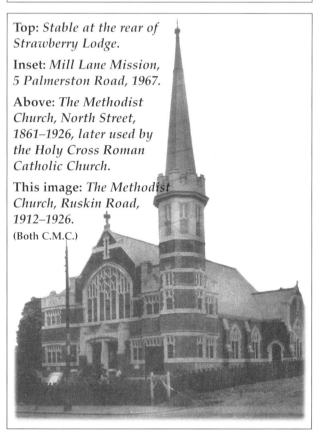

Top: *Stable at the rear of Strawberry Lodge.*

Inset: *Mill Lane Mission, 5 Palmerston Road, 1967.*

Above: *The Methodist Church, North Street, 1861–1926, later used by the Holy Cross Roman Catholic Church.*

This image: *The Methodist Church, Ruskin Road, 1912–1926.*
(Both C.M.C.)

Chapter Twelve

VANISHED BUILDINGS

DAME DUFFIN'S COTTAGE

There is a little building on the corner of Church Hill, opposite the road bridge over the Ponds, that is known as the Engine House, because when it was built in 1836 its purpose was to house the village fire engine. Since then it has been used to keep the bier-carriage, the wheels on which coffins were carried at funerals. It was built by a man called John Weller, who lived at No. 9 West Street, but more importantly owned the Carshalton brickyard or brick-field, halfway up Wrythe Lane by Brookfield Avenue: and in 1828 it was he who built the bridge over the Ponds. His bricks were probably used for the Ponds' retaining walls three years before in 1825. In 1836 John Weller agreed to build a new engine-house to replace the one that was already there; to demolish the old cottage which stood on the corner; and to make good the hole which the demolition would leave in the churchyard wall. He agreed to do all of this for no fee as long as he was allowed to keep the material from the demolished cottage.

This old cottage that belonged to the church, which was described as 'ruinous' in 1835 and demolished a year later, was known as Dame Duffin's Cottage. Dame Duffin was an old lady – legend has it she was as old as her house – who made a small income for herself by selling sweets and apples, which she laid out on the steps of the house. The steps were quite a feature of the building, which was very tall, had three storeys and an attic, as well as steps going up at the side under cover of a lean-to shed. It seems to have been a timber-frame building on a flint-and-chalk block base: and it had the gate to the churchyard path on one side, and on the other side – the Pond side – a stout beam of timber to prevent horses and carts knocking into it.

George Brightling in his *History of Carshalton* called it a medieval house for the priest at the church, in other words a vicarage, which is probably the least accurate description. Dr Peatling said that in his opinion it was a post-Reformation house replacing an old chapel attached to the Boleyn holy well – which is probably nearer the truth. Clearly it was originally a chapel: there are numerous seventeenth-century references to it as 'the chapel', Carshalton Chapel, the Boleyn Chapel, the Chapel House and so on. Mr A.E. Jones, who was particularly interested in the building, was able to prove that it was given to the parish by Nicholas Gainsford in 1497 for the saying of masses for the dead (obits).

Five years earlier, in 1492, Gainsford's daughter-in-law (Joan Brent) left money and altar cloths for the new chapel being built at Carshalton in honour of the Virgin Mary, and called the Chapel of Our Lady of Boulogne (spelt Bolen/Bullen). Mr Jones was also able to show that it must have been sold off after the Reformation, and was then re-purchased for the Church in l619. Presumably it was during this time that the chapel was converted into a three-storey house. It was then used as what is called a 'parish house' or poorhouse: Mr Jones saw it as a sort of workhouse, which was replaced in 1739. It was possibly more of a house provided for poor people to live in, an 'almshouse', as it was called in 1826, which was why Dame Duffin had it.

During the nineteenth century it was also called a 'Chantry House'. Mr Jones has suggested that during the Middle Ages a chantry priest, a special chaplain saying prayers for the dead, had been appointed with his own chapel in the Parish Church, to help the vicar in this increasingly burdensome business. Eventually there was no room for two priests in the church, they got in each other's way and fell out, so that at the end of the fifteenth century it was desirable to build the chantry priest his own separate chapel. This seems to be on the right lines, but not quite accurate. There was another priest besides the vicar, with a separate chapel in the church, which in the 1490s had a new chapel built outside. He was, however, a fraternity chaplain.

One of the most notable features of popular piety in the later Middle Ages was that most towns and villages established fraternities, which were attached to the Parish Church, but which had their own rituals and services, and therefore their own priests. The prime function of the fraternity was to say prayers for the dead, but its function was much more than this: it had feasts and processions of its own, and operated as a sort of club or friendly society. People

Dame Duffin's Cottage, copy of Haydon family oil painting, c.1800.

Dame Duffin's Cottage, a photograph of an engraving by J. Roger, 1831.
Note Ponds Bridge, built in 1828.

would pay money over the course of their lifetime to cover their funeral costs, or to have their bodies brought home if they died elsewhere (like a kind of AA Relay Service). The amount paid depended on the distance covered back to Carshalton in fetching the body – so it was better to break down and die nearer home. Money was then provided to support people's dependants, and make sure they had somewhere to live and were fed. Some fraternities received so many donations that they became real businesses, purchasing their own land and herds of cattle. They were like insurance companies; they were societies for both the quick and the dead.

The Carshalton village fraternity was dedicated to the Virgin Mary – Our Lady of Boulogne. The Gainsford brass in the church includes a figure of the Virgin carrying the dead body of her son, a type known as 'Our Lady of Pity', and the Burton brass does in fact have a scroll to Our Lady of Blessed Pity, so it is probable that the Carshalton fraternity was known as the fraternity of our Lady of Pity. Many of these late-medieval fraternities had friars as their chaplains. Friars could not be parish priests, but they came to specialise in this sort of charitable support work (often much to the annoyance of the incumbent).

There is in the church today a most peculiar memorial to William Quelch, the vicar of Carshalton who died in 1654. He ordered that his body should be buried together with the remains of 'a certain Fryer sometimes Vicar of this place' to symbolise the reuniting of Catholics and Protestants in heaven. This is an impossible inscription. In 1654 they seem to have been unaware that friars could not be parish vicars but what is much more interesting is that they did have a friar buried at the church at Carshalton. This seems to show that there was a fraternity in Carshalton, with its own chapel, where a chaplain who was a friar ministered and probably lived.

MASCALLS

One of the biggest mysteries in Carshalton history is the location of the old medieval manor house called Mascalls, which was still in use in the 1720s, but which appears to be referred to as far back as 1392. The only reference to its location was made in the early-eighteenth century, mention being made of a handsome old house near the church (Aubrey) with fish ponds and reservoirs of water in a garden behind it. This might suggest the area of the Square.

It may be possible, however, to solve one small part of the mystery: why was it called Mascalls? Keith Pryer once reminded me that this was probably a corruption of the Latin word (medieval) marescallus or maraschallus (French, maréchal) meaning 'marshall'. If there was a Marshall family in medieval Carshalton, then it was probably their home.

The name 'Marshall' is not listed amongst the medieval lords of the manor of Carshalton but the

manorial court rolls, and those for Ewell, reveal a family tree going back to the thirteenth century. There was a William Marescall or Marescallus of Mitcham between 1220–40, and a John Marscall of Carshalton, perhaps a brother or son. Curiously enough this was in connection with a grant of land at Beddington and Wallington to St Thomas Hospital at Southwark. The next references to a John Marescal at Carshalton in 1358–60, a century later, are related to a complaint that the Master of St Thomas Hospital had let the Wandle be diverted on his land at Hackbridge, where it had caused flooding. By 1380 John is joined by a Simon Marscal. There is also a reference to a John Marchall holding land at Carshalton in about 1408.

Between 1440–70 there was a John Marshall who became an important official in the royal treasury under the Lancastrian kings, and was turned out of office by the Yorkists in the Wars of the Roses. He was a great friend and colleague of two families – the Iwardbys and the Burtons. The Iwardbys held the manor of Carshalton in the sixteenth century, and the Burtons in the seventeenth century – again there seems to be a connection. The last reference so far is to a Walter Marshalle in 1569, who took gravel out of the Wandle. Obviously there is a lot more work to be done here – but it now seems clear why the old Carshalton manor house was called Mascalls: it was the Marshalls' house.

PULPITS, CRADDOCKS & CALCOCKSHAW

A local resident remembers a tunnel running up from the garage/petrol station in Pound Street into the chalk hill behind it, and as a boy he used to walk up it as far as Ruskin Road and listen to the trams rumbling by overhead. He suggested that the tunnel entrance might be exposed when the new Texaco service station was built in Pound Street (at the junction with West Street, opposite Margaret's Pool). There have been many suspect tunnel stories over the years about Carshalton and Beddington, but sure enough, with the demolition of the old garage a door and a window were revealed that cut into the wall beneath the ceramic tile warehouse behind the garage. Number 4 Carshalton Park Road is the address of the Continental Tile Centre, but it had been part of the garage in the past.

It transpired that there was indeed a tunnel behind this door and window. The door is now blocked up, but one can still get to the tunnel through a trap door in the floor of the tile warehouse and down a ladder. In order to research this section of the book it was necessary to explore the tunnel, in the company of Douglas Cluett of Sutton Library (later to become the Borough Heritage Officer). On entering the tunnel, one first sees a small, roughly square cellar. This is not wildly exciting (very cold and dirty), but it does have two very old timber beams in the ceiling, which suggest that the cellar was once

Pulpits viewed from the corner of Carshalton Park Road and Pound Street, showing the long north-south arm running up the hill. (S.L.S.L.)

Wardill's cycle shop and garage, 33 Pound Street, c.1912. (S.L.S.L.)

two rooms with a timber partition between them, and that this is probably the remains of a timber-framed building. In the south wall, leading into the hillside, there is an arched opening, leading into a passage. The passage is about 30ft long, fairly narrow (5ft) but tall (6ft), so that it is easy to walk along. The walls and ceiling are lined with brick, and there are three shallow arched alcoves and another small one built into the wall along one side. At the far end of the tunnel there is what can only be described as a sort of narrow Gothic/early-English pointed arch 'window' – only bear in mind that it is facing south into the hillside, is perhaps 20 or 30 ft underground, and well beyond the boundaries of the tile warehouse – probably under the house next door (6 Carshalton Park Road). One wonders if they know! Through the 'window' one can just see chalk: we couldn't detect a further passage through it, but it is possible that the chalk has fallen and blocked it. We have no explanation for the tunnel. Why anybody should burrow into the chalk hillside for 30ft seems inexplicable, especially as they went to all the trouble of putting in such a lot of brick work. Someone suggested that a stream might have flowed through it, but there was no evidence of this, and why should anyone make a brickwork channel for an underground river? In any case, the water would simply have run through into the cellar and filled that up.

Although no explanation is forthcoming about the origins of this passage, a little is known about the building to which the cellar once belonged. It was called Pulpits or The Pulpits. Demolished in about 1913/14, only photographs of it remain: but it appears to have been a fairly large, two-storey brick and weather-boarded house with a tiled roof, which by 1850 had been split up into six cottages. The building was L-shaped, with the north-south arm running uphill parallel to the bottom of Carshalton Park Road. It may seem surprising that there was a Carshalton Park Road in 1850, but it was a short road which just ran up to where Doral Way is, leading to a blacksmith's forge at the top (owned variously by the Overy, Maspero and Preen families). Although it seems odd that a smithy should be on top of a very steep slope, which would be difficult for horses, it was built thus because it was not originally serving Pound Street, but Crooked Lane, the old main road to Sutton which ran along the Park wall to Carshalton Park Road and then bent southwards to where Carshalton Park Road now becomes an extension of Ruskin Road/Beynon Road. The east-west arm of this L-shaped building was at the back of the modern garage site, and a good deal of the side of the hill must have been cut away to get the foundations. The age of Pulpits is unknown: it could be anything from medieval to eighteenth century. The property had several small fields attached to it on the west side of Carshalton Park Road, leading up to Ruskin Road – that is, alongside Crooked Lane and the Park wall.

The cellar (and passage) is clearly what now remains of the bottom of that arm of the building which was cut into the hillside. It was part of a terrace of cottages in 1850, and later in the nineteenth century came to be used by Wardill's garage and bicycle shop, the predecessor of the modern garage. Presumably it now belongs to the tile warehouse, previously part of the garage built on top of that arm of the Pulpits.

The Pulpits, although it was divided into cottages, was almost certainly originally one building. The name Pulpits is a corruption of the name of the family which owned it: 'Puplets'. However, the Pupletts were obviously never very clear about what they were called, as the many documents in which they are mentioned reveal the name in many different forms: Pullpets, Pipletts, Poplets, Popletoes, Popelot and so on (if you were a lady called Miss Popelot, you too would want to change your name. Although it sounds worthy of Edward Lear, it's all true!)

The other thing to mention about Pulpits is that it was originally the centre of a larger property. The very helpful abstract of the lands of the manor of Carshalton made by William Lacey in 1714 lists it under the heading 'Pupletts or Pulpets and Popletoes, Cradock('s) West Mead, and Calcocks Haw', and his first entry tells us that in 1530:

Thomas Christmas, the son and heir of Nicholas and Maline Christmas, was admitted to a copyhold tenement in Carshalton belonging to Adam Popletoe, with 10 acres belonging to it in the common field. And a croft (farm) called Craddocks with the water there, two acres at the south end of Westmead, and a close there called Calcockshaw near Crooked Lane on the west.

Apart from these acres in the common fields, there were three main elements, taken separately. Firstly, Craddocks can probably be forgotten about. Mr Jones has already wrestled with the question of whether Craddocks Farm and its water was in Pound Street, or on the other side of Carshalton House in the area of Shorts Road, and has settled, probably rightly, for the far side of Carshalton House. The main reason is an entry in the Carshalton manor court rolls for 1446, which states that there is a toft (house-site) and garden called Craddocks in the west field of Carshalton between Kinnersley (Carshalton House) and West Mead. Just over 200 years later in 1660 this seems to be confirmed when a pasture called Craddocks recently planted with cherry trees was sold to Dixey Long, the occupant of Carshalton House.

Secondly, with Calcockshaw there is no difficulty. It was a large meadow with trees, which stretched from Carshalton Park Road down to the Greyhound orchard. The earliest reference to it appears to be in 1450, when a certain Adam Paris was charged with losing control of his pigs, and letting them run wild and cause damage, first on the Wrythe, and then in

Calcockshaw. It was called Calcockshaw because it belonged to the family of Calcocks or Colcocks. In 1449, it is recorded that Joanna Colcock held by charter a piece of pasture from the manor of Carshalton, that she had died, and that in order to inherit it her son Richard would have to pay a heriot or inheritance tax of his best animal to the lord of the manor. A year later he still hadn't done so, and was sued. In 1565 there was a dispute about inheritance of property, which was solved by separating Calcockshaw from Pupletts: Anthony Wood got an orchard on the east side of Pupletts (and some fields along the road to Banstead). In 1714 it was noted that Calcockshaw was by then included in the Greyhound. In fact in 1850 the Greyhound still owned the land right up to Carshalton Park Road. The first mention of the family in Carshalton is in 1380, when John and Roger Colcock were accused of illegal brewing of ale (really a licensing device).

Finally, the Pupletts or Popelots, spelt in this instance 'Papelots' – Thomas and William – also appear on the same charge in 1380, and in the 1390s, Roger Popelot too. More interestingly, in 1445–49 Adam Popelot was reported because his holding had become very ruinous for want of repair, and he was to be fined 20s.0d. if he didn't mend it. It is not clear from the record what happened next, but some 30

years afterwards in 1482 virtually the same entry appears – only this time it was a barn or storehouse which was falling down, and the fine imposed by the manor court was correspondingly reduced to 6s.8d.

Perhaps the most interesting point about all this is that the Popelot family had a house in the mid-fifteenth century that was old enough to be ruinous and falling down: the Pulpits is a very old-established site. Presumably the old house was rebuilt before 1500 and may be the one in the photographs of 1913 – but certainly there was a house there which continued to be lived in all the way through the sixteenth, seventeenth and eighteenth centuries.

The Christmas family remained as tenants well into the reign of Elizabeth until the inheritance by married daughters in the 1570s led to the disappearance of the name. But the family reappears a century later, in the 1650s and 1660s, as tenants not of the Pulpits, but of the now separated other section, Calcockshaw. From the division of the holding in 1565, Calcockshaw had remained with the Wood family until 1633, and then with members of the Lambert family, who had a house in Carshalton, between 1633 and 1657. The Lamberts were a prominent Banstead and Woodmansterne family. The Oaks was for centuries Lamberts Oaks, and the Lamberts who had a house in Carshalton during

Main: *Pulpits, Pound Street, c.1870.*
Inset: *Far left of Pulpits in Carshalton Park Road, c.1912.* (S.L.S.L.)

The Oaks, seat of the Earls of Derby, an early-twentieth-century photograph.

the seventeenth century owned even more property in Banstead.

The same is also true of the other tenants mentioned. The Calcocks family had a half share of the manor of Woodmansterne from 1364, land at Banstead by 1393, and were well known in Chipstead by the sixteenth century. So too were the Popelots or Pupletts who can be traced at Banstead between the fourteenth and eighteenth centuries, and the Christmas family are a familiar Wealden and Surrey name. This little piece of Carshalton, across the road from Margaret's Pool, seems to have been a colony of Banstead.

THE OAKS

The Oaks is one of the most famous buildings in England in that it gave its name to one of the classic horse races, The Oaks, and The Derby is named after the owner of the building. It is one of the worst-documented well-known buildings in the country. There are hardly any surviving deeds, and the accounts of its history are completely confused and contradictory.

It is just about possible to trace who owned it and lived in it during the nineteenth century, and that the Earls of Derby owned it from about 1770 to the 1820s. It is also known that most of the castellated building which appears in old prints was built by the Derbys. This was an extension to an already existing

building, which had been occupied by Derby's son-in-law, General Burgoyne of Saratoga notoriety – who was also a distinguished playwright, and laid on the famous fête champêtre. Burgoyne apparently leased the building from its constructors, a group known as the Hunters Club, who had built it to make a country sporting house by the Carshalton-Epsom racetrack. It is likely that this group of sportsmen acquired it in about the middle of the eighteenth century, and that the property at that time still belonged to the Lambert family of Banstead: it was called Lambert's Oaks, and the Lamberts had owned it and a great deal of Woodmansterne since around 1200.

The Oaks was demolished in 1958 and all that remains is an outbuilding, a double coach-house, which is very clearly a well-designed eighteenth-century structure, and must be as old as The Oaks itself. There are very old beams set in the flint wall inside the coach-house; and numerous other traces of flint, or flint and chalk-block walls, and timber framing round about. It seems incredible that people in the eighteenth century should deliberately keep these chunks of flint walling, even incorporating them into new buildings, unless they thought they were of special interest. This raises the intriguing question of whether we have here pieces of a medieval building, which the eighteenth century inhabitants preserved as part of a romantic Gothic ruin.

Lavender picking in Carshalton, c.1908.

Cottage of Content

Charrington

COTTAGE OF CONTENT
42 William Street, Carshalton

The Cottage of Content, William Street. (A.C.)

Chapter Thirteen

A MISCELLANY OF MEMORIES

MISS MOODY RECALLS

A certain Miss Moody remembers moving into the Old Rectory in Festival Walk in 1886 when she was six years old. She had been born in Wallington soon after her father came home from Canada (where he was on the Governor-General's staff). He bought one of the new houses in Maldon Road. Even then, she recalls, he found Wallington too suburban for his liking, and he came to live in the Old Rectory.

It appears to have been a very happy household, with lots of children and an army of servants. One of these was the laundress, who came in every other day to do the washing – and she was kept extremely busy because:

There was a lovely garden, with a stream running through it, on which we kept a punt. We fell into the water so often that our Mother ordained that we must change our clothes in the laundry – if we went up to our rooms to change, it made a mess on the stairs, and the servants complained about it. (Obviously one had to be very careful not to offend the servants.)

They were often joined by the rector's children who lived in the new rectory in the High Street. The rector, Lord Victor Seymour, was 'great fun'. And Miss Moody remembers, 'I adored Lady Seymour: she was always having babies' – and every time this happened the elder children came to stay with them. The favourite was the elder son Conway, whom she describes as 'the most awful monkey, and flatly refused to learn anything. He ended up in the Diplomatic Service.'

One lady recalls how the children had to spend their evenings in the bathroom boiling up concoctions of barley water and glycerine. The villagers would queue at the back door with their bottles to receive a ration of this mixture – which was a noted cure for coughs. This was all part of the obligation of the rich families of the neighbourhood to be charitable to the poor of the parish. Another lady remembers that whenever anybody was ill in her house in Carshalton Road the road outside would be covered with straw to reduce the noise of the traffic,

horses and carts. This was the normal custom – and it was still being done in London as late as 1930.

However, the thing which both ladies remember above all was the lavender. All summer long, one of them writes:

Carshalton smelled of lavender, and as far as the eye could see there were lavender fields stretching up towards Banstead – and peppermint too. When it was cut we children would be given as much as we could carry for sixpence – and it was in the house all the year round. But the rest of it went off to the local distillery... The horrible moment came when it all disappeared – and for the next few days there was just one horrible stink.

One may say that these personal reminiscences are not of much historical value. However, not only are they fascinating to read, but they do manage to convey the authentic character and atmosphere of a past age in a way which the ordinary written records cannot.

THE CARSHALTON BEADLE

In the spring of 1879 the parish beadle – the village policeman, Mr Roffey – had died, and it was necessary to appoint a new one. (The person who was appointed at this time would in fact be the last beadle to be appointed: the Vestry system of local government was soon to be swept away, and replaced by the new Urban District Council. However, that was still some 15 years into the future.) In 1879 a new beadle had to be appointed, and the various eminent persons of Carshalton parish were keen to get their man into post. The real competition was between the rector, the Revd William Albemarle Bertie Cator, who lived in the Grove, and everybody else. Would the Rector's nominee be accepted? Extracts from a poem written in April 1879 illustrate this election:

Then rose a sporting doctor, with speech so glib and free
  (Dr Shorthouse)
Explained what kind of personage the beadle ought to be

But by way of a conclusion he begged to raise his voice
For William Edwards, High Street, the beadle of his
*   choice.*
On which the reverend rector, who caters for us all,
Jumps up and hopes the name of Thorpe will not be
*   left to fall.*

One of the leading opponents of the rector was a man called Greenhill, and no sooner had the rector been led to announce his candidate, than Greenhill set to work to discredit him:

Whereon the gruff-voiced
*   Greenhill stood up and said,*
*   said he,*
Your other man to Jericho –
*   Bone's the man for me.*
This motion was supported by Mr
*   Matthew Jones,*
Who o'er the village vestry a deal
*   of power owns…*

Mr Jones was the village corn merchant and was very important to the millers. He lived at Summer House, behind Haydon's, in the High Street; and his brother was the village coal merchant, a successful combination. The rector's nominee was out, and Mr Charles Bone was in, and remained as Carshalton's last beadle until he died on the last day of 1902. Our poet was moved to end:

That dust returns to dust we are
*   called upon to learn;*
In the dread hereafter, our bones
*   to ashes turn.*
But in the present instance – as
*   may easily be shown –*
The ashes of the beadle have crumbled into Bone.

A singularly unfunny remark, but a witticism which apparently convulsed the village for months afterwards, with the exception of the Revd Cator, who did not think it was at all funny either – but that may have just been sour grapes.

Mr Bone had a daughter, Kate Bone, who was born in 1850 and so could very well remember the Carshalton of 100 years ago. In 1920 she very obligingly wrote an account of her earliest memories.

What she remembered best about Christmas was that her father would escort the bell-ringers from the Parish Church round to the houses of all the principal inhabitants, who were regaled with a recital of

Charles Bone, the last Beadle and Crier to the Manorial Court. He died aged 80 on 31 December 1902 and is buried in the churchyard.

Christmas music and carols on hand bells. One hopes that the said principal inhabitants were duly appreciative. In any case the bell-ringers had their reward, since it was traditional that on Christmas Eve itself they came back from ringing their chimes, and assembled in the belfry of the church, where the rector was dishing out free beer. Afterwards they adjourned to the beadle's house, where Mrs Bone the beadle's wife always brought out bottles of her home-made elderberry wine. Her daughter recalls that the results of this mixture were usually disastrous and the bell-ringers had great difficulty in pulling the ropes on Christmas morning. It is probably fair to suggest that the last thing one would want to do with a hangover is to ring one of the church bells, and the parishioners must have been treated to some very odd sounds.

THE COTTAGE OF CONTENT

Frederick John Reeves was a JP and councillor for Carshalton Urban District Council and worked for Hamilton's brewery in Stockwell. He was a drayman but was unfortunately trapped between the back of the horse and the loading cart during the 1930s. He could not work again and for his pension the brewery gave him a thatched cottage pub in Carshalton, The Cottage of Content in William Street (now demolished). Frederick built a dance-hall on the side of the pub, as well as an off-licence, and there were ducks and goats in the garden.

During the Second World War some of the customers at The Cottage of Content were Canadian soldiers, stationed in huts on Mitcham Common where they manned anti-aircraft guns. They were often known to shoot their smaller guns through the pub ceiling.

Frederick kept a parrot in the public bar, which was taught to wolf-whistle and swear by the customers. When Frederick died he left a will in which he bequeathed the parrot to an old ladies' home in Leatherhead, with the instruction that the home should receive seven pints of Guinness a week for a year for looking after the bird.

Chapter Fourteen

PROMINENT FIGURES & EVENTS OF THE TWENTIETH CENTURY

DR A.V. PEATLING

Dr Albert Victor Peatling came from a long-established Cambridgeshire family; his father and his eldest brother were both Mayors of Wisbech. After qualifying as a doctor at Magdalen College, Cambridge, and St Thomas' Hospital, he became a ship's doctor during the 1890s. When the Boer War broke out he went to South Africa as an Army doctor. This explains why he came to England in 1903. He was returning home after the Boer War, although it is still a mystery why he came to Carshalton. What is certain is that if he had not done so a vast amount of local history would have gone unrecorded.

As well as practising as a GP Dr Peatling was a keen photographer and a local historian. His work, the Peatling Collection, is in the care of the Local Studies Library of the London Borough of Sutton. He was also a founder member of the Surrey Record Society in 1913 and one of the first volumes of records to be published (largely financed by him) contained the manorial court rolls of Carshalton in the late Middle Ages.

After the First World War Dr Peatling became adviser to the diocese of Southwark on village war memorials and he represented Carshalton at the unveiling of the Cenotaph by the Ponds. An amateur artist of some distinction, his watercolour paintings and notes on stained-glass windows in Surrey churches were published jointly as a posthumous tribute to him by the Peatling Memorial Fund and the Surrey Archaeological Society in 1931.

On 19 April 1906 Dr Peatling married Muriel Palliser Barrow, daughter of Samuel and Florence Mary Barrow of the Grove, Carshalton. Samuel Barrow was a leather baron with a business in Bermondsey. He was a prominent member of the Leather and Hides Trades Provident and Benevolent Institution – indeed, he was President in 1895 as well as President of the Boot and Shoe Manufacturers Association and of the Leather Trades Protection Society. He was knighted in 1921. Sir Samuel Barrow

was also a great local benefactor and gave land for the extension of the churchyard when his first son Samuel Palliser died in 1910.

The Peatlings had two sons, Tom and Paul, and the practice and family home was at Park View, 35 High Street. When her husband died at the early age of 53 in May 1922, Mrs Peatling moved to Sussex and their two sons eventually went to live in Rhodesia and South Africa. A plaque in memory of Dr Peatling can be seen above the door of his former house in the High Street. This was donated by Mrs Gurner and put up in 1979.

Top and above: *Red Cross card of thanks to Mrs Muriel Peatling for work during the Great War and a Red Cross certificate belonging to Mrs Muriel Peatling for her services in 1916.*

Dr A.V. Peatling with his sons Tom (right) and Paul (left).

Wedding of Dr A.V. Peatling and Muriel Palliser Barrow, 19 April 1906, pictured at the Grove.

The Golden Wedding of Sir Samuel Barrow and Lady Florence Mary (née Palliser), 1934.

Park View, 35 High Street, taken by Dr Peatling between 1906–22.

MAJOR C.P LOVELOCK

The man mainly responsible for piloting through the Carshalton sewerage scheme was the newly-appointed Clerk to the Local Board, Mr C.P. Lovelock. He recalled many years later that when he arrived to be interviewed for the job, it was a cold, wet night in the winter of early 1893. As he walked down the High Street for the first time, not looking forward to being interviewed, he said to himself, 'What a miserable hole Carshalton is.' Nevertheless, he got the job!

In his *History of Carshalton* Mr Jones has asserted that historians look in vain for the name of any single individual who ruled the destiny of Carshalton during the great changes which took place in the early years of the twentieth century. However, when Major Lovelock (as he then was – he did a great deal of training work for the East Surrey Yeomanry and the Territorial Army during the First World War and was awarded the MBE) retired in 1918 after 25 years' service as clerk, first to the Local Board, and then from 1894 to the new Urban District Council, Councillor Parker said of him, as he was presented with a grandfather clock:

If anybody ever writes a history of Carshalton, it will be incomplete without the name of Major Lovelock figuring prominently in it. What Carshalton is today is largely due to him: it is now a very different place to what it was twenty-five years ago.

He ought not to be forgotten. As clerk, he effectively dominated the Council during this period of major change. He was noted for his diplomacy: it was said that he received a great many letters during his life – some pertinent, some impertinent – but everybody who wrote to the Council received a courteous answer. Yet at the same time he would very quickly 'put a stop' to any councillor who was not completely honest or who was a member of the Council for his own ends (although his reminiscences after he retired makes one wonder whether this statement ought not to be taken with a pinch of salt). He nevertheless presided over the lives of Carshalton people from cradle to grave. Besides his Council work, he was Chairman of the day nursery, Secretary of the old-age pensions committee, and Superintendent of the Cottage Hospital. He was also a considerable local historian in his own right, and whilst not in the same class as someone like Peatling, he left a number of articles on the history of Carshalton which still make interesting reading.

However, his real memorial comprises three buildings and two public parks, all of which deserve preservation, and the Carshalton road system, which probably doesn't. In the first place he gave the parish what is undoubtedly the best twentieth-century building constructed in Carshalton. When Lovelock came to Carshalton in the 1890s local government was a very minor affair – there were only nine councillors – and they had little to deal with beyond looking after the roads, some poor relief, and running the fire brigade. The whole thing could be run from a large room, which was by the side of the Public Hall in the High Street. As the role of local government steadily expanded, so new offices became necessary, and it was Lovelock who was mainly responsible for the new combined council offices and fire station – built for £2500 in 1908 in the Square – now known as Carshalton Library. This is the only modern building in the village to be Grade II listed, and very deservedly so.

Although we are grateful for this handsome and useful building, in point of fact Carshalton's miniature Council hardly needed offices except somewhere to file the papers. The real offices were not in the Square at all, but further along the High Street at the Greyhound. Lovelock remarked to one of the councillors (a certain Mr T.F. Jones) that when he had first come to Carshalton he had had difficulty in finding a house to live in, and had put up at the Greyhound for several weeks. As a result, he commented, it had been a second home to him ever since.

This seems to have applied to many of the councillors: they always met there after their official meetings, and according to Lovelock, if they had any important matters of business to discuss they always left them until they got there and felt sufficiently fortified to deal with them. Indeed, after a time, some councillors got so that they could not deal with matters except at the Greyhound, and this affected other local bodies. For instance, the Carshalton Music Society was always presided over by a local councillor, and therefore always had to have its meetings at the inn – they no doubt sang all the better for it.

Lovelock recalled that amongst all the honest councillors he had known, his two favourites were the old veterans who dated back to the old Local Board in the 1890s. One was the huntsman and deerkeeper from Carshalton Park, old Tom King, who was a prominent member of the local fire brigade. One night he went to the Greyhound and enjoyed himself, with the result that when he came out, it was rather dark and he fell straight into the Ponds. He was so used to shouting 'Water' when there was a fire, that on this occasion, having had so much water, he was discovered sitting in the middle of the Ponds bellowing 'Fire'. Ladders were brought to pull him out. On the strength of this, having proved his suitability, he was elected a councillor three weeks later.

The other honest fellow was Old Edwards, as he was known, of Irish Yard, the disreputable slum area at Wandle Mount. He was a noted poacher; he used to take trout out of the Ponds by tickling them. Additionally, said Lovelock, there was not a day that passed without him making sure that some mischief was occurring. He claimed that the exploit of which he was most proud was the occasion when, he claimed, the church paid him to get drunk. He turned up at the Greyhound with 2s.0d., and explained that on the way he had met the rector's mother – 'Lady' Cator as she was popularly called. He told her that the previous night he had had a dream, in which he had died and gone to heaven. 'And do you know, ma'am', he said:

As soon as I got through the Golden Gates, the first person I saw was the rector himself – and he promised me that if I woke up, and told you the good news that he was saved, you would give me 2s.0d. for it.

Lovelock was closely concerned with two other buildings. One is that very pleasant house in Rochester Road, which was opened in 1899 as the Cottage Hospital, and of which he became superintendent. When in due course it became obvious that it was not nearly large enough, Lovelock initiated the scheme for building a second new hospital as a war memorial, and was collecting money for it well before the Armistice in 1918. It was estimated that this would cost £60,000, but by waiting until land values fell after the war, the War Memorial Hospital was eventually built in an area of the old Park in 1923/4 for £25,000 – just ten times the cost of the Council offices. Although Lovelock was retired, he became the first secretary of the War Memorial Hospital until 1931, when he finally resigned and died a year or two later.

Both the War Memorial Hospital and the Library stand on land once belonging to Carshalton Park. In 1913 the Council, with Lovelock as clerk, performed the great public benefaction of buying up most of what was left of the Park (for £5000) and making it into the present public park. Lovelock maintained very close relations with Mr Blake Taylor of Carshalton Park House, so that the Council inherited the lordship of the manor from him. Mr Taylor (also then a Major) in fact returned to Carshalton in 1918 to attend Lovelock's farewell dinner, and from him Lovelock extracted for the Council some important parts of Carshalton, like Wrythe Green and the upper or western Pond (the one with the war memorial).

The other Pond came to the Council with the Grove in 1924/6, but that this happened is again largely due to Lovelock's ability to forge a very close relationship with the leading local landowner, in this case Mr Samuel Barrow (later Sir). Although Lovelock was no longer clerk in the 1920s, he maintained his contact with Barrow. When Lovelock became Secretary of the War Memorial Hospital in 1924, Sir Samuel Barrow became President of it – and this probably had a lot to do with the fact that the Grove became public property very soon after. Lovelock certainly does not deserve to be left out of the history books.

One of Lovelock's bequests which has not survived is the annual Carshalton Dinner, which he

had instituted to enable the leading lights of Carshalton to get together once a year at the Greyhound and make speeches about each other, about Carshalton affairs, and Carshalton history. These dinners were killed off by food rationing during the First World War, although Lovelock tried to revive them after he retired in 1918 by holding a sort of farewell dinner for his friends. In his own speech on this occasion one can see his intense concern for Carshalton. He understood, he said, that the Germans talked about Deutschland über Alles, but for him it was Carshalton above everything, and he wanted Carshalton affairs to be managed by people who felt the same. It was not, he remarked, a political occasion, but he would rather see the hottest radical alive elected to a seat in Parliament, provided he was a Carshalton man, than he would 'the best Conservative who came from Mitcham' – which was greeted with loud laughter, since it was well known that the Conservatives always won the Carshalton seat.

In many ways little has changed since Lovelock's days – a fact of which he would surely have approved. He constantly harped on the theme that Carshalton was a village and not a suburb, and should be treated by village not suburban standards. Yet, at the same time, he had a curiously limited and ambiguous vision of what this entailed. Running alongside village ideals was the notion that Carshalton was close to London, and so had to demonstrate that it was 'making progress' and 'keeping up with the times'. It was a very municipalised outlook in many ways – what Carshalton wanted was good modern buildings and public open space; he had little interest in keeping old buildings or in leaving things as they were because of their rural character and origins. For example, when he came to Carshalton (said Lovelock), there were only 5000 people living there and there were no houses to the south of the High Street. It was all park, with deer running about: one might have been fooled into thinking one was in Devon.

Clearly, Lovelock did not view this with great enthusiasm. However, when he left, the population was, despite the First World War, nearly three times as great, many alterations had taken place, and, he ventured to say, Carshalton had kept pace with the times. The Council had naturally carried out many improvements, especially the widening of many roads, and he wished to thank Major Taylor as lord of the manor, and the man who had made most of this possible. When Taylor was selling up the Park and about to leave Carshalton, he had asked Lovelock what he could do for the place before he went, which would most benefit posterity. Lovelock suggested that he gave land so that the roads could be widened to 40ft because as it stood, 'Park Hill was narrow; the road to Sutton was a village track'. Consequently, Major Taylor surrendered land along the edges of the roads to the Council, which he could otherwise have sold for several £1000s. This land was reserved when houses were built so that the roads could be widened. Ruskin Road is a good example of the result of such actions.

Even after Taylor had left the district, Lovelock reminded him that he had promised to pull down two old cottages at the entrance to Carshalton Park Road, and had gone without doing so. 'If I said I would do it', he at once replied, 'I will do it'. Instructions were immediately given, the cottages were pulled down (presumably Pulpits, a Tudor building), and the road was widened (which was greeted with applause). It was of course the demolition of cottages in the Square which had made possible the building of the new Council offices/library.

There is an oddly equivocal quality about Lovelock: the new Carshalton that was forged during his time of office was achieved very much through compromise. Hundreds of new suburban houses were built, but some of

Major Lovelock. (S.L.S.L.)

the great parklands were kept. High-quality new buildings were constructed; but many old historic buildings were lost. It was declared that Carshalton was a village still, but it worked to accommodate the motor car – it regarded good, new roads as the top priority for the future. There was an irreconcilable dichotomy in this outlook, and indeed years later we

are still paying the price for this attempt to have things both ways. It remains a very open question as to whether present inhabitants of the parish shall be capable of doing any better.

Over his 25 years, said Lovelock, there were four things about Carshalton which had struck him most forcibly. One was the inordinate and quite outstanding honesty of the local Council. Secondly, there was Carshalton's intense conservatism: nobody wanted to listen to new ideas, and you had to say things for ten years before anybody heard what you had to say. (They do say that history repeats itself.) Thirdly, Carshalton only wanted the best: if it was a case of spending a little money, or going the whole hog and doing things properly, Carshalton always said 'Spend the money'. Even if it meant spending more than the income in rates, the money was found, the job was done properly, and the matter did not have to bother the Council again. The last characteristic was that however much people were divided on matters of principle, 'once a question was decided, all was peace and happiness'. It showed the friendliness of a village community – they had their little differences and sacrifices sometimes had to be made, but they usually finished up with something satisfactory to all parties.

CARSHALTON URBAN DISTRICT COUNCIL (1963–64)

from the Official Guide and Handbook

COUNCILLORS

St Helier North
H.W.C. Leach
H.L. Markan
T.W. Turner

St Helier West
P.J. Bassett, C.C.
R. Bunker

St Helier South
L.A. Marchesi
S.G. Reading
C.A. Strick

North-East
G.W. Ballard
Mrs J.S. Buck
Mrs M.E. Chapman

North-West
Lt-Col. T.F. Gadd
A.H. Howell
A. Wilkins

Central
F.C. Finch
J. McMahon
P.A. Rye

South-East
G.F. Everitt
S.F. James
J.R. Truphet

South-West
A.J. Day
Mrs J.M. Mackie
C.C. Sheward, C.C.

Main and right: *Shepley House, c.1870, and another, undated, but early view of the property.*

SHEPLEY

The last owner of Shepley House was Charles Dingwall who drowned when a German submarine torpedoed the *Lusitania* in 1915. In 1916 the break-up of the estate began. The house became the Alf Evans Memorial Convalescent Home belonging to the National Union of Printers and Paper Workers. Some of the land went in the sale of 1926, and the rest in 1932 when the house was demolished. The whole area was soon covered with a modern housing estate: the past is commemorated only by the street names – Shepley Close, Mill Close, the Causeway and River Gardens.

However, there is one part of the Shepley House estate which escaped and has been saved. Around the middle of the twentieth century one of the beauty spots of Carshalton was Watersmeet, the point where the two arms of the River Wandle, the Beddington Wandle and the Carshalton Wandle join up. It belonged to Shepley House, but visitors could readily secure permission to see it, and walk across the white wooden bridge to the island (once called Frog Island), now known as Wilderness Island.

Left: *From about 1970 proper bathrooms were installed on the estate. Prefabricated bathroom units were lifted by crane over the tops of the houses and placed in position at the back. Here a bathroom is lifted by crane at Waltham Road, 1971.*

Below: *Progress of the bathroom over the roof.*

Below left: *The bathroom finally in place.* (All E.B.)

The railway used in the construction of the St Helier estate. Locomotive 0-6-0 saddletank 'Lionheart' is seen here travelling south from Mitcham over Wandle Bridge near Bennett's Hole.

The St Helier Estate & Rosehill Court

The St Helier estate was built by the London County Council on either side of the Sutton bypass (later named St Helier Avenue), so part of it is in Merton and Morden and part in the London Borough of Sutton. The latter part, which is the largest, is in Carshalton. It was named after Lady Mary St Helier who was an LCC councillor and alderman and whose life's work was devoted to the improvement of housing for the poor. Sadly she died in 1931 before the completion of the estate.

The plans were drawn up by G. Topham Forrest and the cottage-style houses were after the style of Sir Ebenezer Howard, founder of Letchworth and Welwyn Garden City. The houses were well built and had internal WCs but no bathrooms as such, although they did have a bath in the kitchen, covered with a board. Roads were named after abbeys and priories because of historic connections. Morden had been owned by Westminster Abbey; Sutton by Chertsey Abbey; and Merton was an abbey in its own right. The roads ran in alphabetical order, north-west to south-west – Canterbury, Titchfield, Tewkesbury, Waltham, Woburn and Westminster, to name but a few. Between 1928 and 1936, 8523 houses were built along with 543 flats. This resulted in the largest estate south of the Thames.

Parts of south London had dreadful slums and St Helier estate accommodated hundreds of people in a slum clearance operation in the early 1930s. People from Camberwell, Stockwell and the Elephant and Castle were allocated to roads beginning with the later letters of the alphabet and those from the East End were housed further over, near the bottom of Middleton Road. Houses numbering some 5000 were to form the 'Garden City', rather like Welwyn Garden City, with rustic fences and gates. These houses were built by the firm of Wills.

When Lord St Helier let the government have the land it was said that he stipulated that open spaces and clumps of parkland trees should remain. Much open space was left for recreational purposes – 130 acres in all. Part of the open space was to provide a strip of land between Green Wrythe Lane and Wrythe Lane in an attempt to secure a green belt from the River Wandle to Sutton. Some of that land was purchased by the National Playing Fields Association and other similar organisations. The relocated people must have felt very lost in what was quite open country. They were grateful, but undoubtedly missed the closeness with their neighbours they had known in Bermondsey. An elderly resident recalled that the Hatfields of Morden Hall were very kind and used to arrange events, particularly for the children. Churches, schools, shopping areas and two public houses were provided, and there was also the Gaumont Cinema at Rosehill, now a bingo hall. St Helier railway station was opened in 1935 and St Helier Hospital was built during the late 1930s.

During the Second World War the Revd Neil Nye of St Peter's Church was believed to be dead. However, he escaped from a prisoner-of-war camp and later turned up in the parish and was returned to St Peter's as vicar. This parish celebrated its 21st birthday in 1956 with all sorts of events – concerts, drama, fêtes, etc.

As a result of the desperate need for housing after the Second World War, the only blocks of flats in the parish were built in Durand Close. In about 1959, 300 flats and maisonettes replaced 100 prefabricated houses which had been erected in 1945. Prefabricated houses were only meant to last ten years but they could last longer and were a great success.

The London Borough of Sutton came into being in 1965 and in 1970 the St Helier estate was handed over to them by the London County Council. Young men came from all over the country to live in Carshalton, seeking work. Some of the estate houses were converted into flats for the elderly. Tenants could buy their homes from the early 1970s before the general 'right to buy' was introduced in 1979. Over the years much work has needed to be done on the houses. Kitchens have been modernised, windows and roofs replaced. Some of the terraces still look exactly as when they were built, which pleases the conservationists who regard them as architectural treasures. There are, of course, no garages or spaces for cars. Unfortunately many of the clumps of trees, mainly elms, were felled due to Dutch elm disease in the 1970s.

*Rosehill Court, built in the 1930s,
showing the Gaumont Cinema to the right.*
(S.L.S.L.)

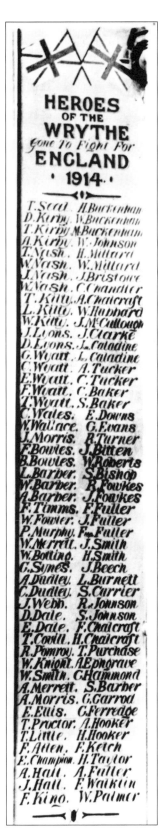

HEROES
OF THE
WRYTHE
Gone To Fight For
ENGLAND
· 1914 ·

T.Seal. H.Buckenham
D.Kirby. W.Buckenham
T.Kirby. M.Buckenham
A.Kirby. W.Johnson
T.Nash. H.Millard
W.Nash. W.Millard
J.Nash. J.Bristowe
W.Nash. C.Chandler
T.Kitt. A.Chalcraft
L.Kitt. W.Hubbard
W.Kitt. J.M'Cullough
J.Lyons. J.Clarke
D.Lyons. L.Caladine
G.Wyatt. L.Caladine
C.Wyatt. A.Tucker
E.Wyatt. C.Tucker
F.Wyatt. C.Baker
T.Wyatt. S.Baker
C.Wales. E.Downs
W.Wallace. G.Evans
J.Morris. R.Turner
F.Bowles. J.Bitten
B.Bowles. W.Roberts
L.Barber. S.Bishop
W.Barber. R.Fowkes
A.Barber. J.Fowkes
F.Timms. F.Fuller
W.Fowler. J.Fuller
P.Murphy. F.Fuller
W.Merrett. J.Smith
W.Botting. H.Smith
G.Synes. J.Beech
A.Dudley. L.Burnett
C.Dudley. S.Currier
J.Webb. R.Johnson
D.Dale. S.Johnson
E.Dale. F.Chalcraft
T.Covill. H.Chalcraft
R.Pomroy. T.Purchase
W.Knight. A.Epngrave
W.Smith. C.Hammond
A.Merrett. S.Barber
A.Morris. G.Garrod
E.Ellis. C.Ferredge
T.Proctor. A.Hooker
T.Little. H.Hooker
F.Allen. F.Ketch
E.Champion. H.Taylor
A.Hall. A.Fuller
J.Hall. F.Watkin
F.King. W.Palmer

List on the wall of the Cricketers of those who went to war from the Wrythe in 1914. (M.F.)

The Willie Bird Memorial Cross of 'Honour to the Heroes of the Wrythe who have died in God for the King and for You. May they rest in peace.' This cross formerly stood outside St Andrew's Church, Wrythe Lane. It is now in Carshalton Churchyard. (J.H.)

The Cenotaph by the Upper Pond.

REFUGEES AND WAR

Some local residents remember seeing Basque refugees in Carshalton during the time of the Spanish Civil War. Mr Mizen, the market gardener, lived at the Culvers then and many of the refugees were housed in the outbuildings. They also lived in a big house at the end of North Street. They were kept busy working for Mr Mizen who owned watercress beds and they bunched up the watercress ready for sale.

In common with the rest of the country there are countless memories of the Second World War as Carshalton received its share of bombs, shrapnel, radar tape and doodlebugs. Local people contributed towards the purchase of a corvette named *Marigold*, and a large model of this ship took up residence on the lower Pond, painted battleship grey. There were shelters in the High Street and the air-raid siren was on top of a large pole at the High Street entrance to the Grove, opposite the Coach and Horses. The King's Arms in the High Street received a direct hit and was demolished. Many gardens sprouted small dug-out Andersen shelters and schools had very large ones, which smelt dank and musty. Some homes preferred the Morrison table shelter, an iron table with removable mesh sides which could be put up when the air-raid activity became more intense. Ration books were issued from the conservatory at the back of the Grove.

The cenotaph had been erected by the Upper Pond after the First World War and a memorial garden was created behind it to commemorate the fallen of the Second World War.

Inset: *Wounded soldiers arriving at Carshalton station to attend a concert in the Grove, 1917.*
(S.L.S.L.)
This image: *Members of the 58th Battalion of the Home Guard in Carshalton Park during the Second World War.*

Street Party in Culvers Way on Victory Parade Day, 1946. (D.Y.)

VE Day Street Party, Whitby Road, St Helier Estate, 1945. (J.E.)

King Edward VII Coronation celebration, August 1902.
Taken in William Street, looking towards Wrythe Lane. (M.F.)

Celebrating the Coronation, 1937, in Fuller's Barn at the corner of William Street and Wrythe Green. (M.F.)

A scene from Carshalton Coronation Pageant, 1911, held in Carshalton Park.

Another scene from Carshalton Coronation Pageant, 1911, held in Carshalton Park.

Lords and ladies dress up for Carshalton Coronation Pageant, 1911.

The opening of Carshalton Park Public Pleasure Ground, 25 June 1913.

Many Carshalton girls can be seen here attending the London May Queen in the mid 1940s.

Councillor Everett, leader of the Carshalton Urban District Council, pouring tea at the Darby and Joan Christmas Tea in 1957. (J.B.)